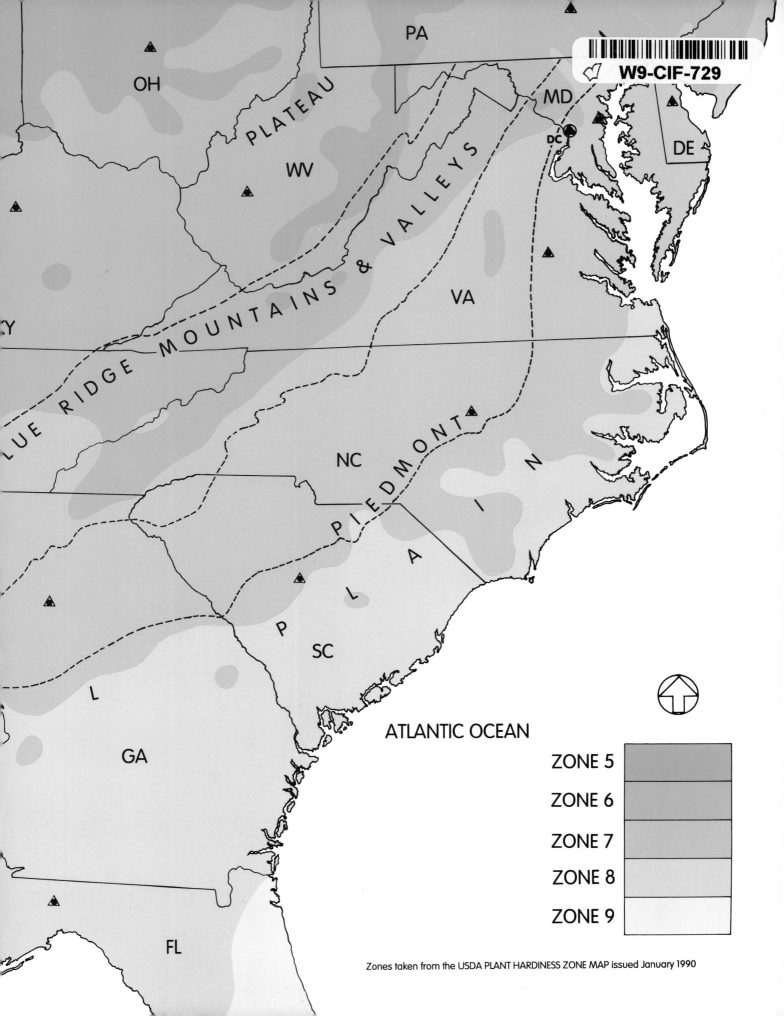

ATLANTIC OCEAN

| ZONE 5 |
| ZONE 6 |
| ZONE 7 |
| ZONE 8 |
| ZONE 9 |

Zones taken from the USDA PLANT HARDINESS ZONE MAP issued January 1990

W9-CIF-729

GARDENING WITH NATIVE PLANTS OF THE SOUTH

GARDENING WITH NATIVE PLANTS OF THE SOUTH

Sally Wasowski

with

Andy Wasowski

TAYLOR TRADE PUBLISHING

Lanham • New York • Oxford

By Sally Wasowski with Andy Wasowski:

Requiem for a Lawnmower

Native Texas Plants: Landscaping Region by Region

Frontispiece: Spigelia and sundrops, backed by a non-native astilbe, bloom under the shade of hardwood trees in this Memphis garden owned by Bickie and Michael McDonnell and designed by Tom Pellett.

Published by Taylor Trade Publishing
An Imprint of The Rowman & Littlefield Publishing Group, Inc.
4501 Forbes Boulevard, Suite 200
Lanham, Maryland 20706

Distributed by National Book Network

Designed by Hespenheide Design

Library of Congress Cataloging-in-Publication Data

Wasowski, Sally, 1946–
    Gardening with native plants of the South / Sally Wasowski with Andy Wasowski.
        p.   cm.
    Includes bibliographical references (p. 189) and index.
    ISBN 0-87833-802-0
    1. Native plant gardening—Southern States.   2. Native plants for cultivation—
Southern States.   3. Landscape gardening—Southern States.   4. Landscape plants—
Southern States.   I. Wasowski, Andy, 1939–.   II. Title.
    SB439.24.S66W37   1994
    635.9'5175—dc20   93-39404
                                                                        CIP

Printed in the United States of America

For my cousin, Hazel Cassel.
Her knowledge of birds, her generosity,
and her marvelous sense of humor have
contributed much to this book.

CONTENTS

ACKNOWLEDGMENTS

"Southern hospitality" is not a phrase dreamed up by some Dixieland chamber of commerce; it is real and it is alive and well. Andy and I encountered it everywhere we went during our two-and-a-half years of traveling, from East Texas across to the Atlantic coast and on up to the Mason-Dixon line.

But before I thank the many people we met along the way who gave us their time, their knowledge, and their friendship, I should acknowledge some people without whom this book would most certainly never have happened—because *I* would never have happened: my Southern ancestors.

My ties to the South go back many centuries; one of my early relations, Joseph Cobb, arrived in Virginia in 1613, and settled for a time in the second Jamestown colony. From there, the family spread out to North and South Carolina, Georgia, Tennessee, and eventually to Texas. Have you ever visited Rocky Mount, in Piney Flats, Tennessee? This restored farm—now a popular tourist attraction—was built by William Cobb in 1770, and stands today as the oldest original territorial capitol in the United States. Young Andrew Jackson was a family friend, and visited often. But enough name-dropping . . .

The fact is, I've probably got long-lost Cobb, Posey, Hudson, Hill, and Heslep kin throughout the South. And even though I am a Texan, and therefore considered (depending on whom you talk to) either a Westerner or Southwesterner, a good portion of my life was spent in the South. I went to college in Decatur, Georgia, at Agnes Scott, and recall those years fondly. And, at various times, I lived in Maryland, Alabama, and Virginia, where my attraction to native plants—dare I say it?—took root. Even my Yankee husband and co-author can claim some ties to the South, having spent several childhood years in Fairhope, Alabama.

As a result, when we packed up our van for the first of many research and photography trips throughout the Southern states, we did so with a genuine sense of homecoming.

We also went with more than a little trepidation. Virtually everyone on our "must-see" list—botanists, landscape architects and designers, nursery owners, as well as knowledgeable weekend gardeners—was a stranger. We were literally at their mercy; if they'd had no time for us, or no interest in our project, we would have been stymied.

This book is ample evidence that such was not the case. Andy and I were touched by their willingness to drop whatever they were doing and take us around to favorite gardens, share their experiences and insights, and even, on many occasions, take us into their homes and treat us like favorite relatives. (We're also very grateful for their numerous tips on local dining; we sampled the best the South has to offer, from Chesapeake crabcakes to Atlanta soul food, from smoked trout in Bucksnort, Tennessee, to Cajun cuisine in Baton Rouge. Clearly, writing a regional gardening book is both fulfilling *and* filling!)

First mentioned must be my dear cousin, Hazel Cassel, of Nashville, to whom this book is dedicated.

Aside from being a lot of fun, she's also one of the most unflappable individuals I know. One autumn day when it was pouring down rain on every garden we'd planned to visit, she provided one of the highlights of our trip by taking us a hundred miles or so ahead of the storm to the Fiery Gizzard hiking trail. A dedicated bird-watcher, Hazel gave us wonderfully specific bird information for this book.

A big thank-you goes to Dr. Ed Clebsch of the University of Tennessee in Knoxville, who checked all our slides to make sure we'd shot what we thought we had shot. For the final determinations on which Latin names to honor, I thank him and Barney Lipscomb of the Botanical Research Institute of Texas.

For reading the early manuscript and catching our goofs, thanks go to Benny J. Simpson of Texas A&M University; Lynn Lowrey of Anderson Nursery in Houston, Texas; Mike and Barbara Bridges, owners of Southern Perennials and Herbs in Tylertown, Mississippi; and Ed Steffek, curator of the H. L. Blomquist Garden of Native Plants at Duke University, Durham, North Carolina.

For help in compiling the plant lists for habitats, thanks go to Bob McCartney of Woodlanders, Inc., a native plant mail-order nursery in Aiken, South Carolina.

Some gardens and gardeners were so helpful that we returned time and again. For the woodland garden, special thanks go to Louise Smith and her gorgeous indigenous garden in Birmingham, Alabama. Other splendid examples of woodland gardens and woodland gardening techniques were provided by Jenny Andrews, curator of the Howe Garden, sponsored by the Garden Club of Nashville, Tennessee, and situated at Cheekwood Gardens; Ed Steffek of the Blomquist Garden at Duke University; both the Mountain Garden and woodland trails at the University of North Carolina at Chapel Hill; and the private garden of Margaret Reid in Raleigh, North Carolina.

For the perennial garden, our gratitude goes to garden designer Kitty Taylor and her husband, Neil, for their magnificent double border in Collierville, Tennessee. Other outstanding perennial gardeners include Barbara and Mike Bridges with their invaluable demonstration perennial and herb garden in Tylertown, Mississippi, and Edith Eddleman, co-curator of the perennial border at North Carolina State University in Durham, North Carolina.

For Atlantic Coastal Plain garden information, we're grateful to the Helen Avalynn Tawes Garden in Annapolis, Maryland; Al Hill of Brookgreen Gardens in Murrells Inlet, South Carolina; and all the staff at Woodlanders in Aiken, South Carolina.

For Gulf Coastal Plain gardens, thanks go to Lolly Jackson's garden, designed by Will Fleming, in Houston, Texas; Robert Poore and his numerous gardens in Jackson, Mississippi; Edward Blake, Bob Bruzek, and Chris Wells at Crosby Arboretum in Picayune, Mississippi; Johnny Mayronne for his home garden in Covington, Louisiana; Marion Drummond and Neil Odenwald for showing us around lower Mississippi plantation country; and Bill and Lydia Fontenot for sharing Cajun country with us.

Others who spent countless hours with us are Gail Barton and Richard Lowery, Gene Cline, Mark Gormel, Kim Hawkes, Carole Cameron, Nell Lewis, Mary Jo Modica, Darryl Morrison, Jim Neal, Carole Otteson, Carl Owens, Tom Pellett, Andrea Sessions, Plato Touliatos, Don and Sue Williams, Larry Wilson, Louise Wrinkle, and Matthew Dew, a charming sixteen-year-old who showed us around his parents' Tennessee mountain garden—in a steady downpour!

Numerous other people also gave generously of their time, talents, and hospitality: Kathy Crye; Richard Evans; John Fairey; Carlene Jones; Lou and Betsy Kellenberger; David Lewis; Julie and Joe Mackintosh; Jane, Larry, and Daniel McGoldrick; Jan Midgley; Ned and Georgene Newland, and their sons Edward and Marc; Elizabeth Newland; Mike Mapstone; Bickie McDonnell; Randy McMullian; Dr. Stephen and Sally Pridgeon; Todd Stephens; James Turner; Pat Wells; Lundy Pridgeon Wilder; and Jim Wilson.

Special thanks to the excellent photographers who shared photos we needed for this book and were unable, for various reasons, to get ourselves: Geyata Ajilvsgi, Ritchie Bell, Barbara Bridges, Albert Hill, David A. Laster, Paul Moore, George Pyne, Benny J. Simpson, and Larry T. Williams.

Thanks also to Chris Holowiak, whose home was the basis for the landscape plans in this book, and to Jay West, who did such a great job turning my rough sketches into finished plans fit for publication.

If, inadvertently, your name is not here and should be, please be as generous with your forgiveness as you were with your time, and blame it on the panic we felt as the publisher's deadline drew closer.

INTRODUCTION

What's the hottest news in gardening? Native plants. And high time, too. Natives have been around for many thousands of years, adapting themselves to their habitats—and most of us have only just recently (in the past ten to fifteen years) begun to appreciate and use them.

When we talk about native plants, we're talking about *common-sense* gardening. Doing it Mother Nature's way. Working *with* her, not against her. Native plant gardening means using the plants that are best adapted to the conditions where you live, and not relying on those non-native plants that have such a hold on the nursery trade—plants that, in many cases, are totally unsuited to the area where they are sold. Keeping these aliens alive often means putting in far more hours in the garden than the average homeowner would like. And all too often these labors are in vain.

I really believe that most folks have lots of other things they'd rather be doing. But they're trapped. Traditional gardening, the kind practiced by the vast majority of American homeowners, calls for an all-out effort: weeding, mowing, edging, watering, and pouring on oceans of chemical pesticides and herbicides.

Native plants offer us a wonderful alternative. We can reduce our workload because natives are remarkably self-sufficient; after all, they've been taking care of themselves for millennia. Natives are friendly to the environment; when you practice some simple and natural gardening techniques, such as allowing fallen leaves to turn into mulch and controlling garden pests with ladybugs, praying mantises, and other animals, you can stop using toxic chemicals. With native plants, you'll be able to create natural habitats that welcome desirable wildlife, such as songbirds and butterflies. And with native plants, your property will have a true *sense of place,* something that is missing from most of our homogenized, look-alike landscapes.

This book is designed to be not just a basic introduction to the wonderful native plants of the South but also a basic primer on how to use them.

Selecting the plants that would go into this book, from the vast palette available to the Southern states, was nothing short of a nightmare. The publisher wisely decided that a twelve-pound tome would not be a best-seller, so I had to get my plant list down to a manageable number. That list was revised countless times as I agonized over what to keep and what to delete. Just when I thought I'd gotten it right, I'd show the list to various local native plant authorities and listen in horror as they said, "Oh, no, you're not dropping the so-and-so, are you? But you *must* include it!"

The native plants that made the cut are the showiest and easiest to buy and grow or they are so important to the basic Southern habitat that it would have been difficult to garden appropriately without them. As for the plants that had to be omitted, you'll be happy to know that many of them are covered in other identification books, with photos and descriptions (see bibliography). And, I understand that many other such reference books are in the works.

My aim here is simply to give you a taste of what is out there, and show you new and exciting ways of putting it all together.

Gardening From a New Perspective

Landscape with native plants and you enter into a wonderful new way of looking at your garden. Instead of trying to make nature conform to rigid rules based, quite often, on what your neighbors think you ought to be doing, you can look at what nature has been doing—successfully—and then modify those concepts to suit your own personal taste. You will come to understand that landscape plants should be looked upon, not as solitary entities unconnected to their surroundings, but as part of a greater community, just as they are in the wild. You'll see how you can trade in your conventional lawn-boxhedge-poodle-shaped-shrub landscape for . . . perhaps a bit of woodland, or a meadow, a delightful shade garden, or one of many other lovely possibilities. These can include dramatically reducing the lawn area around your home, or doing away with it all together.

Even if you continue to have a lawn as part of your landscape, you will be pleased to learn that it doesn't have to be a boring expanse of green; it can contain a number of plants—flowers, mosses, violets and other woodland flora, groundcovers—even other types of grasses used as accents. When you go native, you'll find out that you no longer need toxic herbicides or pre-emergents that can make your skin itch and your eyes water. If it's not good for you, it's not good for your pets or the environment either. You'll also learn that soil is a living substance that consists of millions of helpful organisms, that wasps eat web worms, that mushrooms help tree roots, that beetles feed baby songbirds, and that mice feed owls.

When you copy natural habitats, you are plugging into an ancient system that can cut down on your maintenance considerably. But not completely. Too many pieces of the fabric are already missing, and we, who have disturbed the fabric, now have to do the work of those forces that have been eliminated—fires, grazing animals, and so forth. Still, pruning once a year, weeding two or three times a year,

and watering occasionally during the summer probably don't amount to anything close to the maintenance you're doing right now.

Of course, you may still opt for the more traditional landscape look, and that's fine, too. I'm not doctrinaire. In that case, there are a number of plans in this book to help you—one big difference being that you will be using natives instead of the standard nursery stock you're more familiar with. While these plans concentrate on giving you lots of floral color at particular seasons, there is also an evergreen garden plan for those of you with tiny courtyards, and lots of ideas for making shady areas perk up.

I should also make the point that you do not have to turn your back on old favorites that happen to be non-native. In a beautiful natural habitat, to add non-natives would be, in my opinion, criminal. But, in a neighborhood where established landscapes are already non-native, a mixture of natives and non-natives is often the most sensible approach. There are many perfectly good naturalized plants and some cultivars that do very well in your area. My own landscape is only 60 percent native. The plans that I've included in this book *do* use natives exclusively, but that's because I'm taking the position that most of you will know little or nothing about the native plants in your area. The idea isn't to discourage the use of other suitable materials but simply to expose you to as many native possibilities as I can. Besides, I also want to show that going 100 percent native is not only possible, it can also be very attractive.

The key to success is to use what works. You want *more* choices, not fewer. But a word of warning: evaluate those old favorites carefully. Could they threaten to take over the neighborhood? Many naturalized plants can and do. Do they require too much work to keep them looking their best? Are they vulnerable to disease and insects, and therefore need plenty of doctoring with chemicals? Often, when you compare those old favorites to your local natives, you'll find that the natives look far more attractive. And I don't just mean visually.

I suspect that this book will be a real eye-opener for most of you. I still recall when I first learned about native plants; it was nothing less than an epiphany. I wish the same for you.

DALLAS
MARCH 1993

Woodlands are not just green. One garden that illustrates this particularly well is the home garden of Louise Smith of Birmingham, Alabama. She has combined an artistic eye and a thorough knowledge of native plants to create an exceptionally diverse and colorful woodland garden. Early spring, before the canopy has leafed out, is a time for wild azaleas and woodland flowers. In this scene, in mid-April, a bark mulch path leads up to her extensive early spring woodland flower garden. Fire pink, blue phlox, celandine poppy, Piedmont azalea, and yellow azalea provide the color, while Christmas fern and the leaves of flowers not currently in bloom fill the forest floor. Note the thick, natural mulch of last year's leaves.

1

CREATING HABITATS

To make gardening as easy and as enjoyable as possible, you'll want to make the majority of your landscape a habitat or at least an approximation of one. To do that, you'll first need some idea of what a habitat is. A **habitat** is the native environment of a plant or animal. Habitats are actually communities of native plants *and* animals, and they all interact synergistically, in much the same way that the cells in your body work together to keep you alive. The two main types of habitats are woodlands and grasslands.

Anatomy of a Forest

The natural forest—as opposed to a monocultural (one-species) tree farm—is composed of three basic elements. First, and standing tallest, are the **canopy trees,** so-called because they form a canopy, or umbrella, over the woodland beneath. Most trees that attain heights over 50 feet are classified as canopy trees. Dropping down a bit, we come next to the **understory.** These are the smaller trees and shrubs that measure about half the height of the canopy trees. And then, at ground level, are the very small shrubs and groundcovers, ferns, and wood-

There are woodland flowers and shrubs for summer color also. In mid-June, Louise Smith has a stunning scene near the entrance to her driveway, this time all in yellows. In the shade is golden St. John's wort, and on the other side of the split-rail fence, catching extra sun by the road, are black-eyed Susans, Queen Anne's lace (from Europe), and butterflyweed.

By late fall, a scattering of red leaves remains to lend color to the evergreens. This garden near Jackson, Mississippi, is tucked under a canopy of pines and hardwoods. Mr. and Mrs. Robert Legate had landscape architect Robert Poore design a woodland garden using many plants transplanted from other parts of their property. Visible in this picture are two kinds of evergreen fern, blackgum, flowering dogwood, Florida anise, two-winged silverbell, scarlet buckeye, and partridgeberry.

Life Cycle of a Meadow

You might think a grassland is boring—"just a bunch of old grasses and weeds." But if you stop and spend some time in one, you'll be amazed at how much there is to see, hear, and smell. There is a myriad of flowers that you simply didn't notice driving by. You will be astounded and delighted at the activity of birds, butterflies, bees, and other insects. Every year, every season, every day, is a little bit different.

Gardeners who don't mind mowing a few times a year or burning once a year or every other year can maintain a meadow. It is certainly a great deal easier than maintaining a lawn.

land flowers that, along with fallen leaves, nuts, and cones, make up the **forest floor.**

It is these diverse elements that combine to create a viable habitat for a range of wildlife: songbirds, small mammals, butterflies, and a host of friendly insects that actually help to protect this environment. Conversely, in the monoculture, there is sterility; the singing of birds and chirping of cicadas are rarely heard.

It is the diverse, naturally synergistic woodland setting that we want to recreate in our landscapes.

*This meadow on the Natchez Trace is maintained by mowing. This picture was taken in early summer when black-eyed Susan (*Rudbeckia hirta*) was dominant among a mixture of grasses. Earlier, there had been lyreleaf sage and butterweed, which seem to have been mowed in late spring after setting seed. Fleabane (*Erigeron strigosus*), aster (*Aster*), and goldenrod (*Solidago*) were busily growing leaves and stems, but a long way off from blooming.*

Crosby Arboretum in Picayune, Mississippi, used to be a slash pine plantation. Now it is a laboratory designed by its director, landscape architect Edward L. Blake, and Androprogon Associates in Philadelphia. One third of the site is being burned to be maintained as savannah—at different times in different years to mimic warm-season fires that used to be set by lightning—and the rest is being left to develop into woodland. This picture of a fledgling longleaf pine savannah was taken in March of 1992. The area on the right had been burned three weeks earlier, on the left two years before. The new green growth is mostly sugarcane plumegrass, switchgrass, and broomsedge. The grassy areas were too soggy to walk on, and crawfish houses were visible everywhere.

Taken from another angle, this is the same savannah that we saw burned in March, but this time we are seeing it on the last day of July. Most of the white flowers are Lady's hatpins (Eriocaulon decangulare), with some roundleaf eupatorium (Eupatorium rotundifolium), pineland hibiscus, and yellow daisies called Balduina uniflora.

The same savannah in mid-October. Sugarcane plumegrass towers over swamp sunflower and roundleaf eupatorium.

Habitats for Wildlife

Dr. David Wilcove, senior ecologist for the Wilderness Society in Washington, D.C., writes in *The Nature Conservancy Magazine:* "Early settlers in the eastern United States speculated that a squirrel might travel from the Atlantic Ocean to the Mississippi River without ever touching the ground, so vast was the forest cover. Today, that squirrel could retrace its steps without ever leaving asphalt."

Robert K. Godfrey, in *Trees, Shrubs, and Woody Vines of Northern Florida and Adjacent Georgia and Alabama*, tells us that it is getting harder and harder to find a habitat that is anywhere

close to authentic, because we have messed up our land pretty badly. Godfrey goes on to say that tree farming, clear-cutting, and site preparing (by which he means bulldozing) "greatly alters the topsoil and drastically changes—in some places virtually obliterates—the native flora and fauna, both of which are integral parts of what constitutes a forest."

Unlike tree roaches and fire ants that thrive in man-made environments, songbirds and butterflies—beautiful creatures that we all love and appreciate—depend on functional habitats. Both serve as indicators of ecological distress and are harsh critics of damaged environments. Their numbers, or lack of them, are sometimes used to test the authenticity of a restored habitat or the extent to which one has been degraded. Accordingly, where information has been

Male Cardinal

Eastern black swallowtail on Piedmont azalea.

available, I have indicated which plants are known to help support these creatures.

Numerous studies are documenting major declines in songbird populations. In two parks in Arlington, Virginia, breeding birds have been counted for over 30 years. Many species, such as American redstarts and hooded warblers, have disappeared. Others—red-eyed vireos and ovenbirds—have declined by 60 to 90 percent. These, along with tanagers, orioles, thrushes, and many others, are migratory songbirds who spend the winter in the tropics and raise their babies here. They have a problem: They are losing their tropical forests, their nesting places here, and their roosting and eating places in between.

The other 40 percent of our songbirds, the ones who live here all year, are also in trouble. They, too, are losing habitats, and studies have shown that smaller woodlots have more predators per songbird than are found in a large forest. Songbirds' eggs are being pushed out of the nest by cowbirds. These parasitic birds, which are native to the Midwest, have moved into the Northeast and Southeast where they find cow pastures and rice fields much to their liking. Both the eggs and nestlings of songbirds are being eaten by squirrels and raccoons, blue jays, grackles, and crows, whose numbers are increasing, ironically, because of the food they steal from bird feeders.

Furthermore, when songbirds are raising their young, they need insects for protein, not fruits and nuts, and pesticides are greatly changing the numbers, composition, and dietary value of insects.

Butterflies are also in trouble. The larvae are destroyed by fire ants, systemic poisons, and other insecticides. Bt (*Bacillus thuringiensis*), touted by many organic gardeners as safe, is especially harmful to both butterflies and ladybugs when they are in the larval stage. So is burning when it is done when the larvae are attached to grass stems. Each kind of butterfly is on a different schedule, so it is important not to burn at the same time every year. Summer burns are often best for butterflies.

Besides not actively killing butterflies, it is important to provide food for them if you want them to thrive and multiply. Larval plants are as important as nectar plants, and many butterflies are very picky about where they lay their eggs. Be generous with the leaves of your larval plants. Plant scads of nectar flowers, so the butterflies can easily find them—and your garden. For complete information on Southern butterflies and how to attract them, I recommend Geyata Ajilvsgi's book, *Butterfly Gardening for the South.*

Admittedly, individual native plant gardens—even whole neighborhoods of native plant gardens—are not going to be as perfect for songbirds and butterflies as miles of pristine forest and clearings. But, we do the best we can. We don't want to eliminate birds and butterflies from the scene.

Examples of Habitat Gardens

Along the **coast** where there are dry soils, salt spray, and constant wind, live oaks have proven to be the toughest trees. Hung with Spanish moss, they are found, along with southern magnolia, in landscapes like this one (*top, left*) facing the Gulf of Mexico in Ocean Springs, Mississippi. The understory is typically made up of more evergreens: yaupon, wax myrtle, and dwarf palmetto.

In the **Coastal Plain,** there are pine woodlands that are flat and poorly drained. On such a site, Johnny Mayronne, president of Natives Landscape Corporation in Covington, Louisiana, has designed the home landscape you see here (*top, right*). This is the front entrance in mid-April. Blue phlox and yellowtop are nestled in a mixture of ferns. A red Florida anise is on the left with a younger white one on the right. The red amaryllis is a non-native, old-fashioned garden favorite. The pink shrub you see on the other side of the porch is a Piedmont azalea in almost full sun. Its roots are in a quarter-acre-sized natural wet area filled with native grasses and flowers. In October, this bog is golden and purple with swamp sunflower, wild ageratum, and sugarcane plumegrass.

Dry longleaf pine areas are the most distinct of the Southern habitats because they are *so* dry. Many homeowners buying new houses in such areas are dismayed to have such fast-draining sand and high water bills. In the Carolinas and in Florida also, these habitats are called **sandhills.** This bracken fern (*right*) as a groundcover shows how these landscapes can be attractive and drought-tolerant as well. Other groundcovers you could use are pussytoes, lyreleaf sage, or evergreen blueberry. For fall color in this habitat, plant turkey oaks under the longleaf pines, along with sparkleberry and lanceleaf sumac. For evergreen screening, use American holly, yaupon, mountain laurel, staggerbush, wild olive, redbay, and sandhill rosemary. For flowers, use bigleaf storax, Georgia basil, dwarf huckleberry, St. Andrew's cross, passionflower, Texas or sandhill bluestars, vernal iris, butterflyweed, white baptisia, sundrops,

and silkgrass. In quantity, silkgrass (really a daisy, not a grass) can be used as a groundcover also, as can splitbeard bluestem, broomsedge, wiregrass, or pink muhly.

Hardwood forests have the richest understory. Because they were clear cut in this century, most are immature and contain pines as well. Post oak woods are dry and beech woods are moist. Tulip poplar, maples, oaks, and hickories are usually present. This most typical Southern woodland habitat can be found from hammocks in the Coastal Plain to rich coves in the mountains. The soil is typically acid to very acid, and

rhododendrons, mountain laurel, and blueberries are common. This picture (*below*) shows one of the deciduous Southern rhododendrons—Piedmont azalea— in Louise Smith's garden in Birmingham, Alabama. Scattered in the woods about ten feet apart, their colors range from rose to white. Blue phlox is planted at their feet for contrast.

Limestone occurs throughout the South from the Coastal Plain to the mountains. Because rain is plentiful and leaf mold is too, the surface topsoil is usually acid, but the underlying lime makes the hardwood forests here rather dif-

ferent. Eastern red cedar is common, not pines. Rhododendrons, azaleas, mountain laurel, stewartia, and blueberries do not occur except in particularly acid, rich soils. White ash is common and so are yaupon, wax myrtle, scarlet buckeye, redbud, possumhaw, rusty blackhaw viburnum, bottlebrush buckeye, both hydrangeas, crossvine, wild red columbine, blue phlox, lyreleaf sage, wild ginger, and most ferns. Some special plants are rarely found elsewhere in the South—among them Alabama croton, neviusia, golden St. John's wort, Allegheny spurge, aromatic aster, Short's aster, and American smoke tree (*Cotinus obovatus*).

This autumn scene (*top, right*) shows the native plant garden at Cheekwood Botanical Gardens in Nashville, Tennessee. An eastern red cedar is on the right. White ashes are overhead and their leaves, already fallen, can be seen on the pond. The Short's aster, which covered the garden in purple earlier, is gone also. Flowering dogwood is still red, redbud is yellow, a hickory is bronze, and the flowers in the background are a form of swamp sunflower called *Helianthus simulans.*

The **mountains** have such cool summers that they get a whole range of gorgeous plants that are not native to most of the rest of the South. Of course, considering all the Coastal Plain goodies that are not winter-hardy for them, I guess that's only fair. Hemlock becomes the signature conifer. Rosebay rhododendron, dwarf rhododendron, mountain stewartia, and large fothergilla are some of the plants that cause envy.

The garden in the picture (*right*) belongs to the Whitcomb

family, who have owned this land since before the Revolution. Rosebay rhododendron covers the entire bank above Wolf Creek. A spiderwort blooms under the hemlock shading the bench, and a lizard's tail is in bud by the creek. Some of the other native plants in this garden are mountain magnolia, a huge yellow buckeye (*Aesculus flava*), American holly, red and sugar maples, Jack-in-the-pulpit, and New York fern. And for good luck, there is an eastern red cedar on either side of the front door.

The prettiest landscapes are divided into several smaller gardens. Here is a portion of Lee Moomaw's 50 by 50 foot back yard in Virginia Beach, Virginia. Out of sight to the left are an herb garden, a shady border, and, completely hidden from the house, a surprise garden where overarching evergreens shelter ferns and other shady groundcovers around an inviting bench. In this view we can see two flower gardens and a charming arbor gate. Joepyeweed and orange rudbeckia are dominant in late July. The gate acts as a focal point that visually lengthens the backyard and extends it to the front yard.

Nancy Arrinton's garden in Manassas, Virginia, seen below, is considerably larger, totaling three acres. Sunny areas, shady areas, and natural areas are joined by mowed paths composed of native and non-native herbs that arrived on their own and tolerate mowing and moderate foot traffic. Moss and violets dominate the shady paths, and grasses dominate the sunny ones. Woodland left to its own devices is the backdrop. The sunny areas around the house were cleared to allow in enough sun for two ponds and a butterfly garden; the stump of a tulip poplar is visible where five paths meet in the largest open space. This photo was taken from the path between two shady flower gardens. Almost everything visible in this picture is native to northern Virginia, with the exception of the white buddleia.

2

PLANNING YOUR NATIVE GARDEN

During the question and answer period following our talks on landscaping with native plants, Andy and I seem to get the same two questions over and over: "Where can I find these native plants?" and "How do I get started?" The first question is getting easier to answer every year. While many conventional nurseries are adding natives to their inventory, we're also seeing the establishment of numerous specialty nurseries where 50 percent or more of the stock is native. There are so many in the South already, with new ones appearing every time you turn around, that it would take too many pages to list them here. To find a nursery near you that carries native plants, look in the yellow pages or ask for recommendations from your local native plant society, arboretum, or nature preserve, or consult one of the lists in the resource section.

As to the second question, we can answer that now. The **Getting Started** plan shows a typical small lot, about 65 feet wide. We saw home lots this size from Maryland to East Texas, mostly in older neighborhoods, with big old trees shading at least half the yard, so that lawn maintenance is a major

undertaking. This small lot is the interior portion of the plan—the part around the house.

The bigger picture is for those of you on larger properties. It fades out at the edges, so that you can imagine those portions of the plan extending for acres, if that's how much land you have.

The point is, no matter how much acreage you own, it's the portions immediately around your house where you will probably do your most ambitious gardening. Beyond that small envelope, you can still have gorgeous gardens, of course, but they'll need to be modified imitations of native habitats. That way you can save yourself loads of work, not to mention watering.

All the plans are based on this one layout. It will quickly be obvious to you that you can have a working area (in back, with the firewood, brush pile, and compost pile), a flower garden, an evergreen courtyard, and a shady spring garden, even on a small lot.

Converting your present landscape to a native landscape: Your first step is to quit watering, quit spreading lime and replanting grass every spring, quit fertilizing and spraying, and quit raking

leaves. In other words, quit doing all those chores you don't enjoy anyway. (And you thought this would be hard.) After a full spring and summer on this regimen, you will notice that some plants have died off—or are in the process. Others are doing just fine. And some will actually be doing better! Cut down and remove all those that have declared themselves unhappy and unhealthy.

Now, assess what you have left. You don't have to keep whatever remains alive. Sometimes, a plant you have hated for years is still vigorous and thriving. I give you permission, right now, to get rid of it. If some smaller shrubs and flowers are not where you want them, transplant them—to another spot in your future garden or to a friend's landscape.

If you have plenty of sun, refer to the Sunny Flower Garden, the Fragrance and Herb Garden, the Early Fall Flower, Fruit, and Foliage Garden, and the Flowery Meadow plans for ideas. Where you have shade from one or more huge deciduous trees, look at the other plans. The **Basic Plan** shows you how all the native plant landscapes can fit together.

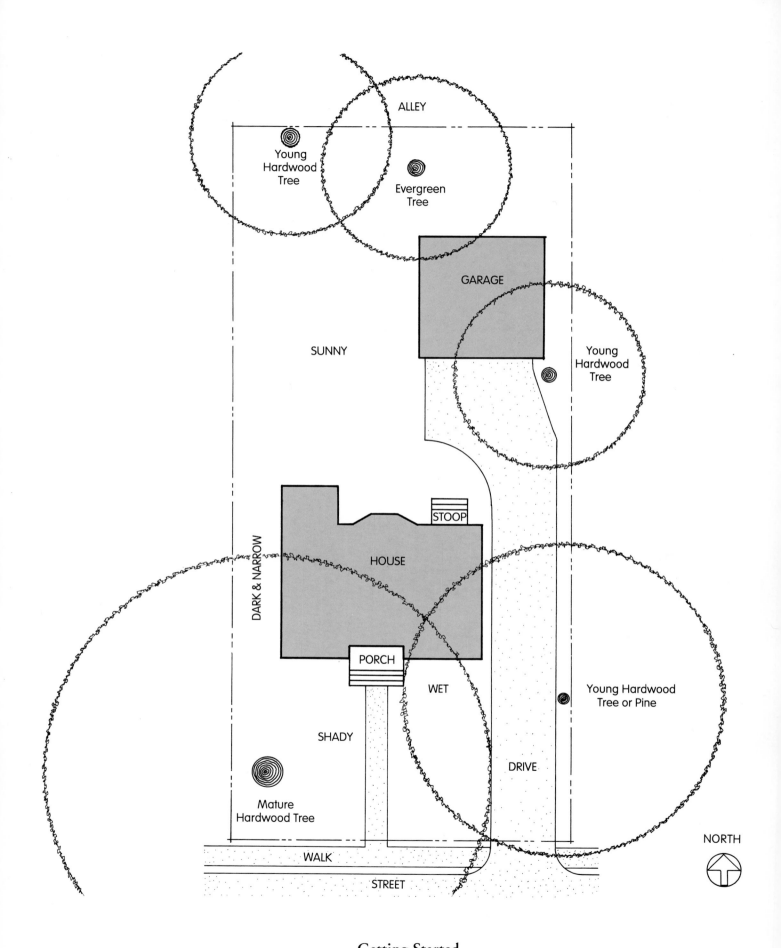

ALLEY

Young
Hardwood
Tree

Evergreen
Tree

GARAGE

SUNNY

Young
Hardwood
Tree

STOOP

DARK & NARROW

HOUSE

PORCH

WET

Young Hardwood
Tree or Pine

SHADY

DRIVE

Mature
Hardwood Tree

NORTH

WALK

STREET

Getting Started

The existing trees will be designated by dark, filled-in circles on the subsequent plans.

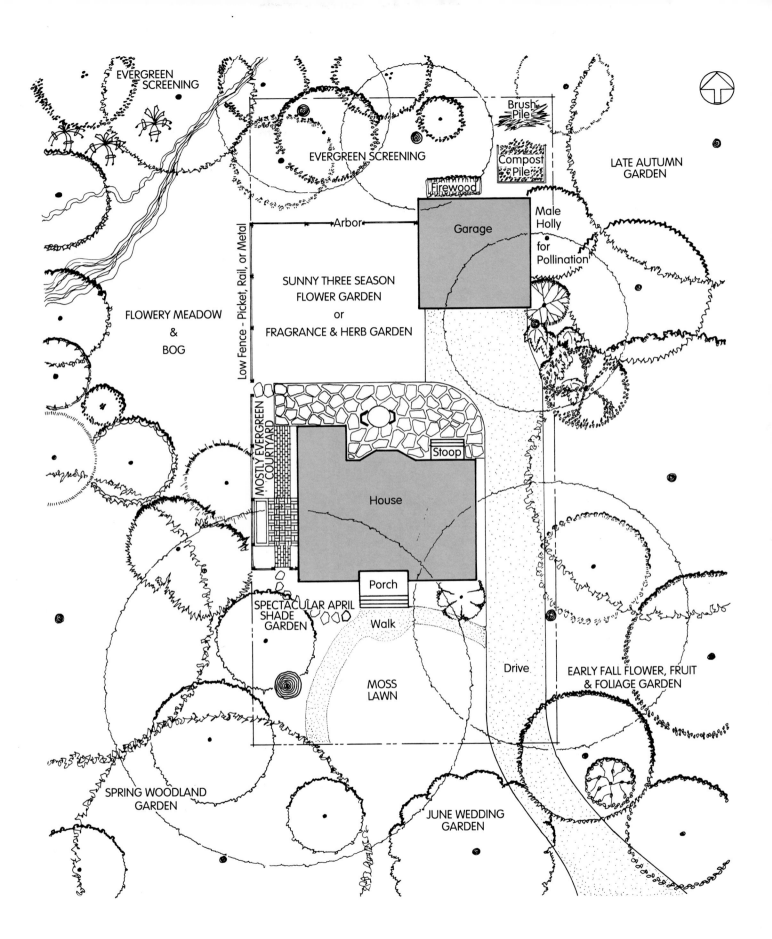

EVERGREEN
SCREENING

EVERGREEN SCREENING

Brush
Pile

Compost
Pile

LATE AUTUMN
GARDEN

Firewood

Garage

Male
Holly

for
Pollination

Arbor

SUNNY THREE SEASON
FLOWER GARDEN
or
FRAGRANCE & HERB GARDEN

Low Fence - Picket, Rail, or Metal

FLOWERY MEADOW
&
BOG

MOSTLY EVERGREEN COURTYARD

Stoop

House

Porch

SPECTACULAR APRIL
SHADE
GARDEN

Walk

MOSS
LAWN

Drive

EARLY FALL FLOWER, FRUIT
& FOLIAGE GARDEN

SPRING WOODLAND
GARDEN

JUNE WEDDING
GARDEN

Basic Plan

Mostly Evergreen Courtyard Garden

Nearly every home has a narrow, dark area that is difficult to landscape but *has* to look good because everyone can see it. In many ways, this type of area is not unlike those wonderful courtyards so typical of Charleston and New Orleans that many of us would love to imitate.

In tiny gardens like this, you usually want plants with the following characteristics: evergreen, pretty, not too big, contrasting textures, healthy, easy to take care of.

This plan introduces you to such plants. You've probably never heard of them, even though they literally used to live in your own back yard.

The garden in this plan is only 10 feet wide. A little brick patio divides up the area, so it doesn't seem too long and tunnel-like. The water feature and bench provide a focus and a purpose to the patio, but they don't block the wheelbarrow path that connects the front and back yards. Moss will probably want to grow on your bricks; don't fight it, enjoy the soft, restful look it contributes. The top (north) third of the courtyard is sunny. The middle third has morning sun, and the bottom third, where the tiny water garden is, receives shade all day.

The temptation for most gardeners, given a narrow, straight bed beside the house, is to plant a line of shrubs along it. This increases the tunnel effect and is extremely boring. Notice how the Christmas fern (your substitute for a short, manicured hedge) is positioned to make curves and clumps. Two are planted so close

to the walk that they cover part of it, softening what would otherwise be straight and rigid.

No single kind of plant will perform the same way in a wide range of sunlight conditions. Christmas fern is used only in the shady two-thirds of the walk. Where there is afternoon sun, there is an inkberry instead, chosen because it is dark green, like the Christmas fern, naturally well shaped and tidy, and it loves sun. I used only one as a specimen to enclose the open end of the courtyard. It will eventually make a dainty 9-foot-tall tree if you prune up the stems to make trunks. Or you can keep it about waist high. If you want a more tropical feel and you live on the warm Coastal Plain, choose a dwarf palmetto.

To give height to the garden, there are two vines on the fence (or wall). In the shadiest area is crossvine, which is fully evergreen. Where morning sun is received, there is coral honeysuckle. In early spring, it will be a shower of red.

The water garden is too shady for waterlilies and the usual water-garden plantings. In the big pot, you might have crinum lily, with its wonderful swordlike leaves, and fragrant summer flowers. It is almost evergreen in mild winters. If you live where it is not winter-hardy, you'll have to carry it inside. It can tolerate regularly moist pot-plant conditions (you don't have to keep it in the bath-tub) and it will remain fully evergreen. Or, you can use lizard's tail, my all-time favorite water plant, with its flowers that resemble white fuzzy tails. For low-growing softness around the big pot, use netted chain fern in the smaller pots. Keep the pots at one end, so

they are set off by a good stretch of water. The crossvine growing on the wall behind the clear water will provide enough ornamentation.

The two very large patio pots on either side of the bench contain itea. This shrub has young green stems, gracefully arching branches, and white tails of flowers in May that are similar to lizard's tails. In fall, a few of its leaves turn yellow, orange, or red, while the rest stay green.

For groundcover in the shadiest spots, use partridgeberry—a very dependable evergreen. It is low-growing, easily makes a solid carpet, has tiny, fragrant white flowers in spring and summer, and red berries in fall and winter. For an accent, plant one smilacina for midspring blooms of fluffy white followed by red berries in the summer.

Where there is more sun, add more flower color. Spigelia's red and gold blooms repeat those of coral honeysuckle. Butterweed provides yellow daisies as a spring accent. The rest of the year it's an evergreen groundcover. Use Wherry's foamflower instead if you prefer white to yellow.

These flowers and groundcovers can also take sun, so they are planted right up to the stone terrace. To give height and color in front of the inkberry, plant three New England asters. If you have chosen the palmetto, use low-growing Stokes aster instead; you don't want to crowd the palmetto leaves.

Beyond the inkberry (or palmetto) is a planting of pink coreopsis. Its fresh, yellow-green foliage sends a definite signal that the garden ahead is sunny.

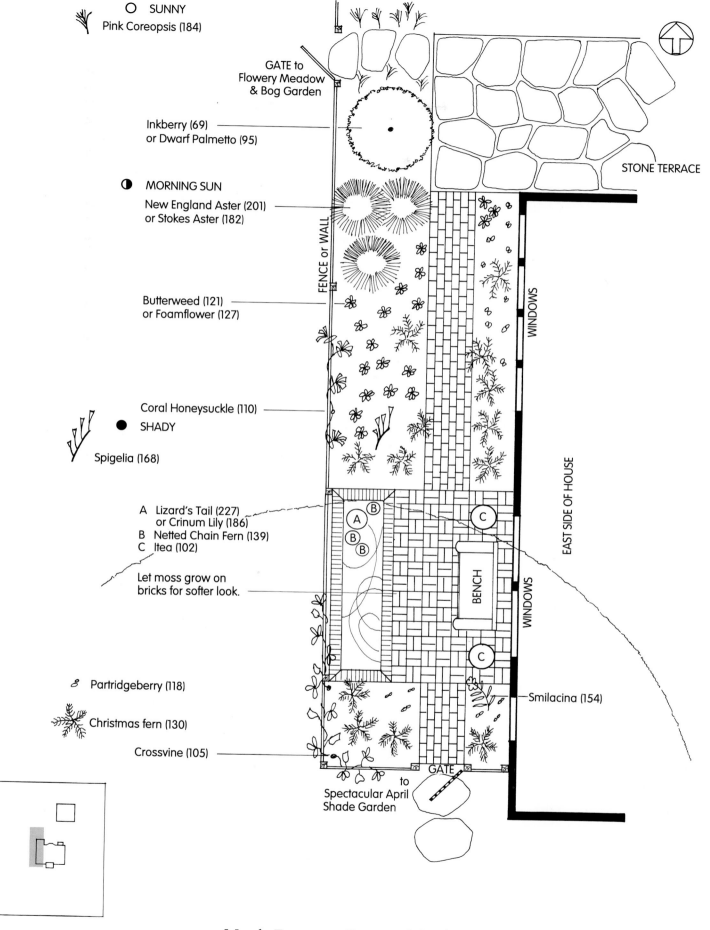

SUNNY
Pink Coreopsis (184)

GATE to
Flowery Meadow
& Bog Garden

Inkberry (69)
or Dwarf Palmetto (95)

MORNING SUN
New England Aster (201)
or Stokes Aster (182)

Butterweed (121)
or Foamflower (127)

Coral Honeysuckle (110)

SHADY

Spigelia (168)

A Lizard's Tail (227)
   or Crinum Lily (186)
B Netted Chain Fern (139)
C Itea (102)

Let moss grow on
bricks for softer look.

Partridgeberry (118)

Christmas fern (130)

Crossvine (105)

STONE TERRACE

FENCE or WALL

WINDOWS

EAST SIDE OF HOUSE

BENCH

WINDOWS

Smilacina (154)

GATE
to
Spectacular April
Shade Garden

Mostly Evergreen Courtyard Garden

Spectacular April Shade Garden

Great news! The front of your house doesn't have to have a mustache of evergreen shrubs around its base. You don't have to put up with that straight walkway that slices your front yard into two halves. And you don't have to maintain a lawn; if your front yard is so shady and acid that you have lots of bare dirt and exposed tree roots, then you're probably fighting a losing battle anyway. So why not have a lovely moss lawn and a shady flower garden instead? It will look a lot prettier, and your neighbors will give you credit for being industrious and talented, when really you're putting in less work. After the initial investment, it will also cost you less to maintain.

The most spectacular time in a shade garden is in April. The flowers on this plan are not dainty and shy. They will knock the socks off anyone just driving by your house. We saw them blooming at the same time just about everywhere we went. The color scheme is white, deep yellow, pure blue, lavender blue, and scarlet, and they are all quite easy to grow. All you need is summer shade under a deciduous tree, soil enriched by years of decomposing leaves or by digging or tilling in 4 to 8 inches of compost, and the ability to water if you're having a drought.

To give height to your shady April flower garden, add some shrubs and trees. Piedmont azalea, yellow azalea, and their hybrids tend to bloom at the same time as the spectacular shady flowers, as do serviceberry and two-winged silverbell. Flowering dogwood also often makes the show, so if you

have an existing, healthy dogwood, count it into the scheme. Let the azaleas get as big as they want. As you can see from the plan, just three shrubs, allowed to reach their full size, make a very pleasing composition. Don't be afraid you'll get burglarized if the shrubs grow up taller than your windowsills; no burglar will want to fight through them. And while these shrubs provide privacy from passersby, your own view out the windows won't be spoiled; you'll be able to look out through the branches to the street just fine.

The flowers are arranged in drifts or clumps, not in rows or as edging. Leave spaces between them. And don't be overly fastidious; there's nothing wrong with seeing decaying leaves and rich earth between their blooms. In those spaces the pink or silver fiddleheads of ferns will be thrusting up, as well as the leaves and buds of smilacina and other flowers that will bloom hard on the heels of this grouping. Foamflower and wild geranium are almost evergreen, so notice that there are no ferns or later-blooming woodland flowers planted on top of them. Look at the **June Wedding Garden** to see how June-blooming white flowers can be worked into this same plan. It and the **Spring Woodland Garden** are larger versions of this garden.

For the moss lawn, see the instructions under haircap moss (119). Don't worry about making this a perfect monoculture. If you look carefully at the ground under the mountain magnolia picture, you will see a lovely mixture of mosses, violets, and other low-growing groundcovers, all of which are mowed occasionally to keep them at an even smoothness.

Three-season Sunny Flower Garden

If I do say so myself, I rather outdid myself designing this flower garden. Of course, I had some help. Our daughter Melissa came up with the brilliant idea of putting the lattice on an angle. She also drew in the snaking path of flagstones. Each bend of the path provides a focal point for a visually delightful scene, and in this small space (approximately 35 feet by 35 feet) there are no less than 13 focal points—the dream of any garden photographer. The upper left corner, with the eryngo and the grasses, is stunning in its textures, and I have Edith Eddleman, co-curator of the perennial border at the arboretum at North Carolina State University, to thank for her good eye and inspiration.

Enter the garden from the stone terrace at the bottom of the page. In **April**, early for a perennial border, there is action at the far end, where two tall gate posts, joined by a rope swag, are entwined with coral honeysuckle. The scarlet trumpets with golden yellow throats are echoed in the copper iris. Deep blue iris and green-and-gold make this a vivid sight.

Then, there will be a lull while the rest of the garden gears up for the big spring bash. This occurs in **May**—early May in the Deep South and late May in the upper South—and continues on until the first part of June. Coming from the swagged archway, along the path toward the house, there is a new scene, now dominated by leaves. The dark green swords of the irises provide a striking contrast to the new growth of grasses, the silvery

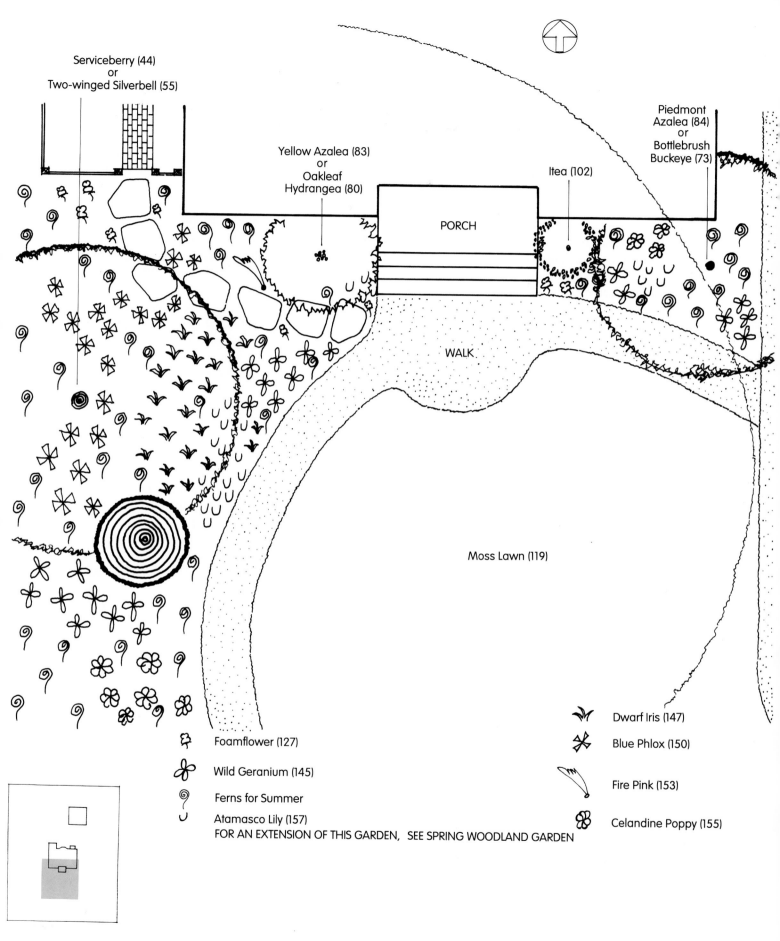

Serviceberry (44)
or
Two-winged Silverbell (55)

Piedmont
Azalea (84)
or
Bottlebrush
Buckeye (73)

Yellow Azalea (83)
or
Oakleaf
Hydrangea (80)

Itea (102)

PORCH

WALK

Moss Lawn (119)

Foamflower (127)

Wild Geranium (145)

Ferns for Summer

Atamasco Lily (157)

FOR AN EXTENSION OF THIS GARDEN, SEE SPRING WOODLAND GARDEN

Dwarf Iris (147)

Blue Phlox (150)

Fire Pink (153)

Celandine Poppy (155)

Spectacular April Shade Garden

grasslike leaves of silkgrass, and the fat, pale, cabbagelike leaves of giant rudbeckia.

Turn the corner, and this subtle beauty is replaced by a crisp scene of dark blue baptisia, bright blue phlox, pale bluestar, and lavender blue Stokes aster, contrasted with the clean white of thimbleweed and the deep yellow of eared coreopsis and sundrops. Turn the corner again, and the orange of butterflyweed accents a scene of whites and the pastel yellows of Carolina bushpea and yellow rudbeckia. The chartreuse of spikerush blends with this color scheme.

As you turn the corner again, that chartreuse is repeated by two plantings of feathery-leafed pink coreopsis, which will not be in bloom until summer. The flowers in this portion of the path are white Mississippi penstemon, white baptisia with its dark, steely gray stems, and the delicate pink of downy phlox and Small's penstemon.

Turn to the home stretch, and the pale pinks have changed to a variety of deeper pinks provided by beebalm. Masses of them are planted on either side of the path, filling the air with their minty sweetness. A spiderlily, with its bold, glossy, straplike foliage and tropical-looking white, fragrant flowers, marks where the stepping stones meet the terrace.

Midsummer—July and August—is dominated by pinks, whites, and yellows. There is not really a clear time line between one set of flowers and the other. Each has its own schedule, and there is considerable overlapping. Furthermore, each year the weather is a little bit different, which also causes bloom times to vary.

Starting from the terrace this time, Barbara's buttons, with its almost evergreen foliage, and redroot both provide white flowers. Threadleaf coreopsis and orange rudbeckia are both yellow daisies, although the latter has dark centers and is sometimes called perennial black-eyed Susan. To the left are three very tall flowers. Seashore mallow is pink, three-lobed rudbeckia is yellow, and joepyeweed is a soft pinkish purple. These three dominate the summer garden. But on closer inspection, there is a second focus—the lattice.

The lattice is covered with large, fancy passionflowers. On its left is a six-foot-tall cutleaf rudbeckia. This plant blooms well into the fall, and its large yellow daisy flowers are unusual in that they have green centers. That green is picked up by the foliage of pink coreopsis, now dotted with tiny pink daisies. Cattail gayfeather with its purply pink spikes provides a vertical accent.

Nearby, but deserving individual appreciation, is pineland hibiscus, with its creamy, scalloped trumpets, which have velvety red centers. There is also pine lily, its orange flowers placed next to the coral honeysuckle, which blooms intermittently all summer. The silvery lightness of narrowleaf mountain mint pulls together both the white flowers and the grassy textures.

Fall is often considered the season when the perennial garden shuts down. Not so. September and October are the heyday of grasses and the sunflower family. Swamp sunflower, goldenrods, wild ageratum, and asters are featured here, but in some parts of the South, other members of the family, such as gayfeather, joepye-

weed, and the rudbeckias, are also part of the fall scene.

The lower right corner, next to the terrace, is dominated by a trio often found blooming together on the Coastal Plain. The plumes of sugarcane plumegrass reach well over our heads; they start off dark red, turn to Indian red, then salmon pink, and finally silver, as all the flowers ripen to seed. Swamp sunflower, half its height, carries a profusion of yellow daisies. At its feet is knee-high wild ageratum—always blue to the eye but pink in photographs.

The upper left corner is all yellows, creams, and silvers. Brushy bluestem has showy, white, fluffy seed heads. Indiangrass has golden plumes of flowers. Both have pale, bluish foliage, which contrasts well with the dark green spears of eryngo, iris, and redroot. That pale color is echoed by the cannalike leaves of giant rudbeckia. Silkgrass pulls everything together. Its silvery leaves are topped by yellow daisies.

Other fall-flowering grasses in the plan are pink muhly and switchgrass. Beyond the back fence, there is a mass planting of inland seaoats. This is an easy grass to use where it is semishady and you don't want to weed. It has lovely lime-green seed heads in the summer, which are great in flower arrangements. In autumn, those seed heads turn either gold, rust, or ivory.

This is a garden for those who love to bring flowers into the house. Most of the flowers and the grasses last well as cut flowers, and cutting makes them bloom more, as they have to try again to make seed.

This is also a great garden for butterflies and hummingbirds.

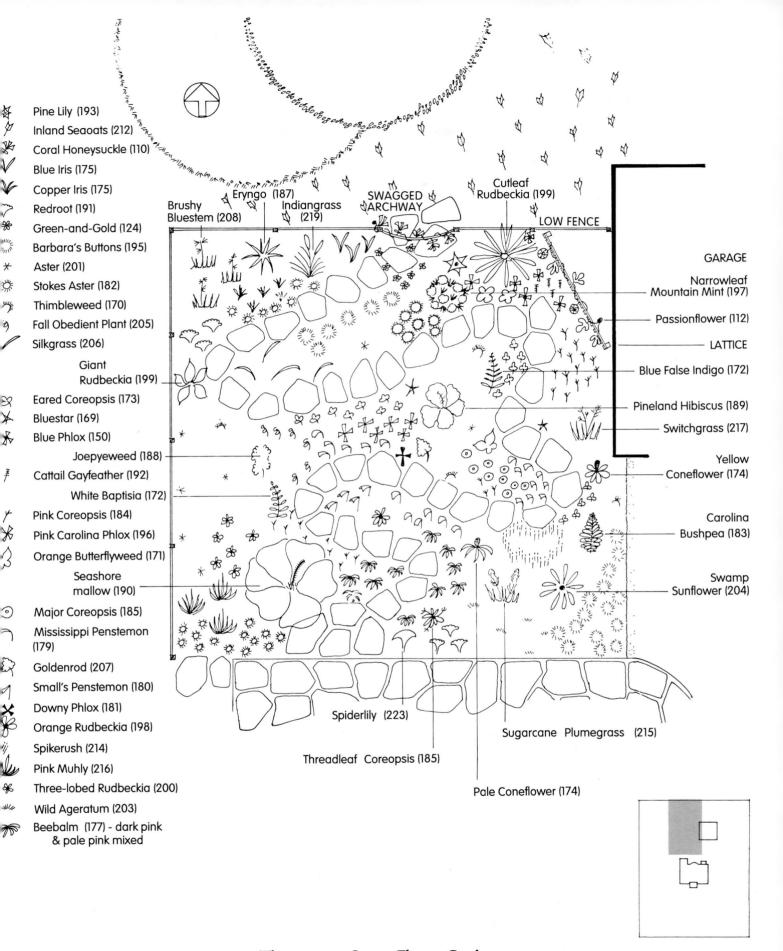

Pine Lily (193)
Inland Seaoats (212)
Coral Honeysuckle (110)
Blue Iris (175)
Copper Iris (175)
Redroot (191)
Green-and-Gold (124)
Barbara's Buttons (195)
Aster (201)
Stokes Aster (182)
Thimbleweed (170)
Fall Obedient Plant (205)
Silkgrass (206)

Giant Rudbeckia (199)

Eared Coreopsis (173)
Bluestar (169)
Blue Phlox (150)

Joepyeweed (188)
Cattail Gayfeather (192)

White Baptisia (172)

Pink Coreopsis (184)
Pink Carolina Phlox (196)
Orange Butterflyweed (171)

Seashore mallow (190)

Major Coreopsis (185)
Mississippi Penstemon (179)

Goldenrod (207)
Small's Penstemon (180)
Downy Phlox (181)
Orange Rudbeckia (198)
Spikerush (214)
Pink Muhly (216)
Three-lobed Rudbeckia (200)
Wild Ageratum (203)
Beebalm (177) - dark pink & pale pink mixed

Brushy Bluestem (208)
Eryngo (187)
Indiangrass (219)
SWAGGED ARCHWAY
Cutleaf Rudbeckia (199)
LOW FENCE

GARAGE
Narrowleaf Mountain Mint (197)
Passionflower (112)
LATTICE
Blue False Indigo (172)
Pineland Hibiscus (189)
Switchgrass (217)
Yellow Coneflower (174)
Carolina Bushpea (183)
Swamp Sunflower (204)

Spiderlily (223)
Sugarcane Plumegrass (215)
Threadleaf Coreopsis (185)
Pale Coneflower (174)

Three-season Sunny Flower Garden

Fragrance and Herb Garden

Imagine yourself sitting in your garden on a balmy evening, surrounded by marvelous scents. Or, picture yourself going out into your garden and gathering spicy leaves and pungent flowers for potpourri, wreaths, garnish, or tea. These are two excellent reasons to consider having a fragrance and herb garden.

Many of the South's most fragrant plants are trees and shrubs, and many have a strong preference for very acid soil, shade, and lots of moisture. Others need lots of sun and super drainage. To have this garden in its entirety and keep everything happy, you'd have to keep it moist but very well drained, and have a pH of 5.0 to 6.0.

If this is not your normal condition, for a less labor-intensive plan, choose whichever quadrant best fits your needs. To the left of the path are those plants that require very acid soil, pH 4.5 to 6. To the right are those that prefer moderately acid soil, 5 to 6.5, and the few, like Alabama croton and Allegheny spurge, that seem actually to like limestone. Near the back fence are plants that will take poor drainage at least once in a while, and near the terrace are those that tolerate or prefer drought. Sourwood, witchhazel, sweetshrub, fothergilla, and Alabama croton like moderate moisture best. Those that are under the two ornamental trees require shade, and those that are not, require sun. And some, like downy phlox, are extremely adaptable.

Witchhazel is the only fragrance you will get in the winter. It really prefers some shade, but will take full sun if you keep it watered. Wild ginger underneath has gingery roots, so it is fragrant only when you disturb the roots by weeding.

Reading from the top of the page to the bottom, those plants that have fragrant flowers are: southern magnolia, swamp honeysuckle azalea, vernal iris, Barbara's buttons, downy phlox, American wisteria, curly clematis, swamp rose, spiderlily, crinum lily, clethra, sourwood, fothergilla, sweetshrub, Allegheny spurge, summer phlox, witchhazel, beebalm, and prairie rose.

Those that have herblike aromatic leaves are: lyreleaf sage (smells great when you walk on it), sweetshrub, Alabama croton, Georgia basil, conradina, Cumberland rosemary, narrowleaf mountain mint, Oswego tea, beebalm, and red basil.

Other plants with sweetly scented flowers not on this plan but described in the book are: gordonia, basswood, sweetbay magnolia, buckwheat tree, sweetleaf, fringetree, yellowwood, titi, eastern persimmon, any of the bigleaf magnolias, sparkleberry, agarista, sandhill rosemary, spicebush, yellow azalea, Piedmont azalea, Alabama azalea, roseshell azalea, Carolina rose, storax, partridgeberry, and fragrant waterlily. They are listed in the order in which they appear in the book. Other plants with aromatic leaves are: eastern red cedar, pines, wax myrtle, redbay, swampbay, sweetleaf, pawpaw, spicebush, aromatic aster, and sweet goldenrod.

Spring Woodland Garden

If you have an eighth acre or more of front yard—or back yard—and you want to make your life a lot easier, then you definitely need to convert at least one of these areas into a woodland garden. The choices on this plan are indigenous for most Southerners, but not for all of you. To make this garden really work for you, use only plants that are native to your specific area.

If you are lucky, you will have enough existing canopy trees to provide dappled shade everywhere. Deciduous hardwood trees are best, but a few old pines with tiny, thin heads won't hurt a bit. You just don't want pine straw so thick underneath that the woodland flowers are smothered, or evergreen leaves so dense overhead that no sunlight can get through to warm the spring buds so they can become flowers.

The canopy trees should average about 50 feet apart where you want to make a graceful woodland garden. If you have too many, cut some down. Leave those that are the most desirable species, or the healthiest, or the best-placed, or those that are providing the most critical shade. If these criteria haven't narrowed down your choices, observe your trees for a whole season and, with flagging tape, mark those individuals that have the prettiest spring flowers (yes, some canopy trees do have spring flowers) or the most vivid fall color. If you presently have no canopy trees or not enough, plant only indigenous trees that will be self-supporting.

You will need at least one evergreen tree. If you have a southern magnolia, plant around it and let it stand as the backdrop for the other colors to play off of. If you don't, plant spruce pine or American holly or some other shade-loving evergreen tree native to your area. Be sure to choose

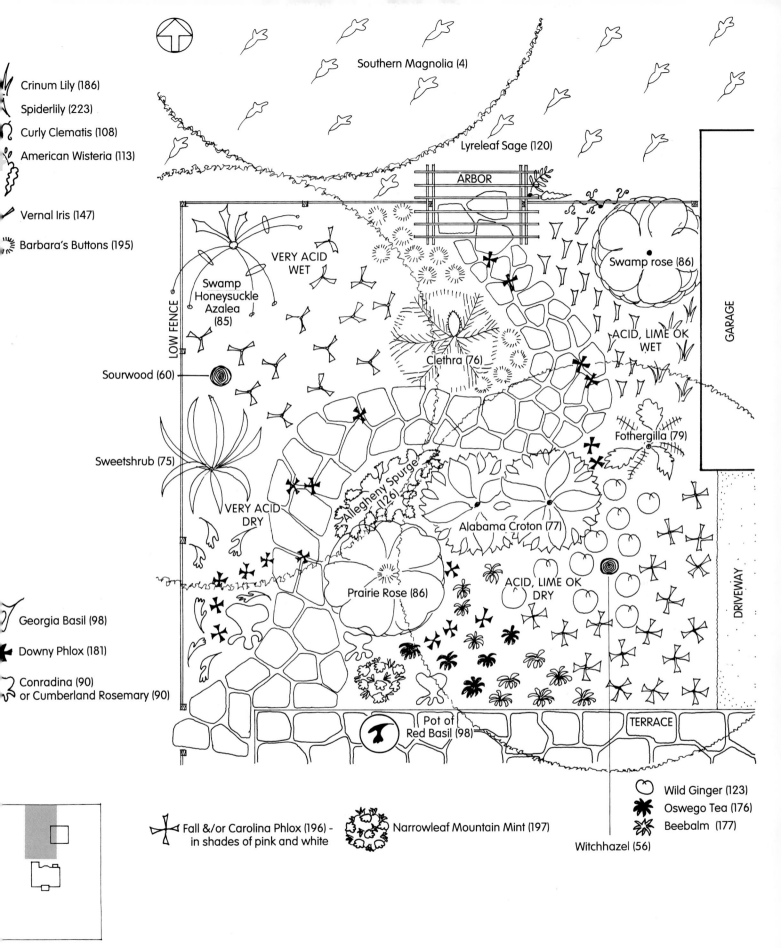

Legend (left column):

- Crinum Lily (186)
- Spiderlily (223)
- Curly Clematis (108)
- American Wisteria (113)
- Vernal Iris (147)
- Barbara's Buttons (195)
- Georgia Basil (98)
- Downy Phlox (181)
- Conradina (90) or Cumberland Rosemary (90)

Labels within the plan:

- Southern Magnolia (4)
- Lyreleaf Sage (120)
- ARBOR
- Swamp rose (86)
- VERY ACID WET
- Swamp Honeysuckle Azalea (85)
- LOW FENCE
- Sourwood (60)
- Clethra (76)
- ACID, LIME OK WET
- GARAGE
- Sweetshrub (75)
- Fothergilla (79)
- VERY ACID DRY
- Allegheny Spurge (126)
- Alabama Croton (77)
- Prairie Rose (86)
- ACID, LIME OK DRY
- DRIVEWAY
- Pot of Red Basil (98)
- TERRACE

Legend (bottom):

- Fall &/or Carolina Phlox (196) - in shades of pink and white
- Narrowleaf Mountain Mint (197)
- Wild Ginger (123)
- Oswego Tea (176)
- Beebalm (177)
- Witchhazel (56)

Fragrance and Herb Garden

one that will not need watering in your woods after you have gotten it established. This whole garden should be drought-tolerant.

As you plan your woodland garden, realize that although you are planting on a scale quite different from a flower garden, the principles are the same. Where you would plant a cluster of three to five phlox to get a good show in a perennial border, plant a cluster of three to five understory trees to make your woodland garden look its prettiest. They should be spaced from 30 to 50 feet apart.

If by any wild chance you have some existing native flowering understory trees, fit them into your scheme. If you or a previous owner already planted a number of healthy flowering dogwoods, use them as your basic understory tree, and add to them if you need to improve the shape of the cluster they make. If your dogwoods are getting some disease or you have no understory trees, use two-winged silverbell or serviceberry instead, as long as they are native to your area. Two-winged silverbell is better for the Coastal Plain, and serviceberry for the mountains. The Piedmont can use either.

After you have planned where your trees go, make a drift of shrubs about 15 to 25 feet apart. The Piedmont azalea is the easiest for most Southern gardeners, and, when massed in varying shades of palest pink to rose pink, it is hard to beat. If you live over limestone and have light shade, choose neviusia. If you have heavier shade, forget early spring color and go for the late spring/early summer color with oakleaf hydrangea or bottlebrush buckeye.

For the flowers underneath, start off with lavender-blue-flowered spotted phacelia and white-flowered isopyrum, as they spread quickly and give you a lot for your money. Southern lady fern, rather aggressive for a small garden, is perfect in this unwatered situation and gives you a fine ferny look for summer. After you have things started, gradually add mayapples, smilacina, Solomon's seal, and other woodland flowers native to your area. They'll multiply slowly, gradually turning your spring woodland into a very complex and satisfying garden.

June Wedding Garden

I suppose we could have called this plan May Wedding. The flowers in this plan bloom the last week in May in the Deep South and the first week in June in the upper South. We went with June because this is the month traditionally associated with weddings.

These flowers are all white, but sometimes have flushes of pink. I don't know why white is so popular this time of year. White flowers normally attract moths and bats, and it could be that these flowers are all pollinated by these creatures. However, being more of a day person, I know I've seen bees and hummingbirds on many of them. Certainly, white shows up best against the dark green of the forest fully leafed out for summer, which is why this makes such a wonderful and romantic garden for balmy June— or May—evenings.

To have white-flowered shrubs up near the house, use bottlebrush buckeye, itea, and oakleaf hydrangea. The idea is to be able to stand on the moss lawn or sit on the porch and be surrounded by delicate white blooms floating in the woods.

This plan is designed mainly for the Piedmont. Three of the woodland flowers—goat's beard, black cohosh, and bowman's root—are native to the upper Piedmont and mountains. Plant them in drifts as shown on the plan, and then let them self-sow and spread themselves wherever they want. The more the better. Where there is a little more sun, use American ipecac and Mississippi penstemon instead, or the palest Small's penstemons you can find. For the magnolia, choose bigleaf magnolia or umbrella tree, both of which have sweetly scented blossoms. The cooler your summers are, the more easily you can have ferns scattered all through this garden.

If you live in or near the mountains and your winters are so cold that oakleaf hydrangea and bottlebrush buckeye are not winter-hardy for you, use more mountain laurels or an early-blooming rosebay rhododendron. You can also use the mountain magnolia.

To make this garden accommodate itself to the Coastal Plain, use southern magnolia. The other magnolias will have finished blooming for you by this time of year. Anyway, one southern magnolia can perfume this whole garden. For the three mountain flowers, which wouldn't dream of enduring your summers, plant even more fly poison, or substitute masses of itea in moist areas and wild hydrangea where it is drier.

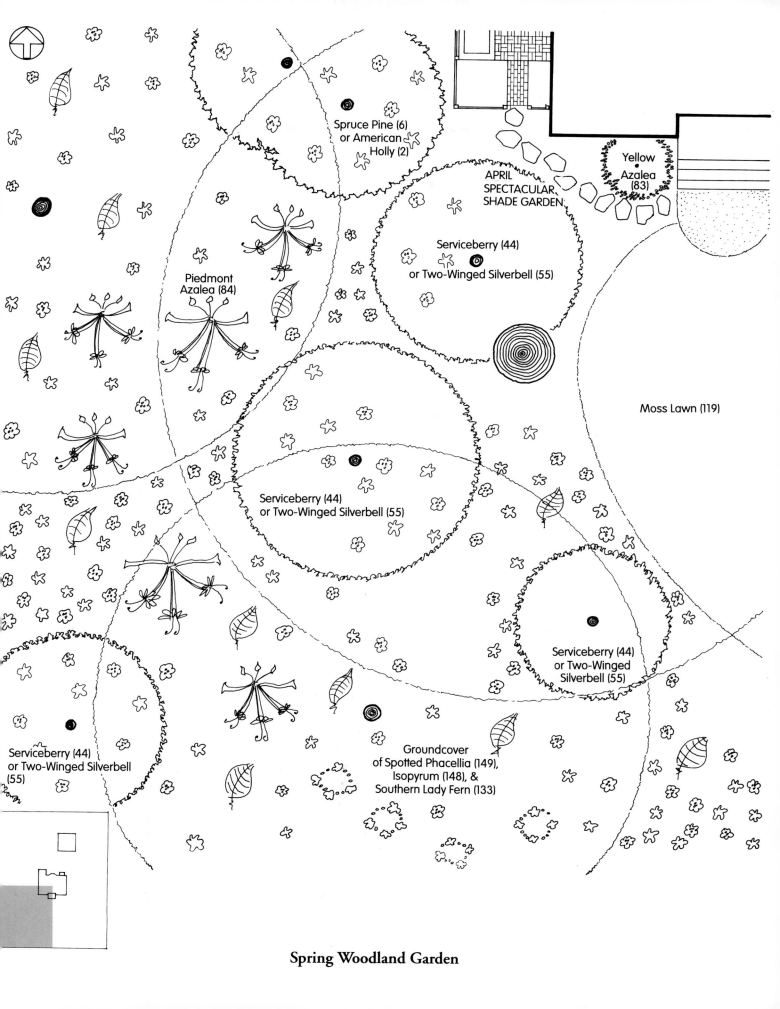

Spruce Pine (6)
or American
Holly (2)

APRIL
SPECTACULAR
SHADE GARDEN

Yellow
Azalea
(83)

Serviceberry (44)
or Two-Winged Silverbell (55)

Piedmont
Azalea (84)

Moss Lawn (119)

Serviceberry (44)
or Two-Winged Silverbell (55)

Serviceberry (44)
or Two-Winged
Silverbell (55)

Serviceberry (44)
or Two-Winged Silverbell
(55)

Groundcover
of Spotted Phacellia (149),
Isopyrum (148), &
Southern Lady Fern (133)

Spring Woodland Garden

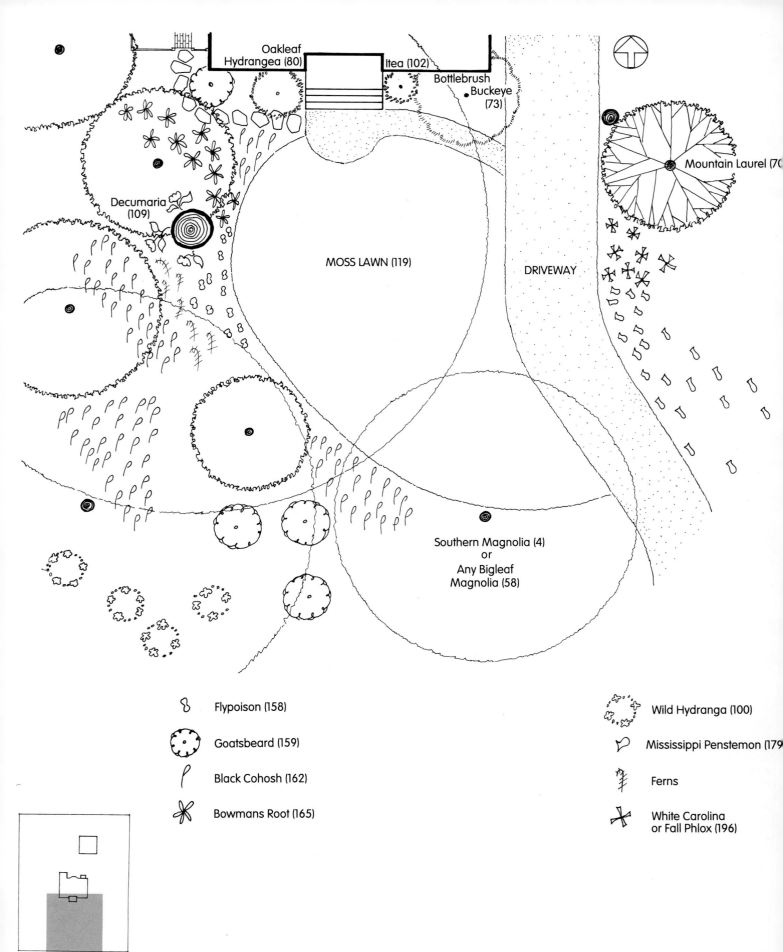

Oakleaf
Hydrangea (80)

Itea (102)

Bottlebrush
Buckeye
(73)

Mountain Laurel (70

Decumaria
(109)

MOSS LAWN (119)

DRIVEWAY

Southern Magnolia (4)
or
Any Bigleaf
Magnolia (58)

Flypoison (158)

Goatsbeard (159)

Black Cohosh (162)

Bowmans Root (165)

Wild Hydranga (100)

Mississippi Penstemon (179

Ferns

White Carolina
or Fall Phlox (196)

June Wedding Garden

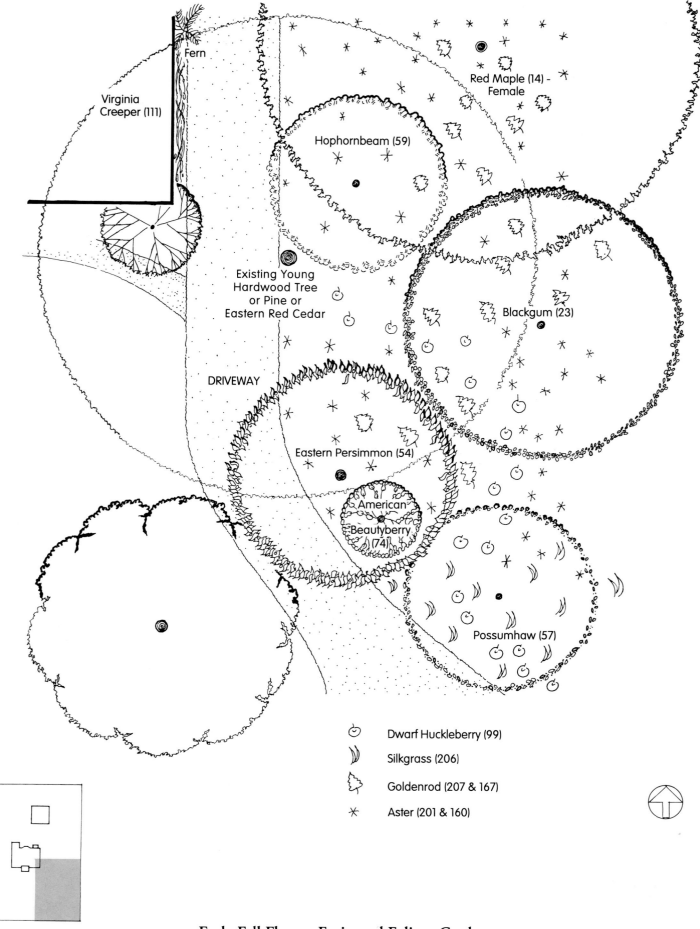

Fern

Virginia Creeper (111)

Red Maple (14) - Female

Hophornbeam (59)

Existing Young Hardwood Tree or Pine or Eastern Red Cedar

DRIVEWAY

Blackgum (23)

Eastern Persimmon (54)

American Beautyberry (74)

Possumhaw (57)

Dwarf Huckleberry (99)

Silkgrass (206)

Goldenrod (207 & 167)

Aster (201 & 160)

Early Fall Flower, Fruit, and Foliage Garden

Early Fall Flower, Fruit, and Foliage Garden

Most gardeners ignore early fall. They're aware of spring and summer, and they know when the maples turn, but everything in between somehow escapes their notice. This is amazing when you start listing all the flowers that bloom and the trees and shrubs whose leaves or fruits turn red or orange in the early fall. Fact is, this is a very active and often even gaudy time of year for the garden.

Another plus for these early fall plants is that they love sun, tolerate poor soil, and are drought-tolerant. Owners of new homes with scraped yards and no topsoil, first-time gardeners, and hopeless black-thumb gardeners can easily find success with these plants. If you have one or two pines or eastern red cedars in your yard and nothing else, that is also a perfect start for this garden.

Plus, if you are a bird-watcher, these plants and the habitat you create by planting them, are worlds better for your feathered friends than store-bought bird feeders.

This entire garden measures 90 feet by 40 feet, but the most intense color is in the lower area that is only 40 feet by 40 feet— a typical size for a small front yard. At the bottom right corner is a possumhaw. Its dry, fleshy red berries are not a treat to most fall-migrating birds. They'll ignore it and eat the juicy blue huckleberries, the orange persimmons, the blackgum drupes, and the purple fruits of American beautyberry. Small birds will pick the seeds out of the papery ornaments of the hophornbeam. But, when the birds return the following spring, they won't pass possumhaw by

this time, especially not the cedar waxwings. Over the winter, what with freezing and thawing, the haws have fermented, making your possumhaw the bird-equivalent of a neighborhood tavern. And now you know why they keep flying into your windows.

There are other wildlife opportunities in this garden as well. Warblers and other songbirds eat red maple seeds in the spring. Winter birds will enjoy the seeds of silkgrass, goldenrod, and aster. Butterflies sip the nectar of these flowers. The hophornbeam hosts several insects vital to the health of songbird nestlings. And raccoons and opossums, as well as humans, are exceedingly fond of persimmons.

Visually, this garden is quite a treat. The red maple usually turns red early, although it might wait and join the late fall garden planted in back of it. Either green or red, it is the backdrop. Hophornbeam has yellow leaves, blackgum has red, eastern persimmon has both leaves and fruit in shades of orange and mauve, and possumhaw is bright red with fruit. Underneath this glory are the tiny green leaves of dwarf huckleberry, setting off yellow goldenrod, blue or white asters, and yellow and silver silkgrass. American beautyberry, a favorite of mockingbirds, provides an accent of bright purple.

If you want to keep grasses out of this garden, you'll have to weed until the silkgrass and huckleberry have formed a solid groundcover. For a larger and really natural version of this garden, refer to the Flowery Meadow Garden.

Late Fall Color Garden

If you have a sweetgum that turns color late in the fall (some turn in early fall) or you've already planted a sugar maple, use it as the starting point for your late fall color garden. By the time these trees turn color, there have already been several frosts and most branches are bare. The flower garden has been cut back and put to bed under a blanket of leaves. This is the last stand in your garden until spring, unless you have a winter-blooming witchhazel.

Most plants that give pleasure in late fall are woodland trees and shrubs that are used to good soil and are able to develop under existing hardwood trees. The viewing angle is from the driveway or terrace. In front is a small, low thicket of shrubbery. Behind that are two small trees, then a canopy tree and an accent shrub. To the left of the thicket is an evergreen shrub for contrast and to block off visibility to the utility yard behind the garage.

To get a beauteous picture, you want to alternate red, yellow, orange, and pink, so that there is always a good contrast.

For the lower South, this is the best combination: Mapleleaf viburnum—the thicket shrub— might be pink, apricot, red, or purple. The musclewood to its right might be orange or scarlet or even yellow. Behind them is a chalk maple, again orange, scarlet, or yellow, with a dark red high-bush blueberry down below and a dark red white oak or swamp chestnut oak up above. Fall color is a matter of genetics, and to choose the shade you want, buy these plants at the nursery when they are in color. You can't always choose the timing of when they

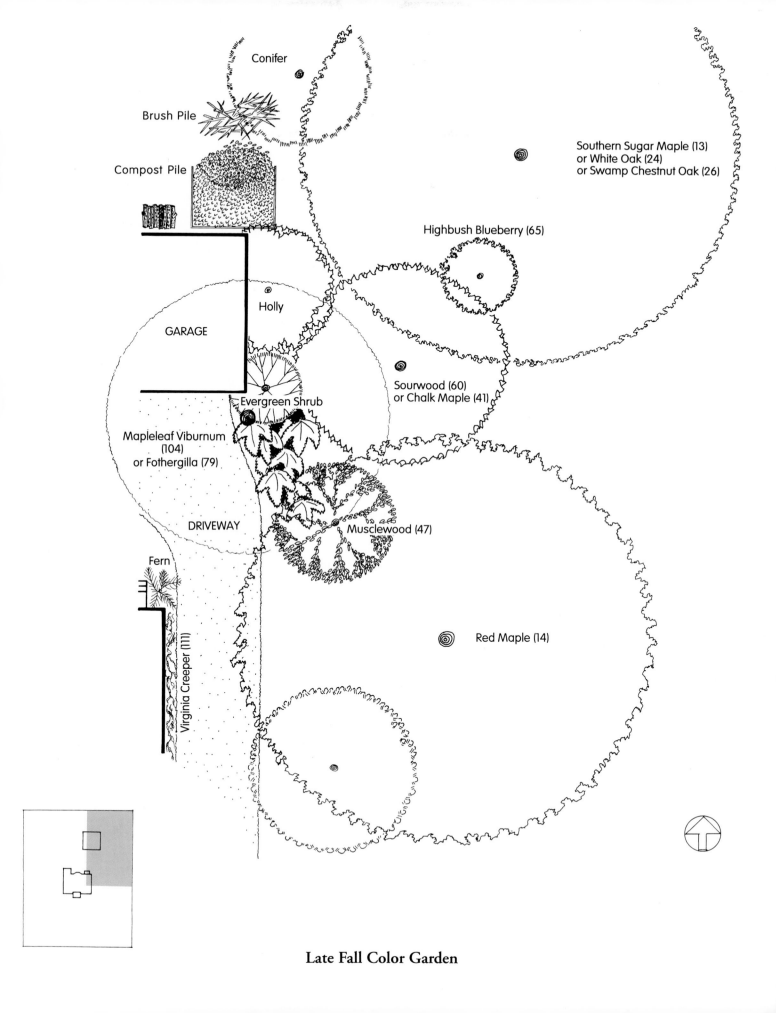

Conifer

Brush Pile

Compost Pile

Southern Sugar Maple (13)
or White Oak (24)
or Swamp Chestnut Oak (26)

Highbush Blueberry (65)

Holly

GARAGE

Sourwood (60)
or Chalk Maple (41)

Evergreen Shrub

Mapleleaf Viburnum
(104)
or Fothergilla (79)

DRIVEWAY

Musclewood (47)

Fern

Virginia Creeper (111)

Red Maple (14)

Late Fall Color Garden

color, because nursery stock often colors early.

For gardeners in Tennessee, North Carolina, and northward, the musclewood and highbush blueberry remain the same. But, although you can still have maple-leaf viburnum, you could also have fothergilla, which is sometimes red, orange, yellow, and green, all on the same leaf. In back of it you could have that wonderful tree, the sourwood, in front of a southern sugar maple or, in really cold areas, the northern sugar maple.

Flowery Meadow Garden

It was on the Coastal Plain that we frequently saw natural grasslands on private property. Almost always, the grasslands were wet in winter and spring and dry in the summer. Where the water table was high, wet areas and pitcherplant bogs were found. Where there were springs, sometimes a narrow channel of water had cut into the soft soil only to spread out into a bog in flat areas and resume its course where the land became rolling again. The stream banks were wooded and shady, but the bog areas were often grassy, sunny, and flowery especially if they had been maintained by fire.

On this plan, imagine the stream, narrow enough to step across, coming out of woodland in the top right-hand corner. At the meadow, it fans out into a bog on one side and grassland on the other. Then, it re-enters woodland.

In early spring, this landscape is abloom in yellow and white.

The meadow itself is golden with yellowtop, an annual that blooms from midwinter to midspring. Surrounding it are some of the South's most beautiful ornamental trees. These trees need to live on the edge of sunlight to be loaded with flowers and fruit. Many of you without a meadow will want to plant these trees around a lawn, patio, parking area, or some other kind of open space.

Starting from the bottom right corner is a fringetree, which is loaded with fragrant white ribbons of flowers just before the leaves emerge. The males of this species might be a tiny bit showier, but I have chosen a female here, because birds love the blue fruits in the fall. Next to it is a sassafras, dotted with tufts of bright yellow, again female for the same reason. The small tree/shrub is spicebush, with flowers similar to those on the sassafras, but intensely fragrant. Then, a sparkleberry hung with fragrant white bells, a parsley hawthorn with white flowers and lime-green trunks, a Walter's viburnum with clusters of white flowers set amid dark leaves, three very fragrant yellow azaleas, a cucumbertree with creamy, pale yellow magnolia blooms, and sweetleaf, whose fluffy yellow flowers smell like not-quite-ripe peaches.

Flowering in the bog are white, fragrant spiderlilies and copper iris set amid a short fuzz of lime-green spikegrass.

In summer, the bog is white with whitetop sedge. If you would like a tree blooming at this time, substitute titi for Walter's viburnum. It has 6-inch spikes of fragrant white flowers in mid-

summer. In the shade are masses of inland seaoats with their dangling green seeds. The meadow is green and grassy, but you could have creamy pineland hibiscus and redroot blooming.

In early fall, the scene is again full of color. Sassafras is golden and orange, spicebush is red with fruit, sparkleberry has red leaves, and pink muhly makes the meadow look like it is covered with a soft pink mist. Arising out of this mist are the golden daisies of swamp sunflower, the blue of wild ageratum, and the tall coppery plumes of sugarcane plumegrass.

Not so showy but well-noticed by the birds are the dark blue fruits of fringetree, sassafras, and Walter's viburnum, and the yummy red haws of parsley hawthorn. Butterflies, bees, songbirds, gamebirds, and mammals all see this kind of habitat as prime. There is shade, sun, trees, grasses, fruits, water—everything these critters want for sleeping, eating, nesting, and drinking.

For those of you in the Piedmont and mountains, substitute bluestems, switchgrass, and Indiangrass for the pink muhly. Choose flowers native to your area from the section on sunny garden flowers. Use alder instead of Walter's viburnum. Realize that you will have damp banks covered with moss and ferns—not a bog. Plant wild hydrangea, wild geranium, loosestrife, and other beautiful woodland plants.

To maintain a meadow, you must plan to mow, burn, or have an animal graze it in order to keep the woody plants from turning it into a forest.

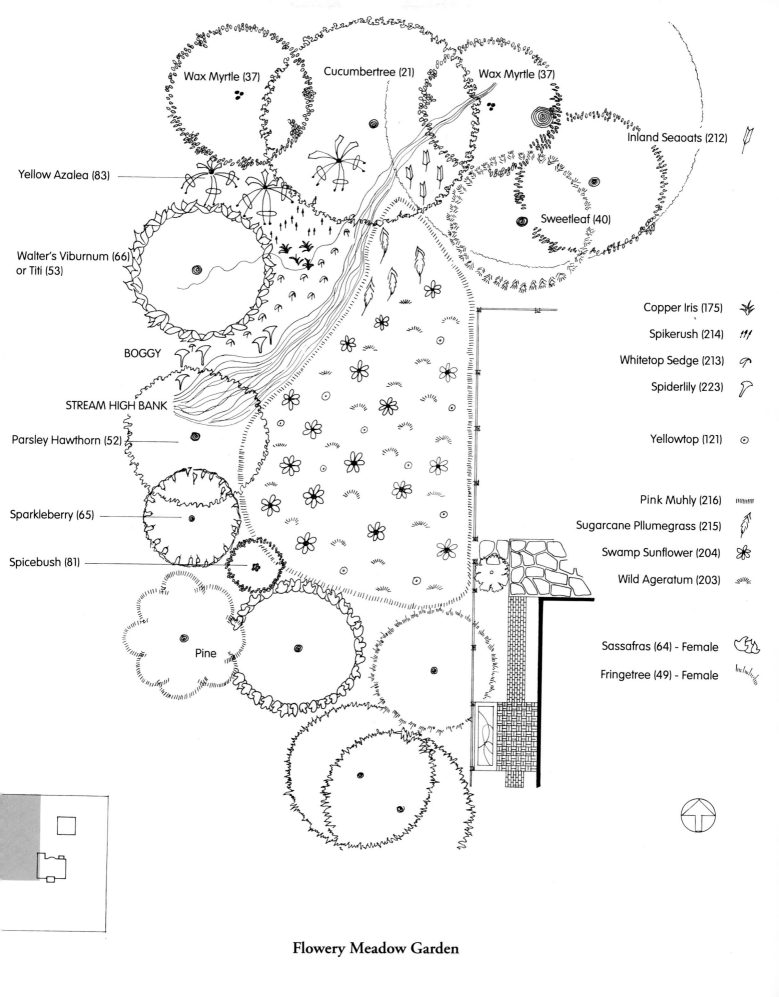

Wax Myrtle (37)

Cucumbertree (21)

Wax Myrtle (37)

Inland Seaoats (212)

Yellow Azalea (83)

Walter's Viburnum (66)
or Titi (53)

Sweetleaf (40)

BOGGY

Copper Iris (175)

STREAM HIGH BANK

Spikerush (214)

Whitetop Sedge (213)

Parsley Hawthorn (52)

Spiderlily (223)

Yellowtop (121)

Sparkleberry (65)

Pink Muhly (216)

Sugarcane Pllumegrass (215)

Spicebush (81)

Swamp Sunflower (204)

Wild Ageratum (203)

Pine

Sassafras (64) - Female

Fringetree (49) - Female

Flowery Meadow Garden

3

PLANT PROFILES: HOW TO USE THEM

The whole point of these profiles is to help you select the right plant for your growing conditions. You may be attracted by the pretty photo and want that native in your garden, but only by consulting the headings in its profiles will you be able to determine if that plant is going to work for you.

Before I tell you what these headings mean, let's look at the order I put the profiles in. I started off with a chapter on tall trees because landscapes are usually designed from top to bottom; the first element we decide on is the tall, or canopy, trees. Then, we get o the chapters on understory trees, then tall shrubs, then very short shrubs, and then vines. The evergreen members of each category of plant come first.

After you've made your decisions on these larger, more durable landscape plants, move on to the chapters that cover those low-growing plants that can be used in the shade: groundcovers, ferns, and woodland flowers. These first chapters constitute the easy-care portion of the book. The next three chapters are for sunnier, more human-contrived growing, and describe garden flowers, grass-

es, and water plants. True, these plants *do* occur in the wild, but normally only in situations where they are maintained by burning and grazing.

The profile headings are designed to give you all the basic information you'll need to make good selections for your area. Additional information, as well as personal observations and insights, can be found in the text that follows the headings.

What follows are definitions of those headings, as well as certain other terms you will run across in the book.

Latin Name
This is usually the most intimidating aspect of gardening for most people. But it's really not all that tough, and it *is* very important in making certain you get the exact plant you had in mind. For instance, let's say you want *Rhododendron austrinum,* which is a deciduous azalea with yellow-to-orange spring blooms that tolerates heat and high humidity. When you get to the nursery, all you remember is *Rhododendron* something-or-other, and you buy *Rhododendron maximum.* Close enough? Not really. The latter is a

taller evergreen shrub with pale pink summer flowers, and it doesn't like hot weather at all.

Plants have been given double Latin names since 1753, when the Swedish botanist Carolus Linnaeus first employed the system. The first name signifies the genus, while the second name signifies the species. These names may change from time to time, but having Latin names is still the most accurate method devised for universal identification. When a botanist from Latvia meets a botanist from Botswana, they can always talk plants.

One last comment: don't worry about pronunciation. Even the pros disagree. And when you add in regional accents, you'd have a tough time finding any two experts to concur. The commonly held opinion is, just pronounce it with a degree of authority and you'll be fine.

Common Name
Most plants have at least one. I've listed only the ones most typically used. Occasionally a common name is used for more than one plant, so knowing the Latin name can help tremendously.

Usual Height

This refers to the height the plant is most likely to reach in your garden. A tree might take thirty years or more to reach that height, a flower only one or two seasons. A woodland plant that reaches for the light might get much taller in a woods than it would get in full sun, where it has no reason to stretch.

Spacing

This measure gives the width of the plant at maturity or how far apart individual plants should be placed in a mass planting or for screening.

Sun or Shade

● Dappled shade all day. This is not the same as the absolute shade cast by a house, but the plants that have this symbol have the best chance of surviving there.

◑ Direct morning sun from 1 to 4 hours and dappled or absolute shade the rest of the day. This is usually slanting sun and the plant is protected from midday sun.

◐ Afternoon sun, which is hotter than morning sun, for 4 to 6 hours. There is often direct, overhead sun for some of this period.

○ Over 6 hours of direct sun or full sun all day.

Bloom

This heading gives you the normal bloom period (which can vary depending on the temperatures in a given year and also on whether you are in Zone 6 or Zone 9), color, size of blooms, and fragrance (if any).

Fiddleheads

See fern chapter introduction for definition.

Fruit

If a plant's landscape value is enhanced by seasonal fruits, I tell you the time of year to expect them, as well as their color and size. If the fruits are not a visual treat but are important for wildlife, sometimes I just give the time of ripening.

Leaves

Evergreen is green for at least a year. Some evergreens, such as live oak and sweetleaf, change leaves all at once in early spring. A few do this in August. Many evergreens lose and gain a few leaves off and on or at set times during the year, but always have enough leaves to look full.

Deciduous trees and most **herbaceous** flowers, groundcovers, and grasses lose their leaves in the fall and get new ones in the spring. Often these plants have wonderful fall color or lovely new spring growth.

Glossiness, summer shades of green, and size are included in this area when aesthetically relevant.

Trunk

Low or high branching—although almost all canopy trees are high branching in a woodland setting. Color and texture are given where visually significant.

Attachment

See vines chapter introduction for definition.

Native Range

Where the plant evolved or arrived on its own and grows without interference from us. Choose plants that are native to the habitat where you live, and your gardening experience will be more pleasurable and less hard work.

Zones are based on the 1990 USDA Plant Hardiness Zone Map.

Coastal Plain is the comparatively flat area by the Atlantic and Gulf coasts.

Piedmont is the rolling area that makes up the foothills for the Blue Ridge Mountains.

Mountains are the Appalachians, which include the Blue Ridge Mountains and the Great Smoky Mountains. The Ozarks and Ouachitas, which have many of the same plants, are not specifically covered in this book.

Mississippi River Basin includes the rich, dense, alluvial soils that you find for miles on either side of the Mississippi River.

Habitats:

A **bluff** is a slightly drier hammock in the Coastal Plain, often kin to post oak woodland in the Piedmont.

A **bog** is wet all year, but is flooded only part of the year. Usually a bog is a small area around a seep. Trees and shrubs are rare; grasses, herbs, or sphagnum moss are common. Sometimes in the Coastal Plain, the wet area is very large and spreads over claypan. In this case, it becomes a grassland dotted with trees, and is called a savannah.

Coves are sheltered areas in the Great Smoky Mountains where the hardwood forests are unusually rich in diversity. Some botanists speculate that they are similar to the very ancient forests that once covered most of the northern hemisphere before the last ice age.

Cypress swamps are wet all year and are dominated by trees. Pond cypress is in acid, peaty swamps. Bald cypress is usually in soil that is just slightly acid or almost alkaline, such as is found in river floodplains.

Flatwoods are pine savannahs that have not been burned for so long that the grasses have been shaded out by trees and shrubs. Flatwoods, like the savannahs, are flooded winter and spring because hardpan is close to the surface.

A **hammock** (also called hummock) is a moist area that is well-enough drained so that it is never wet. A Piedmont-style hardwood forest can grow in the Coastal Plain if it is on a hammock. A **calcareous hammock** has limestone for its bedrock, but the topsoil is generally acid in pH. A **coastal hammock** is alkaline, because its elevation is composed of limestone or shell middens left by Native Americans. Live oak, cabbage palm, and southern red cedar, along with yuccas, are typical vegetation.

A **hardwood forest** usually has some pines present—at least nowadays—but it is primarily composed of the most enduring deciduous trees, called hardwoods, and a great variety of beautiful woodland flowers and ferns.

A **marsh** is wet all year, but is composed of grasses instead of trees. Marshes might be fresh water, salt water, or in between, that is, brackish.

Meadows are grasslands, with flowers and no trees, that exist on soil that is moist or dry but not marshy. With few exceptions, meadows seem to be artificial to the forested southeastern United States. Most are maintained by the highway or parks departments by mowing or burning. Some people like to give meadows more dignity by calling them prairies.

An **old field** is recently abandoned farmland or other land that was denuded and then ignored. First annuals, then broomsedge and perennial flowers appear to make a meadow. Then, very quickly, pines and sweetgum start to grow to make a secondary woods.

Pinelands include savannahs, flatwoods, and secondary woods.

Pocosins are wet places where the water table intersects the surface in the sandhills. Where dependably wet, sphagnum peat bogs or pitcherplant bogs develop, or sometimes there is even enough water for waterlilies.

Post oak woodland is dry woodland. Most of it today is mixed with loblolly, shortleaf, Virginia, or longleaf pines. The soil is usually sterile and highly acid with little ability to retain water, although a fair amount of water-retaining clay sometimes exists.

Sandhills is longleaf pineland that is very dry with an understory of turkey oak. These are very old plant communities dating from the Cretaceous period. The soil is usually sterile and highly acid. Water runs through unless it hits a clay subsoil or hardpan that holds water close to the surface. In the Carolinas, Sandhills is a proper name for those communities at the fall line where Piedmont and Coastal Plain meet.

Savannah means grassland dotted with trees. In the southeastern United States, savannahs are usually flooded, or at least squishy-wet, in winter and spring and are very dry in summer and early fall. West of the Mississippi, this wet period becomes greatly reduced or nonexistent. Savannahs are dependent on fire to survive. Without fire, the grasses are shaded out and a forest, called flatwoods, forms.

Secondary woods were once old fields that have turned into forest. These woods are pinelands and quite different from the hardwood forests that the native Americans managed, the early European explorers described, and the European settlers cut down to make into fields.

Swamp is forested wetland bordering a bog or pond and often bordered itself by flatwoods. Swamps are usually very acid and peaty. Titi, pond pine, sweetbay, slash pine, and gordonia are the principal trees in a southern Coastal Plain swamp. Bald cypress swamps are common along the Mississippi River and other major rivers where the soil is less acid.

Soil

Where there is sufficient humus and leaf mold, all soils in the South are acid, even those that are over limestone. Acidity and its opposite, alkalinity, are measured in pH on a scale from 0 to 14, with 7 being neutral.

Very acid, pH 4 to 5. Sphagnum moss, hemlock, heaths (azaleas, mountain laurel, blueberries, etc.), and most pines require acid soil. Bogs, titi swamps, and sandhills are usually very acid habitats. The high acidity makes iron readily available and easy to assimilate.

Acid, pH 5 to 6. Most soils in the South fall in this range and nearly all Southern native plants will grow in this pH.

Acid to neutral, pH 6 to 7. This pH is found most often in alluvial soils—that is, soils left by river flooding.

Subsurface lime OK. When conditions are just right, acid or even very acid surface soil might exist over a substrate of limestone or beside limestone rocks. Many very acid-loving plants can grow on a marble or limestone hillside if their roots are in pockets of soil sufficiently deep, rich, and acidic for the plants to absorb the iron they need or where drainage is good enough for them to get sufficient oxygen.

Lime OK, pH 6.5 to 8. A few Southern plants show a preference for limestone areas, although most prefer rich, acid surface soil.

Clay OK. Some plants are moderately tolerant of a heavy soil consisting of clay loam or silt.

Drainage

Many gardeners think that drainage is more important than pH. How wet or dry a soil is has a lot to do with how much oxygen is available to the roots. Even wet soils must have some oxygen. Coarse, sandy soils have lots of spaces for oxygen. Silty or clay soils are denser and have less room for air.

Wet means the soil can be soggy at all times, but it has to be wet with well-oxygenated water. Water needs to be moving to pick up oxygen, although a brisk, running stream is not necessary. Even swamps move and you can see them do it if you look long and patiently. However, a sour, muddy spot in your yard can be entirely

devoid of oxygen, and no plant will live in such a spot.

Moist is ideal for most plants.

Dry in the South is a term reserved for coarse sugar sand such as is found in post oak woods or in the sandhills or in coastal dunes. Yuccas grow there, as do other relatives of desert plants. However, if you live outside the South, be warned that "dry" to a Southerner does not mean what it does to a Western gardener or even to a Midwesterner. Rainfall averages 40 to 60 inches a year or more in the South. Furthermore, it usually falls at least twice a month, even in the summer, which is the driest season.

Seasonal Flooding usually occurs in winter or spring in the South, although it might occur any time of year. Many Southern plants can tolerate being wet during a flood, although they can't survive being wet all the time.

Root System

Shallow roots are within the top 6 inches of soil. Plants with shallow, fibrous roots are usually easy to transplant and easy to get established.

A **taproot** usually signifies a deeper root system. These plants need more babying to get established, but then are more drought-resistant.

Colonizing is discussed extensively in the pertinent chapters.

Companion Plants

Each plant evolved as part of a community, a cell in a larger

organism. There are benefits to wildlife in imitating plant communities. Grouping plants according to their needs also makes gardening a lot easier and the plants much healthier. This heading lists a few of the plants that are most simpatico with the plant being profiled.

Propagation

This is a very complicated subject, and can only be touched on here. The serious amateur grower will want to consult more-detailed manuals.

Wildlife

Almost all native plants are important to native animals. Conversely, native animals are important to the plants; they aid in fertilization and distribution of seed, and they even divide roots when they dig up bulbs to eat or churn up muddy soil with their hooves. Generally, the most common plants are the ones used by the greatest number of species, or by species that are present in very large numbers. Because our songbirds, hummingbirds, and butterflies are declining in numbers, I have concentrated on information to help you attract them. There is more information on this in the chapter on attracting wildlife.

Related Species

Sometimes there is a closely (or distantly) related species that is also desirable in the landscape, and might be more appropriate or available in your area. If it is not profiled elsewhere in the book, it will be listed under this heading.

4

TREES OVER 50 FEET TALL

I had considered labeling this category "Canopy Trees," rather than going by height. But the over-50-feet category doesn't include only canopy trees in much of the Southeastern United States. Here the soils are often loose and deep, rainfall is usually ample all year round, and forests are created with canopy trees that grow to well over 100 feet tall. As a result, you can find some understory trees that reach over 50 feet high—southern magnolia being a prime example.

I'm writing this, not from nature's perspective, but from the perspective of you, the homeowner. I figured that you'd be most interested in knowing just how big that tree you're planting is going to get. So, all the trees in this category are likely to exceed 50 feet, and have a commensurately large trunk of at least one and a half feet in diameter.

For most of you, these trees will get a good deal taller, although probably not for 40 years. These large trees have the ability to live at least a century, and many species normally live two to three times that long.

If you are creating a woodland landscape and you plant your trees no more than 50 feet apart,

they will grow tall and slender and join at the top to form a continuous canopy of leaves. But, if you plant just one tree—a **specimen** tree—and it gets all the sunlight and elbow room it needs to reach to its full potential, then it will not become as tall, but it will become broader and fuller. Either way, you'll eventually get lots of shade. It's just that the woodland will cover over in 25 years or less, while the solitary specimen will take 50 to 75 years to deliver maximum shade.

Soil is a major factor in how tall a tree will grow. If you live on the kind of rich, tight clay where corn and other grasses grow better than trees, or if you live on very thin soil over rock, your canopy trees may reach only 50 or 60 feet—even though these same species get up to 120 feet tall over in the next county.

One place where you can see a dramatic example of this is on the Natchez Trace, where the Chickasaw Indian Village once existed. Here you'll find rich prairie clay—and scrubby trees. Sweetgum and white oak grow shorter here than they do a few miles down the road, and pines are replaced by smaller eastern red cedars. You see a lot of sky here,

and redbuds bloom passionately in the spring sunshine. Wildflowers and grasses provide nectar and pollen for bees and butterflies from spring to October.

But on either side of the village site, the Natchez Trace runs like a tunnel through a forest of sweetgums, oaks, and pines that are so tall, the sky is almost hidden, and big-leafed magnolias and hydrangeas (understory) line the road, jostling for a bit of sun. In early spring, before the deciduous canopy trees have leafed out, there are carpets of woodland flowers, replaced in the summer by ferns or, more often, a rich duff of fallen leaves.

The trees in this chapter are the basic **building blocks** for either scene. The canopy trees are what set the tone for the entire landscape. They determine the height and scale, their leaf fall rebuilds the soil so that the most desirable of the woodland species can eventually be planted, and the spread and density of their crowns determine the amount of shade.

They are also the least flexible members of your landscape. Because their root systems are so wide and deep, and because they are so long-lived, they must be perfectly adapted to the soil, rainfall, temperature swings, and other quirks of nature that can occur over their one- to three-century lifespans.

Select your canopy trees wisely. The trees that would most likely be growing natively on your site are the ones you want. Check these headings in the profiles: native range, hardiness zones, soil types, amount of moisture, and companion trees should tell you what you'll need to know to match the tree to the site successfully.

If you plant a canopy tree that is ill-suited to its environment, it will become stressed, sickly, and a target for unwanted insects and diseases that will affect your entire landscape. If it requires more water than normal rainfall can provide, making it necessary for you to make up the difference, then all the plants underneath will be overwatered and unhealthy. Once established, a canopy tree *must* be able to exist on what nature alone provides. (This is something I wish members of those plant-a-tree organizations would understand; too often they encourage the planting of trees that are not adapted to the areas where they are distributed.)

The canopy trees that I've elected to include had to meet one or more of these three criteria: (1) they had to be *the* important element of their habitat, the linchpin without which the plant community would fall apart or be drastically changed, (2) they had to be beautiful, or (3) they had to be easily obtained in the nursery trade.

The hickories have been slighted in comparison to the oaks, because they are, unfortunately, so rarely grown commercially. American chestnut (*Castanea dentata*) used to be a linchpin in southern hardwood forests, but it was attacked by a chestnut blight that arrived in New York in 1904. Genetic engineering may be close to finding a solution to the problem, but as of this writing, chestnut sprouts from ravaged stumps die back every year from renewed infections. So, it was not included. I also left out the elms. The prettiest one, American elm (*Ulmus americana*), has been decimated by another imported fungus, Dutch elm disease. A biological control is being implemented and a single clone, 'Liberty,' has been developed.

Planting

It's much better to plant a native tree in native soil. Use organic matter only as a **top mulch,** renewing it periodically. Eventually, your tree will produce enough leaves of its own to provide sufficient top mulch, which will decompose into rich humus, just the way nature does it in the forest.

After placing the tree in the hole and backfilling with the soil you dug out, water the tree thoroughly to remove all air pockets from the soil around the root ball. Then, give the tree a long, slow drink; leaving the hose on overnight at a bare trickle. During the first summer, if you don't get rain for two weeks, repeat this watering process. At other times during the first year, repeat when there is no rain for a month. Use good sense here. Actually feel the ground with your fingers. If the soil is moist, don't water. If your tree is looking thirsty and the soil is dry more than an inch down, *do* water.

After two summers, your tree should be home free and able to survive without any more help from you. Unless, of course, you planted the wrong tree for your site.

EVERGREEN TREES OVER 50 FEET TALL

Evergreen trees, because they stay green all winter, are the backbone of a garden's design. They serve as a backdrop for the flowers of spring and summer and as a foil for the colorful leaves of fall. But, they are not just aesthetically important, especially in winter. Then they provide essential shel-ter from wind and cold for birds and butterflies that are wintering over—as well as other insects and small mammals. The seeds and sap of pines and other conifers withstand the rigors of winter to provide food for many of these creatures.

Native plants make a pleasant parklike atmosphere at these apartments in Ponte Vedra Beach, Florida. Pictured are four indigenous evergreens: longleaf pine, wax myrtle, redbay, and dwarf palmetto.

1. **Latin Name** *Gordonia lasianthus*
   Common Name Gordonia, loblolly bay
   Usual Height 30 to 60 feet, champion at 84 feet
   Spacing 30 feet, a narrow crown
   Sun or Shade ◑ ◐ ○
   Bloom White, 2 to 3 inches across, fragrant, July (May to September)
   Fruit Tan, hard and dry, fall
   Leaves Evergreen, 3 to 6 inches, dark, glossy, leathery, with a few turning red and dropping now and then during the year
   Trunk Dark brown or gray, furrowed
   Native Range Wet habitats, flatwoods, low hardwoods, cypress swamps, coastal North Carolina to Mississippi, Zones 8 to 9
   Soil Acid, rich preferred
   Drainage Wet to moist
   Root System Shallow
   Companion Plants Longleaf, slash or pond pines, bald or pond cypresses, sweet bay, swampbay, sassafras, wax myrtle, sweetleaf, staggerbush, highbush blueberry, fetterbush, inkberry, saw palmetto
   Propagation Seed or greenwood cuttings
   Wildlife Browsed by deer; host insects important for feeding songbirds and their babies

   Gordonia can be used as a canopy tree, doing very well with full to partial sun, or as an understory tree, tolerating a fair amount of shade. If you plant it as understory, you'll find that it does best under those trees that are open enough to allow in lots of light. Gordonia starts blooming while it is still very small. Instead of bursting into bloom all at once, the gordonia's flowers open one at a time, giving you an extended bloom period of two to three months.

2. **Latin Name** *Ilex opaca*
   Common Name American holly
   Usual Height 40 to 50 feet, occasionally 100 feet
   Spacing Needs 30 to 45 feet at base, top is pyramidal and fits under canopy trees
   Sun or Shade ● ◑ ◐ ○
   Bloom Yellowish white, tiny, spring
   Fruit Red, sometimes orange or yellow, opaque, on female trees, late fall to spring
   Leaves Evergreen, glossy, dark green, spiny
   Trunk Single or multitrunked, light gray, mostly smooth, pale with lichens
   Native Range Floodplains and uplands, with hardwoods and pines, eastern U.S., Zones 6 to 9
   Soil Acid, rich or poor
   Drainage Wet, moist, or dry
   Root System Shallow
   Companion Plants Under any canopy trees with musclewood, pawpaw, flowering dogwood, sourgum, rhododendrons, blueberries, huckleberries, titi, redbay, sweetbay, hawthorns
   Propagation Stratified seed or cuttings taken in late summer; sex of seedlings cannot be determined for 5 to 12 years
   Wildlife Fruit eaten by bluebird, robin, catbird, flicker, thrush, cedar waxwing, mockingbird, woodpecker, brown thrasher; larval plant for Henry's elfin butterfly

   American holly is one of the South's most versatile evergreens. It grows in almost every habitat from sandhills to swamps to mountain coves. It's the female that has the lovely red berries, so that is the one you'll want in your landscape. But you'd better plant a male as well to assure a good berry crop—unless, of course, there are plenty of males in the immediate neighborhood. The males are good landscape trees, too, being tall and evergreen, with pretty pale trunks; they just won't provide bright red fruits to attract birds and cheer up the winter scene.

3. **Latin Name** *Juniperus virginiana*
   Common Name Eastern red cedar
   Usual Height 40 to 50 feet, maximum of 90 feet
   Spacing 10 feet for screening, 30 feet for specimen
   Sun or Shade ○
   Bloom Male and female on separate plants, winter
   Fruit Female has blue "berries" in winter for wildlife
   Leaves Evergreen, bluegreen to yellow-green
   Trunk Straight, silvery or reddish
   Native Range Well-drained, sunny sites, all over South except in high mountains, eastern half North America, Zones 5 to 9
   Soil Any, but neutral to alkaline preferred
   Drainage Dry
   Root System Taproot
   Companion Plants Post oak, black oak, white ash, persimmon, redbud, sparkleberry, sourwood, loblolly pine, shortleaf pine
   Propagation Seed sown outdoors in fall, or scarified and stratified
   Wildlife Fruit eaten by cedar waxwing, purple finch, bluebird, other songbirds, squirrel and opossum; provides nesting for hummingbirds, juncos, myrtle warblers, mourning doves, and small mammals; a larval plant for great purple and olive hairstreak butterflies
   Related Species Some recognize the coastal *J. silicicola*, southern red cedar, as different

Eastern red cedar is tolerant of alkalinity, salt, and urban pollution. European settlers planted cedars on either side of their front doors as a good luck charm—possibly because they are so long-lived. Many cultivars of eastern red cedar are available, but they are mostly northern forms. The South needs to develop its own cultivars with blue-green foliage, lacy weeping foliage, and other lovely attributes. However, the winter color of even the most ordinary cedar is extraordinarily rich in the depths and highlights of its greens.

4. **Latin Name** *Magnolia grandiflora*
   Common Name Southern magnolia, bull bay
   Usual Height 60 feet, may get over 100 feet tall
   Spacing 50 feet for specimen, 20 for woodland, 10 for screening
   Sun or Shade ● ◐ ◑
   Bloom Late May and June, creamy white, 6 to 9 inches, fragrant
   Fruit Shiny red seeds in cone, early fall
   Leaves Evergreen, heavy, shiny; old leaves fall as new ones appear in spring
   Trunk Smooth, gray, knobby if branches cut off when mature
   Native Range Lowland woods, swamp margins, dunes, Coastal Plain from East Texas to North Carolina, Zones 8, 9
   Soil Any, but deep, rich, preferred
   Drainage Moist
   Root System Shallow, prefers 2- to 4-inch leaf mulch to groundcover
   Companion Plants Beech/maple, or live oak/palmetto, or pine/hardwood forest
   Propagation Fresh seed sown in fall, stratified seed
   Wildlife Good nesting and shelter for many animals; seeds eaten by yellow-bellied sapsucker, red-cockaded woodpecker, and red-eyed vireo

This stately, fragrant **southern magnolia** symbolizes the plantations of the Deep South. When a magnolia grows in shade, the lower branches shed and a smooth, pale gray trunk is exposed. If yours grows in full sun, allow its lower branches to remain as protection for the root system. That's why most homeowners plant their southern magnolia away from the house, where it can dominate one corner of the yard. To screen high utility wires, plant your southern magnolias ten feet apart so they'll grow tall and narrow. For a magnolia woods, plant them about twenty feet apart with beeches or live oaks.

5. **Latin Name** *Pinus echinata*
   Common Name Shortleaf pine
   Usual Height 50 to 100 feet, occasionally 120 feet
   Spacing 30 feet for a specimen, 15 feet for a cluster
   Sun or Shade ◑ ◐ ○
   Bloom Lavender male flower, pink female flowers, early spring
   Fruit Small 1- to 2½-inch cones remain for years
   Leaves Evergreen, blue-green, 2- to 5-inch tufts of needles, 2 to 3 per bundle
   Trunk Straight, red-brown plates
   Native Range Upland sites and old fields, eastern U.S., Zones 6 to 9
   Soil Acid, sandy
   Drainage Dry
   Root System Taproot
   Companion Plants Post oak, black oak, southern red oak, eastern persimmon, sassafras, sparkleberry, flowering dogwood
   Propagation Fresh untreated seed sown in fall
   Wildlife Seed eaten by ground dove, quail, wild turkey; pine needles eaten by grouse and used for nests by songbirds

Shortleaf pine is ideal for sugar sand and other dry sites where many Southern trees cannot grow without lots of extra watering and care. It has a somewhat open texture, with short tufts of needles and a profusion of tiny cones high up in the branches. This allows plenty of sunlight down below so you can have a colorful garden of ornamental grasses and flowers. Sassafras, sparkleberry, flowering dogwood, and eastern persimmon might be used to provide color in the spring and fall. Young oaks of the right kind (see above) should be planted among the pines.

6. **Latin Name** *Pinus glabra*
   Common Name Sprucepine
   Usual Height 60 to 100 feet, occasionally 120 feet
   Spacing 20 to 30 feet
   Sun or Shade ● ◑ ◐ ○
   Bloom Male flowers yellow, early spring
   Fruit Tiny, ½- to 2-inch pinecones, often holding 3 to 4 years
   Leaves Evergreen, dark green, pairs of 3- to 4-inch needles, slightly twisted
   Trunk Pale to dark gray, ridged
   Native Range Rich woods and hammocks, Coastal Plain from eastern Louisiana to South Carolina, Zone 8
   Soil Acid, rich, sandy loam preferred
   Drainage Moist to dry, shallow flooding for a short duration
   Root System Taproot
   Companion Plants Beech, southern sugar maple, white oak, tulip poplar, basswood
   Propagation Fresh seed sown in fall
   Wildlife Seeds eaten by birds and mammals, needles used to build nests, branches used for nesting and cover

A gloriously dark and lustrous green, **sprucepine** is a wonderful backdrop for the pinks and whites of spring flowering understory trees—or the golds and scarlets of fall foliage. Most pines grow only on raw, abused land. They are pioneers. Sprucepine likes to grow in a rich, established woodland under the shade of old oaks and other hardwoods.

7. **Latin Name** *Pinus palustris*
   Common Name Longleaf pine, Georgia pine
   Usual Height 80 to 125 feet
   Spacing 50 feet for woodland, 20 feet for a cluster
   Sun or Shade ○
   Bloom Male and female flowers purple, early spring
   Fruit Big cones, 6 to 10 inches long
   Leaves Evergreen, medium to dark green needles 8 to 18 inches
   Trunk Tall, straight, high-branching, with thick, fire-resistant bark
   Native Range Sandhills, scrub oak, flatwoods, savannahs, Coastal Plain from North Carolina to eastern Texas, Zones 8 to 9
   Soil Acid, sandy, some clay mixed in OK
   Drainage Wet in winter-spring, dry in summer
   Root System Taproot, plant one-year-old seedlings
   Companion Plants Turkey oak, post oak, wiregrass, little bluestem, wax myrtle, yaupon, blueberry, staggerbush, Carolina jessamine
   Propagation Fresh seed sown in fall
   Wildlife Extensively used by wildlife. Especially important to the red-cockaded woodpecker

Longleaf pine is the linchpin of sandhill, flatwood, and similar plant communities found in the Southern Coastal Plain. For a small home landscape, plant plenty of bracken fern beneath these trees, along with yaupon, wax myrtle, staggerbush, and other flatwoods evergreens. For a large property, you can use fire to maintain a longleaf pine savannah. Fire keeps the evergreens out so there is plenty of sunlight under the pines for scrub oaks, grasses, wildflowers, and longleaf pine seedlings. Seedlings spend their youth looking like large clumps of fine-leafed grass. After developing a giant root system, they shoot up six feet in one season.

8. **Latin Name** *Pinus taeda*
   Common Name Loblolly pine, old field pine
   Usual Height 60 to 100 feet
   Spacing 10 to 50 feet
   Sun or Shade ○
   Bloom Male and female flowers yellow, early spring
   Fruit 3- to 6-inch cones
   Leaves Evergreen, 6- to 9-inch needles in bundles of 3
   Trunk Reddish, short with low branches if in sun
   Native Range Widespread under 2000 feet elevation, eastern U.S., Zones 7 to 9
   Soil Acid
   Drainage Wet to moist
   Root System Taproot
   Companion Plants Sweetgum
   Propagation Fresh, untreated seed sown in fall
   Wildlife Seeds eaten by cardinal, goldfinch, Florida jay, nuthatch, tufted titmouse, brown thrasher, and meadowlark. Used as nesting by mourning doves and roosting for migrating robins

Loblolly pine is the fastest-growing and most widely used of the southern pines. On old abandoned farmland or vacant lots, it will usually team up with sweetgum, and together these two pioneer species will, in three to five years, begin the process of reforestation. A loblolly can live to be more than 200 years old. It is often found in old forests where the trunk can be a yard across and tower high into the sky with a scrawny tuft of sun-seeking branches at the very top. When you see an old, solitary loblolly in full sun, the look is quite different; it is broad and handsome with a short trunk. If you want a windbreak or screen of loblollies, don't just line them up like soldiers; scatter and cluster them as if they'd been planted naturally by birds and squirrels, and allow hardwoods to grow up among them.

9. **Latin Name** *Pinus virginiana*
   Common Name Virginia pine, Jersey pine
   Usual Height 30 to 40 feet high, can reach 100 feet
   Spacing 30 for a specimen, 15 feet for screening
   Sun or Shade ○
   Bloom Cinnamon male flowers, pale green female flowers, spring
   Fruit Small 2-inch cones that cling tightly for years
   Leaves Evergreen, dark, yellow-green, 1^1/$_2$- to 3-inch needles in bundles of 2
   Trunk Dark brown with orange tints
   Native Range Old fields, burned land, dry sites, New Jersey along Appalachians to Alabama, Zones 6 to 7, usually under 3000 feet elevation
   Soil Acid, poor, deep
   Drainage Dry
   Root System Taproot
   Companion Plants Red maple, blackgum, sourwood, sassafras, flowering dogwood, mountain laurel
   Propagation Fresh seed sown outside in fall
   Wildlife Seeds eaten by towhee, pine siskin, red-bellied woodpecker; nesting and cover for many birds and mammals

Very slow-growing and somewhat small, **Virginia pine** is a good choice for small home landscapes in the upper Piedmont and the Appalachian Mountains. The short, dark needles and low, drooping branches create a somewhat sheltering feeling. This pine must be planted in full sun in conjunction with trees of similar height; it just hates standing under another tree's branches. Along with the companion plants listed above, you might consider using blueberries, huckleberry (*Gaylussacia ursina*), vernal iris, and bracken fern. With a little water, it is easy to also use galax or partridgeberry as groundcovers. Virginia pine is often a pioneer species for a tulip poplar forest, and sometimes it blends with shortleaf pine and loblolly in a post oak/hickory forest.

10. **Latin Name** *Quercus virginiana*
    Common Name Live oak
    Usual Height 40 to 50 feet, rarely 60 to 80 feet
    Spacing 100 to 150 feet for a specimen, 50 feet for a woodland
    Sun or Shade ○
    Bloom Pale yellow, 2 to 3 inches long, spring
    Fruit Acorns
    Leaves Evergreen, small, firm, shiny
    Trunk Short, dark gray-brown, rough
    Native Range Dry sites, dunes, areas where fire doesn't occur, Coastal Plain from Virginia to Texas, Zones 8 to 10
    Soil Any, including saline
    Drainage Dry
    Root System Shallow and spreading
    Companion Plants Southern magnolia, wild olive, cabbage palmetto, dwarf palmetto, redbay, American beautyberry, wax myrtle
    Propagation Fresh acorns planted as soon as ripe in fall
    Wildlife Warblers in spring migration; acorns stashed by squirrels and bluejays and eaten by wild turkey, grackle, nuthatch, woodpeckers, and tufted titmouse; larval plant for white M hairstreak butterfly

Draped in Spanish moss or wreathed with resurrection fern, this is the majestic **live oak** that you see along the streets of New Orleans, Charleston and Savannah. In many old Southern gardens, it has grown so large that its branches rest on the ground a full fifty feet distant from the trunk. To show off this graceful form to best advantage, I'd suggest surrounding the trees with a mowed area of moss, violets, grasses, and wildflowers such as spiderworts, butterweed, and lyreleaf sage. In a natural landscape, this live oak is found growing in a fringe alongside beachfronts with other salt-spray-resistant plants, or in a very dense forest.

11. **Latin Name** *Sabal palmetto*
    Common Name Cabbage palmetto, palmetto
    Usual Height 40 to 50 feet, rarely 80 to 90 feet
    Spacing 10 to 20 feet apart for clusters, 30 feet for a specimen
    Sun or Shade ● ◑ ◑ ○
    Bloom White, 2-foot cluster on long stem, June
    Fruit Black, ½ inch, in huge clusters, late fall
    Leaves Evergreen, 5 feet long and 7 feet broad on 2- to 7-foot spineless stems, about 40 leaves per tree
    Trunk Columnar, up to 2 feet in diameter, shaggy with discarded-leaf bases unless pruned
    Native Range Dunes, hammocks, flatwoods, brackish areas, within 75 miles of the coast from the Florida Panhandle to islands off southern North Carolina, Zones 8 to 10
    Soil Acid, sand preferred, saline OK, lime OK
    Drainage Wet to dry
    Root System Stem grows underground 5 to 6 feet before turning upward; roots are orange, tough, and can be 6 inches thick
    Companion Plants Live oak, dwarf palmetto, slash pine, wax myrtle, yaupon
    Propagation Fresh or stratified seed
    Wildlife Fruit eaten by robins, fish crow, raccoon; food plant for monk butterfly

Cabbage palmetto used to be popular in home landscapes and along public boulevards in towns by the seashore. It is smaller, friendlier (that is, spineless), and far more winter-hardy than the foreign faster growing Washingtonia that has largely replaced it in planned landscapes. If you buy a nursery-grown cabbage palmetto, it will look much like *Sabal minor* for a number of years. The more nutrients and water it gets, the faster it grows. If its growing tip is damaged, it will branch. If you buy an adult tree, chances are it was not grown in a nursery, but was dug up in the wild—a practice that can be damaging to the environment.

12. **Latin Name** *Tsuga canadensis*
    Common Name Eastern hemlock
    Usual Height 60 to 70 feet, rarely 100 feet high
    Spacing 30 feet for a cluster, 50 to 100 feet for a specimen
    Sun or Shade ● ◑ ◑
    Bloom Pale yellow male flowers, pale green female flowers, early spring
    Fruit Tiny, ½-inch cones, fall to winter
    Leaves Evergreen, dark, yellow-green, ½ inch long, glossy
    Trunk Cinnamon to dark gray, furrowed
    Native Range Moist woodlands, occasionally dry, open places, southern Appalachians to Canada, Zones 3b to 7
    Soil Acid, rich
    Drainage Moist
    Root System Shallow, fibrous
    Companion Plants Tulip poplar, sugar maple, red maple, basswood, umbrella tree, cucumbertree, rosebay rhododendron, mountain laurel, leucothoe, wild hydrangea
    Propagation Stratified seed, cuttings with hormones
    Wildlife Fruit eaten by pine siskin, chickadee
    Related Species *T. caroliniana*, Carolina hemlock

Eastern hemlock is one of our loveliest conifers, with a pyramidal form and graceful, drooping branches. In Southern states, it feels most at home in the mountains, liking cool, moist, wind-sheltered, and unpolluted conditions. Unlike most conifers, this one is really happy to find itself tucked away in a woodland or under a mature shade tree. The shorter **Carolina hemlock,** on the other hand, will tolerate a little more sun and summer heat, drier soil, and a small amount of air pollution, which makes it useful in urban settings. Folks who live in the upper Piedmont can use hemlocks, provided these trees get lots of shade from sheltering trees and a rich soil spongy with leaf mold. There are many cultivars available, but it looks to me like they are all of northern stock.

DECIDUOUS TREES OVER 50 FEET TALL

(Paul Moore)

Deciduous shade trees, those that lose their leaves in the winter, such as oaks and maples, are called **hardwoods,** and they give you a lot more color throughout the year than you probably realize. Everyone appreciates the golds and reds of **autumn,** but not many have taken the time to notice the pinks, silvers, limes, and yellows of **spring.** A cloud of strange little flowers or the unfurling leaves turn the woods into a misty luminescence of pastels. **Winter,** unexpectedly, has its beauty. Often the twigs are purple or orange, and the entire tree takes on these soft shades.

The rich golds of hickory and sugar maple glow in the enhanced woodland on the south side of Paul and Nancy Moore's house near Nashville, Tennessee. On the lawn, their leaves join those of white ash, which was the previous week's contribution.

13. **Latin Name** *Acer barbatum* (*A. saccharum* subsp. *floridanum*)

   Common Name Southern sugar maple, Florida maple

   Usual Height 25 to 50 feet, occasionally 100

   Spacing Half as wide as tall

   Sun or Shade ● ◐ ◑ ○

   Bloom Pale green with new leaves

   Fruit Two-winged, brown, ripening late summer

   Leaves Scarlet to orange to salmon to gold to cream in late fall, even deep in the woods

   Trunk Gray, smooth to lightly furrowed

   Native Range Rich, well-drained woods, Southeastern U.S., Zones 7 to 9

   Soil Acid, rich or poor, acid over lime OK

   Drainage Moist

   Root System Shallow and fibrous

   Companion Plants Tulip poplar, white oak, willow oak, white ash, shagbark hickory

   Propagation Fresh seed sown when ripe, one seed to each pair of wings

   Wildlife Sap used by yellow-bellied sapsucker, bees; seeds eaten by oriole, song sparrow

   Related Species *A. saccharum*, northern sugar maple; *A. leucoderme*, chalk maple

For great fall color, the **southern sugar maple** is the one to use throughout the South (except in the mountains, Kentucky, West Virginia, and Maryland). It prefers a northern exposure on a slight slope with soil rich in fallen and partially decomposed leaves. It doesn't care for flooding, dry compacted soils, or salt or chlorine. To keep it happy and avoid extra work, use a leaf mulch beneath the tree. If you must have groundcovers, ferns, or woodland flowers growing there, establish a regimen of regular applications of compost and watering.

14. **Latin Name** *Acer rubrum*

   Common Name Red maple

   Usual Height 50 to 120 feet high

   Spacing 50 to 100 feet for a specimen

   Sun or Shade ◐ ◑ ○

   Bloom Red flowers on males, early spring

   Fruit Red winged seeds on females, midspring

   Leaves Color in early fall, generally orange-red to purplish red, but often pure yellow in Mississippi

   Trunk Gray, furrowed

   Native Range Wet to dry, woodlands or fields, eastern North America, Zones 3 to 9

   Soil Acid, rock, mud, or dry sand, acid topsoil over lime OK

   Drainage Wet to dry

   Root System Shallow, fibrous, easy to transplant

   Companion Plants Hemlock or river birch or post oak or bald cypress

   Propagation Seed fresh off tree

   Wildlife Nesting and food for warblers, chickadee, purple finch, goldfinch, bobwhite, grosbeak, vireo, and squirrels

   Related Species Sometimes *A. rubrum* var. *drummondii* is considered to be separate

As you can see from its companion plants, **red maple** can be happy just about anywhere: with hemlock on fertile moist sites in the mountains, along stream banks wherever you find river birch, with post oak on dry, difficult sites, and in cypress-tupelo swamps. It can be one of the first to reforest a site, or part of the climax community. And it can withstand moderate amounts of modern urban pollution. The only other tree with this range of adaptability is sweetgum. Red maple is cleaner, healthier, and prettier than its better-known cousin, silver maple (*Acer saccharinum*), and grows almost as fast. It colors early in the fall, so to get a great show combine it with blackgum, sassafras, fringetree, and eastern persimmon.

15. **Latin Name** *Betula nigra*
   Common Name River birch
   Usual Height 50 to 90 feet
   Spacing 80 feet for specimen, 30 feet for grove
   Sun or Shade ○
   Bloom Pale yellow-green before leaves
   Fruit Brown catkins in summer, messy over a patio
   Leaves Light green, drooping, briefly yellow in fall
   Trunk Beautiful, salmon to peach exposed under peeling silver, multitrunked or often branching about 20 feet up
   Native Range River and pond banks, floodplains, lowlands, eastern U.S. except mountains and Maine, Zones 4 to 8
   Soil Acid, clay OK
   Drainage Wet to moist, but can be dry in summer
   Root System Shallow, fibrous, easy to transplant
   Companion Plants Bald cypress, sweetgum, swamp chestnut oak
   Propagation Seed sown in fall, tissue culture, softwood cuttings
   Wildlife Seeds eaten by chickadee, goldfinch, purple finch, and pine siskin, redpoll, tanager, titmouse, vireo, grouse, nuthatch

When you think of **river birch,** you think mostly about its beautiful bark. But it has other virtues. It can tolerate compacted clay (within reason) and the kind of overwatering it can get on a typical sprinkler-systemed landscape. The one thing it can't handle well is reflected heat off a parking lot or building. Put one under a bright street light, and you can confuse it; it won't know when to go dormant for the winter. River birch grows very quickly for its first fifty years, then starts a gentle decline. It rarely makes it to its hundredth birthday. The big mistake gardeners make is planting it too close to a house. The trunk gets to be three feet wide sooner than you think. In a natural landscape, river birch should go into a sunny spot next to a stream, river, or pond.

16. **Latin Name** *Carya ovata*
   Common Name Shagbark hickory
   Usual Height 70 to 90 feet, occasionally 120 feet
   Spacing 50 feet for specimen or in a woodland
   Sun or Shade ◑ ◐ ○
   Bloom Pale green catkins as leaves emerge
   Fruit Hickory nuts in fall, edible
   Leaves Palest green velvet in spring, old gold in fall
   Trunk Tall, straight; shaggy with huge, thick plates, branches often black
   Native Range Mostly well-drained woods, eastern U.S., Zones 4 to 8
   Soil Slightly acid, rich, silt and clay OK
   Drainage Moist to dry
   Root System Taproot grows 3 feet first year
   Companion Plants White, black, Shumard, and willow oaks, tulip poplar, white ash, basswood, beech, red and sugar maples
   Propagation Fresh seed sown in fall or stratified seed in spring
   Wildlife Nuts eaten by humans, squirrels, turkey, wood duck, nuthatch; wood used by woodpecker
   Related Species *C. cordiformis,* bitternut hickory; *C. aquatica,* water hickory; *C. myristiciformis,* nutmeg hickory; *C. laciniosa,* shellbark hickory; *C. tomentosa,* mockernut hickory; *C. glabra,* pignut hickory; and others

Hickories are fine, long-lived trees that are almost totally neglected in Southern landscapes. **Shagbark hickory** has sweet nuts, ruggedly attractive bark, and a dramatic way of unfolding its leaves each spring. You can use it in most normally moist home landscapes. Another hickory for moist sites is the **bitternut hickory.** On wet sites in the Coastal Plain, use water or **nutmeg hickory.** For wet sites in the Piedmont and mountains, pick **shellbark hickory.** And for dry sites all over the Southeast, go with the **mockernut** and **pignut hickories.**

17. **Latin Name** *Fagus grandifolia*
    Common Name Beech, American beech
    Usual Height 70 to 80 feet, rarely 120 feet
    Spacing 75 to 100 feet for a specimen, 50 feet apart in woodland
    Sun or Shade ● ◑ ◐
    Bloom Small, yellow-green clusters in spring
    Fruit Beech nuts in fall, spiny outer coat
    Leaves Glossy, dark green in summer, yellow, then copper in fall, brown in winter
    Trunk Smooth, pale gray bark, fat trunk with low branches in sun
    Native Range Rich, moist, well-drained woodlands, eastern North America, Zones 4 to 8
    Soil Acid, rich
    Drainage Moist
    Root System Shallow, fibrous, might colonize
    Companion Plants Southern magnolia, tulip poplar, most fine hardwoods
    Propagation Stratified seed
    Wildlife Nuts eaten by bluejay, chickadee, tufted titmouse, squirrels, and chipmunks; nesting for wood thrush and pileated woodpecker

I'd describe **American beech** as elegant—and picky. It prefers a loose soil, rich with decomposing leaves, and well shaded from the hot summer sun. If you plant a beech seedling in the abused soil found in most home land-scapes, and give it full sun to boot, you probably won't get it to thrive—even with regular watering. Once established, however, it does beautifully even in full sun. I've heard it said that the European beech is better adapted to the South; not true. Michael Dirr, in his *Manual,* says that he has seen the two species planted side by side in the Southeast (Zones 7 through 9), and the native American beech is clearly superior. It handles urban pollutants (ozone and sulfur dioxide) pretty well.

18. **Latin Name** *Fraxinus americana*
    Common Name White ash
    Usual Height 50 to 120 feet
    Spacing 50 to 75 feet
    Sun or Shade ● ◑ ◐ ○
    Bloom Purple, before leaves
    Fruit Pale green, then tan, winged seed like fringe on female tree
    Leaves 7 (5 to 9) leaflets, gold, orange, and purple in early fall
    Trunk Dark gray-brown, fissured, tall and straight
    Native Range Bluffs, river banks, better-drained floodplains, eastern half of North America, Zones 3 to 8
    Soil Acid, rich, deep preferred, lime OK
    Drainage Moist, tolerates brief flooding
    Root System Shallow, easy to transplant
    Companion Plants Southern sugar maple, shagbark hickory, beech, tulip poplar, basswood
    Propagation Fresh or doubly stratified seed
    Wildlife Great for nesting songbirds and butterfly larvae of tiger swallowtail and mourning cloak; seed eaten by purple finch and pine grosbeak, browsed on by porcupine, rabbit, and deer

White ash is named for its white wood. Remember those pale-colored baseball bats—those of you old enough to remember when baseball bats were made of wood? Well, that was white ash. In the fall, on sunny limestone slopes around Nashville, the whole tree glows like a candle flame. White ash turns from the inside out, first yellow, which deepens to orange, then rosy purple. At some point you get all three colors on the tree at once. Wow! In a woods, the top turns first, with the color working its way down, until, finally, the bright leaflets carpet the forest floor with shades of gold, pumpkin, and mauve.

19. **Latin Name** *Liquidambar styraciflua*
    Common Name Sweetgum
    Usual Height 60 to 120 feet, can reach 140 feet
    Spacing 75 feet for a specimen
    Sun or Shade ◑ ○
    Bloom Chartreuse, in 3-inch clusters
    Fruit Spiny sweetgum ball in fall
    Leaves Star-shaped, glossy, fall color in yellow, orange, red, and burgundy, often all on the same tree
    Trunk Straight, dark gray, ridged and furrowed
    Native Range Old fields, floodplains, uplands, Southeastern U.S., Mexico and Guatemala, Zones 6 to 9
    Soil Acid to neutral, deep
    Drainage Moist to wet
    Root System Fleshy rather than fibrous, taproot turns sideways in wet soil, and the whole root system is shallow, might sucker
    Companion Plants Pines, willow oak, blackgum, white ash, red maple, river birch, alder, and post oak
    Propagation Fresh or stratified seed
    Wildlife Seeds eaten by cardinal, chickadee, goldfinch, purple finch, junco, mourning dove, towhee, white-throated sparrow, chipmunk, and squirrel

Sweetgum comes up everywhere in Southern lawns and gardens, driving the tidy gardener mad. But sweetgum's purpose in life is to turn bare earth or grassland into forest. Take advantage of this if you would like to start a woodland garden on the cheap. Select a number of your sweetgum seedlings. Use a tomato cage or some other device to protect them from the mower until they get large enough to shade out your lawn. From seedling to shade can take as little as five years. The other great landscape advantage of sweetgum is that, being a swamp tree, it tolerates compacted, low-oxygen soil.

20. **Latin Name** *Liriodendron tulipifera*
    Common Name Tulip poplar, tuliptree
    Usual Height 75 to 100 feet, occasionally 200 feet
    Spacing Half the height
    Sun or Shade ◐ ◑ ○
    Bloom Yellow-green "tulip" with orange center, after leaves mature in late spring or early summer
    Fruit 3-inch "cone" in fall
    Leaves Glossy, bright green, white undersides, yellow in late fall
    Trunk Tall, straight, pale to dark furrowed bark
    Native Range Moist woodlands, hammocks, stream banks, bottomland woods, fields, eastern U.S. except East Texas, Zones 5 to 8
    Soil Acid to neutral, deep, rich
    Drainage Moist, but never flooded
    Root System Fibrous, fleshy, and poorly branched
    Companion Plants Hemlock, musclewood, sourwood, basswood, umbrella tree, cucumbertree, white oak, beech, hickory, red maple, sugar maple, gordonia, sprucepine
    Propagation Softwood cuttings, root cuttings, stratified seed
    Wildlife Flowers visited by hummingbirds and butterflies, seeds eaten by cardinal, purple finch, and squirrel; leaves host tiger and spicebush swallowtail butterfly larvae

The stately **tulip poplar** is a deciduous member of the magnolia family and, in my opinion, is one of the most beautiful trees in the South. If you'd like to add one to your landscape, be sure that its roots are not in soggy ground. They also get distressed if the ground is too hard and dry in the summer. This will cause your tree to defoliate as early as July or August. Put in your tulip poplar only after you have rebuilt your soil with several years' worth of decomposing leaves. This will keep your soil moisture fairly even all year round.

21. **Latin Name** *Magnolia acuminata* var. *subcordata*
    Common Name Cucumbertree
    Usual Height 60 feet, might get 90 feet tall
    Spacing As broad as tall for a mature specimen
    Sun or Shade ◑ ◐
    Bloom Creamy yellow, mildly fragrant, 4 inches long, never fully open, April, as leaves half out
    Fruit Cucumber-looking while green in June, turning red by August
    Leaves Dark green, silky silver underneath, 4 to 10 inches long
    Trunk Straight, gray, roughly furrowed
    Native Range Upland coves, stream banks, hammocks, Piedmont and adjacent Coastal Plain near Gulf of Mexico, Zones 7 to 8
    Soil Acid, deep, rich
    Drainage Moist
    Root System Broad, deep, and fleshy
    Companion Plants Tulip poplar, basswood, mountain magnolia, umbrella tree
    Propagation Stratified seed
    Wildlife Seeds eaten by yellow-bellied sapsucker, towhee, red-eyed vireo, red-cockaded woodpecker, and eastern kingbird, who takes them on the fly; leaves used in nests
    Related Species *M. a.* var. *acuminata,* some recognize *M. a.* var. *ozarkensis*

Cucumbertree is a high-quality, long-lived ornamental that comes in two universally recognized varieties. *Magnolia acuminata* **var.** *subcordata,* most commonly found in the Piedmont and the Coastal Plain, is the one I saw most frequently planted in Southern gardens. It is slow-growing and sometimes multitrunked (which results in a lower height and broader crown), but it's a myth that it never gets over 30 feet tall. *Magnolia acuminata* **var.** *acuminata,* which gets quite big, is found more often in the mountains and westward. It has greenish rather than yellow flowers and lacks the silky leaves and twigs of its lowland cousin. Give it regular watering in full sun.

22. **Latin Name** *Magnolia virginiana*
    Common Name Sweetbay Swampbay (Swampbay denotes *Persea* in this book)
    Usual Height 60 feet, occasionally 100 feet
    Spacing Half the height
    Sun or Shade ◑ ◐ ○
    Bloom Creamy white, fragrant, 3 to 6 inches across, spring to early summer
    Fruit Dark red cone with bright red seeds
    Leaves Medium green with flashing white undersides
    Trunk Straight, might get 3 feet in diameter, or multitrunked, smooth, pale gray bark
    Native Range Flatwoods, swamps, coastal sloughs, mostly Coastal Plain and outer Piedmont from Delaware to Texas, Zones 7 to 9
    Soil Acid, poor to rich
    Drainage Wet to moist
    Root System Shallow
    Companion Plants Gordonia, swampbay, bald cypress, red maple, American holly
    Propagation Stratified seed, semihardwood cuttings in summer
    Wildlife Seeds eaten by yellow-bellied sapsucker, towhee, red-eyed vireo, red-cockaded woodpecker, eastern kingbird; larval plant for swallowtails

Sweetbay is unique among the southern magnolias in that it will not only tolerate soggy soil, it actually likes it. Since it's always found in swamps or along streams and other wet places, it can handle full sun, even in the wild. The silvery white undersides to the leaves make the tree seem to sparkle in a breeze. In Zone 9, sweetbay is evergreen most winters. Some nursery people recognize two varieties: *M. virginiana* var. *australis,* the more dependably evergreen; and *M. virginiana* var. *ludoviciana,* which has a straighter trunk and larger, more numerous flowers.

23. **Latin Name** *Nyssa sylvatica* (*N. sylvatica* var. *sylvatica*)
    Common Name Blackgum, black tupelo, sourgum
    Usual Height 50 to 75 feet, rarely 140 feet high
    Spacing Half the height
    Sun or Shade ◑ ◐ ○
    Bloom Greenish, with new leaves
    Fruit Shiny, dark blue, rather dry
    Leaves Glossy, brilliant red in early fall
    Trunk Straight, corky
    Native Range Thin woods or fields, Eastern North America, Zones 5 to 8
    Soil Acid
    Drainage Dry, cannot endure prolonged flooding or overwatering
    Root System Thick, hard roots with few rootlets, hard to transplant
    Companion Plants Longleaf pine, post oak, sourwood, sassafras, fringetree, flowering dogwood, sweetgum, willow oak, white oak, red maple, post oak, eastern persimmon, white ash, mockernut and pignut hickories, serviceberry
    Propagation Fresh or stratified seed
    Wildlife A bee tree; fruits eaten by wood duck, bluebird, purple finch, yellow-shafted flicker, hermit thrush, red-eyed vireo, woodpeckers, opossum, gray squirrel, and white-tailed deer
    Related Species *N. biflora*, swamp tupelo; *N. aquatica*, water tupelo; *N. ogeche*, Ogeeche-lime

Blackgum dependably turns red early in the autumn, at the same time eastern persimmon is golden orange. It is a nice size for small landscapes, and a very fast grower when given a little fertilizer. As long as it gets fairly good sun and the soil isn't so soggy, your blackgum should do very well. It is more resistant than most trees to air pollution, so plant it along parkways. In a woodland, it colors best when planted at the edge so it gets plenty of light.

24. **Latin Name** *Quercus alba*
    Common Name White oak
    Usual Height 50 to 100 feet high
    Spacing Grows wider than tall when uncrowded
    Sun or Shade ◑ ◐ ○
    Bloom Yellow, as leaves unfold
    Fruit Large, sweet acorns in fall
    Leaves Unfold rose to peach and then silver, green and glossy with rounded lobes in summer, orange-red to deep red in late fall, sometimes brown in winter
    Trunk Whitish bark, straight, single trunk
    Native Range Moist, well-drained woodlands, eastern U.S., Zones 4 to 8
    Soil Acid, deep rich
    Drainage Moist, well drained
    Root System Taproot and strong laterals
    Companion Plants Red maple, basswood, hickory, tulip poplar, beech, white ash, hemlock, sugar maple, willow oak, eastern red cedar, post oak, red oak, black oak; loblolly, shortleaf, and Virginia pines
    Propagation Fresh seed sown immediately
    Wildlife Acorns a favorite winter staple for white-breasted nuthatch, tufted titmouse, bluejay, turkey, deer, squirrels, grackle, woodpeckers, bobwhite; also provides cover and nesting materials

White oak has lovely pale bark, expansive branching, and rich red fall color. You can plant a white oak fairly close to your house—about 6 feet out—because the roots go very deep and shouldn't present a problem to your foundation. And it's unlikely the branches would ever fall on your roof; they're very strong and hold up well to wind and ice. However, white oak is sensitive to concentrated levels of ozone and wet, compacted soil. If you have any construction going on, make very sure the builder gives it a wide berth.

25. **Latin Name** *Quercus falcata* complex
    Common Name Southern red oak
    Usual Height 70 to 80 feet, occasionally 125 feet
    Spacing 50 to 150 feet
    Sun or Shade ◑ ○
    Bloom Reddish, 3 to 5 inches long in spring
    Fruit Small acorns in fall
    Leaves 4 to 10 inches long with 3 to 13 lobes, usually tawny and fuzzy undersides, drooping, brown fall color
    Trunk Straight, fissured bark, gray to brown
    Native Range Dry upland fields and woodlands, Southeastern U.S. from New Jersey to Texas, Zones 6 to 9
    Soil Acid, sand, or clay, rich to poor
    Drainage Dry to moist
    Root System Deep
    Companion Plants Post oak, black oak, live oak, hickory, eastern persimmon, longleaf or shortleaf pines, willow oak, beech
    Propagation Fresh or stratified seed that has never dried out
    Wildlife Used extensively for nesting, cover, and food by birds and mammals
    Related Species *Q. falcata* can be divided into 4 varieties: *Q. f.* var. *falcata* (southern red oak), *Q. f.* var. *leucophylla* (true cherrybark oak), *Q. f.* var. *pagodifolia* (swamp red oak), *Q. f.* var. *triloba* (three-lobe red oak); but some botanists use other Latin names for this group

Southern red oak is very common, especially on dry sites. The leaf shapes vary quite a bit from tree to tree and sometimes even on the same tree. What the leaves usually have in common are spiky edges, a drooping habit, and a tendency to show their light-colored undersides. Some people think this gives a somewhat shaggy appearance to the tree, but others love the distinctive texture. This is an easy, fairly fast-growing oak for the beginning gardener who is working with soil that is less than ideal.

26. **Latin Name** *Quercus michauxii*
    Common Name Swamp chestnut oak, basket oak
    Usual Height 60 to 100 feet, occasionally 130 feet
    Spacing 50 to 100 feet
    Sun or Shade ● ◑ ◑ ○
    Bloom Yellow-green, in spring
    Fruit Large, sweet acorns in fall
    Leaves Yellow in spring; in summer, chestnut-shaped, large (6 to 9 inches long), dark green, glossy with pale undersides; rich red in late fall
    Trunk Straight, tall, silvery, thin plates or shaggy
    Native Range Floodplains, hammocks, Southeastern U.S. except West Virginia, Zones 6 to 9
    Soil Acid, rich, subsurface limestone OK
    Drainage Moist, winter flooding OK, but flooding during the growing season must be of short duration
    Root System Shallow
    Companion Plants Willow oak, blackgum, white oak, Shumard oak, beech, red maple, arrowwood viburnum, ferns, dwarf palmetto
    Propagation Fresh acorns sown in fall
    Wildlife Acorns eaten by woodpeckers, yellow-bellied sapsucker, tufted titmouse, Carolina wren, deer, and small mammals, larval plant for Juvenal's duskywing butterfly
    Related Species *Q. montana* (*Q. prinus* by some), rock chestnut oak; *Q. prinoides* and *Q. muhlenbergii,* both Chinquapin oak

It's easy to spot a **swamp chestnut oak,** even deep in the woods. Its pale, silvery gray trunk stands out handsomely. In late fall—usually after Thanksgiving—you'll be attracted to its vivid red foliage. Placed in a parklike setting, this tree can become huge and spreading. When it grows in moist—but not flooded—places, the ground beneath is especially rich in ferns and spring woodland flowers.

27. **Latin Name** *Quercus phellos*
    Common Name Willow oak
    Usual Height 70 to 90 feet, occasionally 120 feet
    Spacing 30 to 60 feet, old specimens can be 100 feet
    Sun or Shade ◑ ◐ ○
    Bloom Yellow in early spring
    Fruit Small acorns in fall
    Leaves Pink in spring, willowlike, glossy light green in summer; pale yellow to orange in late fall
    Trunk Straight, grayish brown, smooth when young
    Native Range Floodplains, rich uplands, Southeastern U.S. except West Virginia, Zones 6 to 9
    Soil Acid
    Drainage Moist to wet, tolerates inundation all year
    Root System Fibrous, easy to transplant
    Companion Plants Sweetgum, musclewood, shagbark hickory, pond cypress, pond pine, slash pine, water oak
    Propagation Fresh or stratified seed, cuttings
    Wildlife Acorns eaten by pintail, wood duck, mallard, wild turkey, woodpeckers, yellow-bellied sapsucker, brown thrasher, bluejay, and small mammals

28. **Latin Name** *Quercus shumardii*
    Common Name Shumard red oak
    Usual Height 50 to 120 feet
    Spacing 50 feet in woodland, 100 feet for specimen
    Sun or Shade ◑ ◐ ○
    Bloom Light brown, 6 to 7 inches long, spring
    Fruit Medium-sized acorns in fall
    Leaves Pink in early spring, glossy green in summer, red in late fall, brown in winter, sharply lobed
    Trunk Straight, brown, lightly furrowed
    Native Range Southeastern U.S. except Delaware, Zones 5 to 9
    Soil Acid, lime OK, deep and rich preferred
    Drainage Moist
    Root System Taproot
    Companion Plants Swamp chestnut oak, southern red oak, sweetgum, loblolly
    Propagation Fresh acorns sown in fall
    Wildlife Acorns eaten by wild turkey, Carolina wren, woodpeckers, and mammals; larval plant of white M hairstreak butterfly
    Related Species *Q. coccinea*, scarlet oak; *Q. nuttallii*, Nuttall oak; *Q. palustris*, pin oak; *Q. rubra*, northern red oak

Willow oak doesn't have the charm of either white oak or swamp chestnut oak, but it is an extremely sensible tree to use. It's fast-growing and will take almost any abuse, especially compacted soil and overwatering typical of street-planting sites. That's why it is so popular with landscape architects and city planners. Its narrow leaves are easy to sweep up and fast to decompose, so it is a good choice for places where it will hang over pavement or groundcovers. The fine texture and light color of the foliage make it an excellent contrast plant in a woodland garden.

Shumard red oak is a high-quality tree that doesn't get used nearly enough—especially in the Coastal Plain, and in limestone areas where the northern red oak is rarely suitable. Shumard's kin, **scarlet oak,** is useful for poor, dry upland areas up to about 5000 feet. **Nuttall oak** works for those areas in the Mississippi floodplain where soils are soggy and oxygen-starved; **pin oak** serves the same function for Zone 6 and northward. The latter two are the ones most often sold in nurseries, because their shallow, fibrous root systems are easy to transplant. But they are water-guzzlers. Fall color varies in all species, so buy and plant your red oak in late fall when it is in color and you can see what you're getting.

29. **Latin Name** *Quercus stellata*
   Common Name Post oak
   Usual Height 40 to 60 feet, occasionally 90 feet
   Spacing 50 to 90 feet for a specimen, 50 feet in woodland
   Sun or Shade ○
   Bloom Yellow before leaves, 3 to 4 inches long, quite showy
   Fruit Small acorns in fall
   Leaves Rose to red in spring, thick and glossy green in summer with tawny fuzz underneath, brown in fall and winter
   Trunk Straight, with very thick bark, brown
   Native Range Dry uplands, rocky slopes, Southeastern U.S., Zones 5 to 9
   Soil Acid to neutral, poor
   Drainage Dry
   Root System Thick, few rootlets, hard to transplant
   Companion Plants Longleaf, shortleaf, or loblolly pines; persimmon, flowering dogwood, sassafras, blackjack and turkey oaks; pignut, mockernut, and shagbark hickories
   Propagation Fresh acorns in fall
   Wildlife Acorns eaten by bobwhite, meadowlark, wild turkey, bluejay, red-cockaded and other woodpeckers, deer and small mammals; leaves by larvae of Juvenal's duskywing butterfly

It's hard to find a **post oak** in a nursery, yet it is one of our most common oaks—a vital element in the dryland forests of the Southeastern United States. Perhaps the prettiest time of year to see post oak is in very early spring when the tree is covered in a delicate mist of yellow blossoms. Look around. If the timing is right, you'll see post oak combining with the yellow of sassafras, the whites of flowering dogwood and plum, the dark greens of eastern red cedar and pines, and the light greens of new spring grasses. It's a truly splendiferous sight.

30. **Latin Name** *Quercus velutina*
   Common Name Black oak
   Usual Height 50 to 80 feet, occasionally 150 feet
   Spacing 50 feet, more for a specimen
   Sun or Shade ◑ ○
   Bloom Yellow-green, 4 to 6 inches long in spring after leaves
   Fruit Medium-sized acorns in fall
   Leaves Red to silver in spring; glossy, rich green in summer with velvety undersides; yellow to gold in late fall
   Trunk Straight, bark nearly black and very thick
   Native Range Dry uplands, eastern North America, Zones 5 to 8
   Soil Acid, coarse, rich or poor, clay subsoil OK
   Drainage Moist to dry, intolerant of flooding
   Root System Taproot and deep lateral roots, hard to transplant
   Companion Plants Pignut and mockernut hickories, tulip poplar, red oak, white oak, blackgum, white ash, red maple, beech, shortleaf pine, eastern persimmon, longleaf pine, post oak, southern red oak, and live oak
   Propagation Stratified seed, planted in spring
   Wildlife Acorns eaten by birds and mammals; larval plant for Juvenal's duskywing butterfly

Black oak is especially pretty in spring. Its new leaves start out a deep rose and fade through shades of pink to silver. Its yellow fall color is fairly marvelous, too. In those moderately dry locales where it grows alongside white oak with its own wonderful wine-red foliage, the two form a knock-out combination. Black oak is for those of you on dry sites where the soil is too sterile or too contaminated with industrial wastes for most forest trees. It is not a good choice where road graders and bulldozers have compacted the soil. Black oak can survive in rotten conditions, but give yours rich, moist soil on a shady slope, and it will not be ungrateful.

31. **Latin Name** *Taxodium distichum*
    Common Name Bald cypress
    Usual Height 70 to 100 feet, rarely 150 feet
    Spacing 100 feet for a specimen
    Sun or Shade ◑ ○
    Bloom 4 to 5 inches long, silvery in winter bud,
      purple in spring
    Fruit 1 inch, brown
    Leaves Feathery needles, yellow-green, turning
      coppery in late fall
    Trunk Straight, buttressed, often hollow at base,
      thin, reddish bark
    Native Range Floodplains, swamps, brackish
      tidewater, Coastal Plain from Maryland to Texas,
      up the Mississippi River to Illinois, Zones 7 to 9
    Soil Acid, lime OK, brackish OK, clay OK
    Drainage Wet, can be inundated all year or in an
      irrigated landscape
    Root System Shallow, fibrous, conical knees up to 6
      feet tall
    Companion Plants Water tupelo (*Nyssa aquatica*),
      tupelo gum (*Nyssa biflora*), red maple,
      swampbay, sweetbay, gordonia
    Propagation Seed (remove resin, then sow in fall or
      stratify); cannot germinate in water
    Wildlife Seeds eaten by mallards, gadwalls, sandhill
      cranes
    Related Species *T. ascendens,* pond cypress, Zones 8
      to 9 along the coast from Southern Virginia to
      Western Mississippi

Bald cypress is fast-growing and can tolerate heavy,
soggy, oxygen-poor soils that many other trees can't.
When young, it is shaped like a pyramid, with drooping
branches. As it gets older, it develops middle-aged spread.
Pond cypress, with its ascending branches, looks more
delicate and is not as tall. It requires more acidic water and
blooms later than bald cypress, but the two do form
hybrids.

32. **Latin Name** *Tilia americana*
    Common Name Basswood, American linden
    Usual Height 30 to 70 feet, rarely 130 feet
    Spacing 30 to 50 feet
    Sun or Shade ● ◑ ◐ ○
    Bloom Pale yellow to lime, drooping 4-inch cluster,
      fragrant, late June to early July
    Fruit Small, fuzzy ball attached to leafy crescent
    Leaves Heart-shaped, pale yellow in fall
    Trunk Tan, furrowed, occasionally multitrunked
    Native Range Bluffs, hammocks, coves, mixed
      woodlands, old fields, eastern half of North
      America, Zones 3 to 8
    Soil Acid, lime OK, rich preferred
    Drainage Moist, does not tolerate flooding
    Root System Deep, spreading, might sucker
    Companion Plants Hemlock, tulip poplar,
      umbrella tree, cucumbertree, red oak, beech,
      sugar maple, white oak
    Propagation Green seed, scarified and stratified seed
    Wildlife Nectar used by bees and butterflies; larval
      plant for red-spotted purple and mourning cloak;
      seeds eaten by squirrels and chipmunks
    Related Species *T. americana* is the only species in
      the U.S. recognized by most botanists, but some
      divide it into 3 to 16 species

Sweet, fragrant **basswood** will grow quickly if
conditions are right. What it likes best is a deep, rich soil
on a slight slope that stays moist—not wet. It also likes to
have other forest trees nearby, to keep its roots well shaded
and the air cool. But, if your site happens to be a little
drier than ideal, the basswood will make do. The height
of this species varies all over the South; some trees are
reported to top-out at under 50 feet. Perhaps because
basswood is less common in the Coastal Plain, it seems to
be healthier there than it is up north, where it falls prey to
the parasites and diseases that attack the widely used
European linden, *Tilia × europaea.*

5

SMALL TREES
15 TO 40 FEET TALL

This chapter is devoted to small trees, and some large shrubs, that normally grow 15 to 40 feet tall, although some get over 50 feet tall on rare occasions. Sassafras and eastern persimmon, for example, are usually classified as small trees (sometimes as shrubs), but if they live long enough and don't get shaded out, they can grow well over 50 feet tall. Much of what determines the height a tree attains is simply a matter of the tree's longevity. Sassafras and eastern persimmon usually live about fifty years, but big old specimens have managed to reach their 75th or even 100th birthdays. Most of the trees in this chapter can live 40 or 50 years.

The question of whether these trees are, in fact, trees or shrubs is endlessly debated. Clearly, when a woody plant has a single trunk that is 8 to 14 inches in diameter, it is definitely tree-like. But when it is multitrunked or multistemmed, many people want to call it a shrub, even though it may be taller than a two-story house. Others say that if a woody plant is large enough for an adult to walk beneath the branches, it's a tree. Personally, I belong to this latter school, but as far as I'm concerned, the choice is yours to make.

The trees discussed here are grown chiefly for their beauty. They've been chosen because they put on a big show or because there is such a strong sentimental association with them, as with pawpaw, that I'd be very unpopular with many of you if I had left them out.

All of these trees will grow under canopy trees, but not all of them will bloom, fruit, or get lavish fall color while growing in that kind of dense shade. Redbud, for example, is found by the score in old, many-layered woodlands where it grows as a small tree with a trunk up to an inch or so in diameter, and with nary a bud or seed to be seen. Obviously, this is not where you'd plant your redbud on purpose. You'd place it in the sun where it will grow into a tree with a trunk a foot in diameter, and where it will put on an extravagant spring show. The sun signs that you'll find in the tree profiles indicate where the tree will thrive, not just where it will endure.

There is another heading called Root System. One comment you may find there is, "colonizes to form a thicket." Another name for this is "suckering." It means that the tree sends out roots, which, in turn, send up shoots that can become other trees. The reasons for this have been largely unexplored, but obviously it is a very effective way to reproduce. If the tree prefers sunlight, as many of these trees do, then suckering gives it a chance to keep moving out into sunnier spots when larger trees start to shade it out.

Sometimes these suckering trees are fast-growing and short-lived. It's rare for an individual trunk in a thicket to be over 20, or 30, or 40 years old, depending on the species. When you see a huge sassafras with an 18-inch trunk, straight and solitary, does this mean the sassafras never suckered and led a charmed life? Or does this mean that it was once a thicket, and only the stem that got the best light, or some other advantage, outgrew and eventually outshaded and outcompeted all its colonial mates? As far as I know, there has been no research on what triggers a tree's colonizing tendencies. The stimulus might be genetic or environmental, or a combination of the two.

52

new sucker as it develops until the suckers give up and you have just the one to five trunks you want. This can take two or three years, however, and I must add, sometimes the suckering never ends. My yaupon holly sends up about six shoots each year. It resides in a bed of groundcover that I don't want to mow, so each year I cut them back by hand—really, no big deal! We're talking about only ten minutes or so out of my life each year.

If you want a grove, cutting down the original stem will usually force the roots to sucker. If you want a dense thicket for screening, mowing a young grove can sometimes make it thicken up.

When transplanting a tree that might be a sucker, the best method is to use a sharp shovel to cut the roots all around to the size rootball you think you can manage. It isn't necessary to cut beneath the tree; what you are doing is separating this tree from the mother tree. Then, before you actually move the tree, wait two or three months for the tree to establish an independent root system.

I hope you're not thinking that suckering trees are too much trouble to use. First of all, you're probably already using and enjoying a number of colonizers. Lilacs, crape myrtles, and rose-of-Sharon come quickly to mind. Second, using a colonizing tree can be an advantage. Not all the trees in this chapter are colonizers, but those that are give you a choice of four different looks. You can have a single-trunked tree, a multi-trunked tree (my favorite), a grove, or a thicket.

Gardeners have learned that there are specific things you can do to maintain a tree, and other things you can do to encourage a thicket. To keep a single or multi-trunked tree from colonizing, protect the base of the tree from deer or mowers. If your tree is already colonizing, you can cut off each

EVERGREEN TREES OVER 15 FEET TALL

Medium-height evergreens are most useful for providing screening and privacy from your neighbors. But when their branches have been beautifully pruned, they can also be used as single specimens to ornament the front of your home. Like the evergreen shade trees, they are extremely important for providing shelter for birds, small mammals, and beneficial insects that winter over. Many are also sources of fruits and seeds to feed these critters.

A wild olive in bloom at Brookgreen Gardens in Murrells Inlet, South Carolina, provides a graceful, see-through divider between a formal garden and a rough, low meadow.

33. Latin Name *Cliftonia monophylla*
Common Name Buckwheat tree, buckwheat bush
Usual Height 30 feet, occasionally 40 to 50 feet
Spacing 30 feet
Sun or Shade ● ◑ ◐ ○
Bloom White, usually fragrant, early spring on current year's twigs
Fruit Buckwheat-shaped, palest lime until yellow in late summer
Leaves Evergreen, 2 inches, leathery, glossy
Trunk Crooked, branching 12 to 15 feet above the ground, with dark brown scaly bark and red branches
Native Range Wet, nonalluvial soils, acid swamps, bogs, flatwood depressions, Coastal Plain, Savannah, Georgia, and Jacksonville, Florida, to Mississippi River, Zone 8
Soil Very acid, sand, peat preferred, no mud, lime, sulfur, or salt
Drainage Moist to wet
Root System Usually colonizes to form a thicket
Companion Plants Atlantic white cedar, pond cypress, pond pine, redbay, sweetbay, fetterbush, clethra, inkberry, cinnamon fern
Propagation Seed and semihardwood cuttings
Wildlife Nectar for bees, occasionally browsed

In the wild, **buckwheat tree**'s multiple trunks can get all jammed together. Yet properly pruned, it can be a single-trunked or multitrunked tree with character and charm. It has a long season of ornamental fruits and flowers. When in full bloom, and again when the seed clusters are about to ripen, the tree takes on a lovely misty look. If you don't remove the suckers, buckwheat tree will form a thicket, which can be useful for erosion control on stream or pond banks. Although native only to acid swamps along the coast, it seems to be adaptable to gardens along the Mississippi floodplain.

34. Latin Name *Ilex vomitoria*
Common Name Yaupon, yaupon holly
Usual Height 20 to 25 feet, occasionally 45 feet
Spacing 20 feet
Sun or Shade ● ◑ ◐ ○
Bloom White, tiny, in spring
Fruit Red or orange, rarely yellow, translucent, on females, late fall to spring
Leaves Evergreen, 1 to 2 inches, dark green, glossy
Trunk Usually multitrunked, pale gray, smooth
Native Range Dunes, maritime woods, pond margins, swamps, thin upland woods, fencerows, south coastal Virginia to Texas, north to southeastern Oklahoma, Zones 7 to 9
Soil Acid, lime OK, saline OK
Drainage Wet, moist, dry
Root System Shallow, easy to transplant, will colonize to form a thicket
Companion Plants Live oak, palmetto, southern red cedar, turkey oak, post oak, American holly, wax myrtle, sparkleberry
Propagation Fresh seed, scarified (optional) and double-stratified seed, semihardwood cuttings
Wildlife Larval plant for Henry's elfin butterfly; seed eaten by cedar waxwing, mockingbird, and other songbirds after several freeze-thaw cycles
Related Species *I. cassine*, dahoon; *I. myrtifolia*, myrtle holly

Yaupon is a first-rate screening plant; on its own, it forms thick masses of long-lived, hardy, evergreenery. Used as a small specimen tree, pruning once a year maintains its graceful form. Get the female for her outstanding berries. Give her plenty of sun to ensure a bumper crop for winter viewing pleasure. As for the males, put them in dark spots, such as under live oaks where you need some foliage to fill in blank spaces. **Dahoon** and **myrtle holly** are equally attractive, but are less adaptable than yaupon—they require constant moisture and are less cold-tolerant.

(Bob McCartney)

35. **Latin Name** *Illicium floridanum*
Common Name Florida anise, anise-tree, stinkbush
Usual Height 15 to 25 feet
Spacing 10 to 20 feet
Sun or Shade ● ◑ ◐
Bloom Maroon to red, 1 to 1¹/₂ inches, early spring
Fruit Brown, whorled, dry, fall
Leaves Evergreen, 3 to 6 inches, leathery, dark green, glossy; they discolor, droop, and fall as new leaves appear in spring
Trunk Crooked or multitrunked, dark brown, smooth
Native Range Rare, swamps, wooded streams, western Florida Panhandle to southeastern Louisiana, northeastern Mexico, Zones 8 to 9
Soil Acid, rich
Drainage Moist to wet
Root System Shallow, does not seem to colonize
Companion Plants Sweetbay, redbay, swamp azalea, yaupon, American holly, pawpaw
Propagation Fresh seed, cuttings
Wildlife Foliage and fruit are poisonous to cattle
Related Species *I. parviflorum*, star anise, Georgia coast to Florida

The red flowers of **Florida anise** are so dark that you could miss them. As for the fragrance—"wet dog" or "sweaty socks" are common descriptions. Crush the leaves for another aroma—something like fish or turpentine. In spite of all that, or maybe because of it, everybody who has Florida anise in a landscape raves about it. It is glossy, well-mannered, and doesn't sucker. One nursery selection has white flowers. Its cousin, **star anise** (Zones 8b and 9), always has creamy white flowers, along with lime-green foliage. More drought-resistant, it grows to 30 feet on sandy ridges in swamps with agarista, cabbage palmetto, dwarf palmetto, needle palm, sweetbay, and redbay.

36. **Latin Name** *Lyonia ferruginea*
Common Name Staggerbush, tree lyonia
Usual Height 20 to 25 feet, rarely 40 feet
Spacing 20 feet
Sun or Shade ◑ ○
Bloom White, on previous year's growth, early spring
Fruit Small, tan, fall
Leaves Evergreen, 1 to 3 inches, pale green, glossy, stiff, new leaves bronze colored
Trunk Crooked, leaning, smooth red-brown bark, up to 10 inches in diameter
Native Range Post oak and pine/oak scrub, dry hammocks, dunes, coastal South Carolina and Georgia to Florida, Zones 8 to 9
Soil Acid, sandy, rich preferred, shrubby in poor soil
Drainage Dry to moist
Root System Might colonize to form a thicket
Companion Plants Sweetbay, redbay, sassafras, wax myrtle, gordonia, sweetleaf, inkberry, leucothoe, clethra, highbush blueberry, saw palmetto
Propagation Fresh seed, division, cuttings
Wildlife Flowers visited by bees

Staggerbush grows in those warm coastal habitats that, while mostly evergreen, can still deliver lots of flowers and color. This particular evergreen can be definitely eye-catching in early spring as long as it gets at least a half day of sun. The dry fruits aren't very exciting—not even to birds. That's why they'll still be on the tree when the flowers appear. If they bother you, don't let them form; prune off spent blooms in the spring. Staggerbush will eventually develop into a small tree with lots of character, but it takes a few years. To speed up the process, cut off any suckers and encourage all the growth into just one or two trunks.

37. Latin Name *Myrica cerifera*
   Common Name Wax myrtle, southern bayberry
   Usual Height 15 to 20 feet, occasionally 40 feet
   Spacing 20 feet
   Sun or Shade ◑ ◐ ○
   Bloom Tiny, before new leaves appear
   Fruit Pale blue, waxy, on females only, fall and winter
   Leaves Evergreen, 1 to 4 inches long, olive-green, aromatic
   Trunk Up to 10 inches in diameter, usually multitrunked, pale gray, smooth
   Native Range Outer dune swales, flatwoods, pine savannahs, swamps, bogs, hammocks, Southeastern U.S., Zones 7 to 9
   Soil Acid to neutral, deep
   Drainage Wet to dry
   Root System Might colonize to form a thicket
   Companion Plants Sweetbay or post oak, yaupon, sparkleberry, inkberry, dwarf huckleberry, beautybush, swamp azalea
   Propagation Stratified seed, softwood or semihardwood cuttings, root cuttings, layering
   Wildlife Fruit eaten by tree swallow, bluebird, catbird, red-bellied woodpecker, brown thrasher, white-eyed vireo, Carolina chickadee, myrtle warbler, and 13 other species of birds
   Related Species *M. inodora,* odorless bayberry

For fast, easy-care screening, turn to **wax myrtle.** This shrub or small tree is nonfussy and fast growing, and has attractive light olive-green foliage. Combine it with glossy-leaved, dark green yaupon or inkberry. To get a soft, natural look, plant the shrubs in a random, nonlinear pattern, and don't shear them. To maintain wax myrtle as a small tree, give it an annual pruning. Wax myrtle is winter-hardy but not dependably evergreen. At 0 degrees F the leaves tend to drop off and they don't come back until the following spring.

38. Latin Name *Osmanthus americanus*
   Common Name Wild olive, devilwood
   Usual Height 15 to 25 feet, occasionally 60 to 70 feet
   Spacing 30 feet
   Sun or Shade ◑ ◐ ○
   Bloom Creamy white, early spring
   Fruit Dark blue, not juicy, early fall to spring
   Leaves Evergreen, 4 to 5 inches, leathery, olive-green, glossy
   Trunk Often multitrunked, a single trunk can be 18 inches in diameter, bark is thin, pale gray, with cinnamon underbark
   Native Range Coastal Plain from southeastern Virginia to southeastern Louisiana, Mexico, Zones 8 to 9
   Soil Acid, coarse, poor to rich, saline OK
   Drainage Dry to moist
   Root System Shallow, moderately fibrous
   Companion Plants Live oak, palmetto, beech, pines, redbay, southern magnolia
   Propagation Seeds come up second year, semihardwood cuttings
   Wildlife Fruits eaten by birds and small mammals

If pruning isn't one of your favorite chores, you'll love **wild olive.** Mother Nature gave this small evergreen tree a naturally beautiful shape that won't need much help from you. Which is a good thing, because its wood is very tough. It holds up wonderfully well to gale winds, but it's a devil to work with for woodworkers and pruners alike. Wild olive has exceptionally attractive bark—smooth, silvery gray with coppery undertones. It does best in light shade or full sun. It tends to get scraggly in heavily shaded spots where buckwheat tree and yaupon are more at home.

39. **Latin Name** *Persea borbonia*
   Common Name Redbay
   Usual Height 15 to 40 feet, rarely 70 feet
   Spacing 30 feet, champion is 68 feet broad
   Sun or Shade ◑ ○
   Bloom Pale yellow to white, tiny, May to June
   Fruit ¹/₂ inch, blue to black, not juicy, early fall
   Leaves Evergreen, 3 to 4 inches long, red in spring, glossy in summer with an orange midrib, a few red or yellow and dropping in spring or summer, wonderfully aromatic when crushed
   Trunk Brown, furrowed, might get 2 to 3 feet in diameter, single or multitrunked
   Native Range Dunes, maritime woods, calcareous hammocks, scrub, Coastal Plain from Delaware to Texas, Zones 7 to 9
   Soil Very acid, acid, lime OK, sand preferred
   Drainage Moist to dry
   Root System Yellow, fleshy
   Companion Plants Live oak, longleaf pine, southern magnolia, wild olive, staggerbush, yaupon
   Propagation Seed in fall
   Wildlife Larval plant for Palamedes and spicebush swallowtail; fruit eaten by fish crow, songbirds, turkey, and quail; leaves browsed by deer and used in cooking by humans
   Related Species *P. palustris*, swampbay

Good thing I don't have a **redbay** in my yard; I'd defoliate it as far up as I could reach. The leaves are so wonderfully aromatic I'd be snatching off a leaf to crush and sniff every time I passed by. The only problem with redbay is its susceptibility to a leaf gall, which is not attractive and which renders new tender leaves unusable for butterfly larvae. **Swampbay** is so similar that most botanists make it a variety of redbay. It tolerates much wetter conditions, and is frequently found growing with sweetbay and gordonia.

40. **Latin Name** *Symplocos tinctoria*
   Common Name Sweetleaf, horsesugar
   Usual Height 15 to 35 feet, rarely 55 feet
   Spacing 20 feet
   Sun or Shade ● ◑ ◑ ○
   Bloom Yellow to cream, fuzzy, fragrant like not-quite-ripe peaches, early spring as leaves change
   Fruit Small, brown, dry, late summer
   Leaves Evergreen until spring as new leaves appear in Zones 8 and 9, deciduous in Zone 7, 5 to 6 inches, dark green, glossy, drooping, sweet-tasting, aromatic
   Trunk Gray, sandpaper smooth with striations, straight, single or multitrunked, 6 to 14 inches in diameter
   Native Range Sandhills, flatwoods, post oak woods, stable dunes, stream borders, floodplains, Southeastern U.S., Zones 7 to 9
   Soil Very acid, acid, rich, poor OK
   Drainage Moist to dry, tolerates seasonal flooding
   Root System Aromatic
   Companion Plants Shortleaf pine, blackgum, post oak, red maple, sourwood, sassafras, sparkleberry, longleaf pine, redbay, southern magnolia, sweetbay, cabbage palmetto
   Propagation Seeds probably need to be double-stratified
   Wildlife Foliage browsed, seeds eaten by phoebe

Catch **sweetleaf** in early spring when the old leaves are mostly off and the new ones are not fully out; it's a visual treat. The branches will be covered with a cloud of fragrant yellow fuzz. The rest of the year its large, dark, glossy leaves can be counted on to stay healthy and attractive in a wide range of conditions throughout the South. Some authorities state that sweetleaf can grow into a fine, airy tree even in heavy shade, such as you'd find in a southern magnolia-beech woods. However, don't expect it to bloom well there.

FLOWERING AND FRUITING TREES OVER 15 FEET TALL

Small native flowering or fruiting trees are some of the most beautiful plants in the South. Some bloom in early spring before leaves appear, others bloom in late spring, still others in summer. Several provide vivid fall color, and the deciduous hollies (the possumhaw is my favorite) glow with red, orange, or yellow fruit all winter. The fruits and seeds on these trees provide food for songbirds, while the flowers—many of which are fragrant—provide nectar for butterflies, hummingbirds, and bees.

Sourwood shows off its outstanding clear red fall foliage, backed up by the gold of a sugar maple. This award-winning combination was planted by Melba Jones in Nashville, Tennessee.

41. **Latin Name** *Acer leucoderme* (*A. saccharum* subsp. *leucoderme*)

Common Name Chalk maple

Usual Height 20 to 25 feet, occasionally 40 feet

Spacing 30 to 40 feet for specimen, 10 to 15 feet for understory

Sun or Shade ● ◑ ◐ ○

Bloom Pale yellow in early spring as the leaves appear

Fruit Brown-winged samaras in late summer

Leaves Drooping, green (not pale) beneath scarlet, orange, and gold in late fall, brown in winter

Trunk Multistemmed, dark gray and furrowed at base of old trees, pale gray and smooth on younger stems

Native Range Understory in moist, well-drained hardwood forests, North Carolina to southeastern Oklahoma, Zones 7 and 8

Soil Acid, rich

Drainage Moist

Root System Shallow, fibrous

Companion Plants Tulip poplar, beech, southern sugar maple, basswood

Propagation Fresh seed

Wildlife Used by woodpeckers, bees, mammals, for nesting and food; seed eaten by oriole, grosbeak, cardinal, vireo

Chalk maple is almost always multitrunked with a broad crown. If you use it as an understory tree, you can get good fall color, although the richest colors appear when it gets at least a half day of sun. In drier conditions than it likes, chalk maple may reach only 15 feet, and the leaves might get sunburned. Each maple grows from seed, so you won't know exactly what shade of fall color you'll get. Don't worry. They're all pretty. And a grouping of several different tints is more interesting.

42. **Latin Name** *Aesculus pavia*

Common Name Scarlet buckeye, red buckeye, dwarf red buckeye

Usual Height 15 to 25 feet, occasionally 40 feet

Spacing 25 feet

Sun or Shade ◑ ◐

Bloom 4- to 8-inch spikes of red flowers, early spring after new leaves

Fruit Tan husks filled with one or two buckeyes, early fall

Leaves 5 (sometimes 7) leaflets, dark green, glossy, drop in late summer

Trunk Single or multitrunked, 4 to 10 inches in diameter, smooth bark, sometimes covered with white lichens

Native Range Sandhills, shell mounds, bluffs, North Carolina to Texas and up the Mississippi to southern Illinois, Zones 6 to 8

Soil Acid, lime OK, rich preferred, but will grow even on shell mounds

Drainage Moist, tolerates only very brief flooding

Root System Shallow

Companion Plants Beside or under deciduous canopy trees or pines

Propagation Fresh seed, dormant root cuttings

Wildlife Flowers used by hummingbirds and bees; nuts eaten and spread by squirrels

Related Species *A. glabra,* Ohio buckeye

Folks obviously hold **scarlet buckeye** in high regard; we found at least one in every native plant garden we visited throughout the Southeast. You need to know, though, that its branches might be bare of leaves from August to April. Being a fairly short-lived tree and not wanting to waste precious time, scarlet buckeye starts blooming fast, when it is just 3 feet high. It's easy to grow as long as you don't overwater it. **Ohio buckeye,** with greenish yellow blooms, is not nearly as attractive.

43. **Latin Name** *Alnus serrulata*

    Common Name Alder, common alder, hazel alder

    Usual Height 10 to 20 feet, occasionally 40 feet

    Spacing 15 to 20 feet

    Sun or Shade ◑ ◐ ○

    Bloom Male catkins, 4 inches long, yellow, winter and early spring

    Fruit Brown, female cones useful in flower arranging, fall

    Leaves 2 to 4 inches, dark green, glossy, yellow and orange in fall

    Trunk Usually multitrunked, dark, smooth bark, up to 1 foot 5 inches in diameter

    Native Range Banks, swamps, eastern North America, Zones 5 to 8

    Soil Acid to neutral

    Drainage Wet to moist

    Root System Likely to colonize to form a thicket, nitrogen-fixing

    Companion Plants Black willow, sweetgum, white ash, red maple, river birch, musclewood, buttonbush, possumhaw, lizard's tail

    Propagation Seed, root cuttings, tissue culture

    Wildlife Fruit eaten by many species of birds

Alder is very attractive, with bright yellow catkins in the spring, golden fall color, and female winter fruits that attract a wide array of feathered friends. Still, this tree probably won't figure in your landscape plans unless you have a creek, stream, river, pond, pocosin, or some other natural water feature. If that's the case, you'll definitely want a thicket of alder to help hold on to your banks. Its roots are the best erosion control you could hope for. Plant it in full sun—that's where it grows best. Once established, it can handle moderate shade. In the wild, you'll normally find it in the shade of a river birch or some other taller tree, standing in mucky conditions where it is subjected to periodic floods.

44. **Latin Name** *Amelanchier arborea* var. *arborea* (*Amelanchier canadensis*)

    Common Name Serviceberry, shadbush, Junebush

    Usual Height 15 to 25 feet, occasionally 35 feet

    Spacing As wide as high

    Sun or Shade ● ◑ ◐ ○

    Bloom White, or flushed with pink, before leaves appear in spring

    Fruit 1/3 inch, red, early summer

    Leaves Silvery as they unfold, 2 to 4 inches, lime in summer, yellow to apricot to mauve in fall

    Trunk Often multitrunked, up to 18 inches in diameter, gray bark, smooth when young

    Native Range Rocky slopes, balds, eastern half of North America, Zones 4 to 8, but rare in the southern Atlantic coastal plain and the Mississippi River floodplain

    Soil Acid

    Drainage Moist to dry

    Root System Deep

    Companion Plants Hemlock, beech, tulip poplar, flowering dogwood, sourwood, blackgum

    Propagation Stratified seed, cuttings, tissue culture

    Wildlife Nectar for butterflies; fruit eaten by bluebird, oriole, yellow-shafted flicker, scarlet tanager, hermit thrush, eastern kingbird, downy woodpecker, chickadee, mammals, including us

    Related Species *A. arborea* var. *laevis*, Allegheny serviceberry

Serviceberry is fairly common in the South, although it prefers cooler climates to reach full size. It is one of the first understory trees to bloom in the spring. As the blossoms disappear, the silver leaves unfold, giving you an extended period of beauty. Most of the cultivars available in the nursery trade are *Amelanchier* × *grandiflora*, reportedly a hybrid of our two native varieties. The pure *A. arborea* var. *arborea*, if propagated from a Florida colony, should have more heat tolerance.

45. Latin Name *Aralia spinosa*

    Common Name Devil's walkingstick, Hercules club

    Usual Height 15 to 20 feet, rarely 50 feet

    Spacing 15 feet

    Sun or Shade ◑ ◐ ○

    Bloom White in 3- to 4-foot clusters, midsummer

    Fruit Blue-black, juicy, early fall

    Leaves 3 to 4 feet long with 2- to 3-inch leaflets and prickles, bronze green as they unfold and pale yellow to orange or purple in early fall

    Trunk Straight, up to 6 to 8 inches in diameter, dark brown, armed with orange prickles

    Native Range Upland and lowland woods, bogs, swamp margins, stable dunes, eastern U.S., Zones 6 to 8

    Soil Acid, rich, poor OK

    Drainage Moist, tolerates seasonal flooding

    Root System Shallow, likely to colonize

    Companion Plants Anything that grows streamside with hemlocks in the mountains to woodland on stable dunes by the seashore

    Propagation Stratified seed, root cuttings

    Wildlife Flowers used by bees, wasps, tiger swallowtail; foliage browsed by white-tailed deer; fruit eagerly eaten by cardinal and many other birds and by mammals

Devil's walkingstick has a marvelous way of standing out in a garden and saying, "Hey, look at me!" Huge leaves composed of leaflets and prickles, an enormous mass of white flowers that bees and butterflies really home in on, and large, showy clusters of blue-black fruits all make it hard to ignore. Plant it in a lawn or along the edge of a mowed area, where the suckers can be mowed off and just one or two trunks can be easily maintained. This tree survives in dense woods, but needs several hours of direct sun each day to flower.

46. Latin Name *Asimina triloba*

    Common Name Pawpaw, Indian banana

    Usual Height 5 to 20 feet, rarely 40 feet

    Spacing 20 feet

    Sun or Shade ● ◑ ◐ ○

    Bloom Maroon, 1 to 2 inches, pollinated by flies, before leaves

    Fruit Pawpaw, 3 to 5 inches long, yellowish green, ripening to a fragrant dark brown in early fall

    Leaves 6 to 12 inches long, light green in summer, golden yellow in fall, aromatic

    Trunk Single- or multitrunked, straight, up to 1 foot in diameter, 12 to 20 years being the average life of any one stem

    Native Range Moist, well-drained woodlands, eastern U.S., Zones 6 to 8, mostly in Piedmont and mountains

    Soil Acid, lime OK, rich preferred

    Drainage Moist

    Root System Might colonize to form a thicket

    Companion Plants Beech, willow oak, American holly, umbrella tree, musclewood, red maple, strawberrybush, spicebush, sweetshrub, mapleleaf viburnum

    Propagation Stratified seed

    Wildlife Larval plant for zebra swallowtail, fruits eaten by raccoons and other mammals

    Related Species *A. parviflora*, dwarf pawpaw, smaller and better adapted to the Coastal Plain

Born and bred Southerners grew up singing "Pickin' up pawpaws and puttin' 'em in a basket." Visually, **pawpaw** is not very exciting, but it is adaptable to nearly every moderate habitat of the Southeast. Its foot-long leaves can give your garden a tropical look. If you are planting one for the fruits, give it at least a half day of sun. Also, choose a cultivar; the sweetness and flavor will be more consistent.

47. **Latin Name** *Carpinus caroliniana*
    Common Name Musclewood, ironwood, hornbeam, bluebeech
    Usual Height 20 to 30 feet, rarely 50 feet
    Spacing 25 feet
    Sun or Shade ● ◐ ◑
    Bloom Green, as leaves emerge, in very early spring
    Fruit 5- to 6-inch ornamental clusters, papery tan
    Leaves 2 to 4 inches, blue-green in summer, orange and scarlet in late fall
    Trunk Single, pale gray, smooth, gently twisting like muscles, up to 1 foot in diameter in the South
    Native Range Floodplains, bluffs, stream banks, coves, eastern North America, Zones 5 to 9, Mexico to Honduras
    Soil Acid, lime OK, rich preferred
    Drainage Moist to occasionally wet
    Root System Deep
    Companion Plants Hemlock, red maple, tulip poplar, red oak, Shumard oak, swamp chestnut oak, white ash, river birch, willow oak, shagbark hickory, flowering dogwood, sassafras, pawpaw, American holly, spicewood, strawberrybush, storax
    Propagation Barely ripe seed, double-stratified
    Wildlife Larval plant for tiger swallowtail and red-spotted purple butterflies; seeds eaten by wood duck, myrtle warbler

Musclewood's chief ornamental value is found in its pale, smooth, rippling trunk. With a little imagination you can see "muscles" under the "skin." The tree's clusters of tan, papery fruits are also visually interesting and stand out in the understory. Musclewood is found in most of the South's finest woodlands. It is adaptable, slow-growing, and therefore long-lived (150 years). It can also tolerate lots of shade. The wood is so fine-grained and strong that it was once highly prized as timber for house foundations.

48. **Latin Name** *Cercis canadensis* var. *canadensis*
    Common Name Redbud, eastern redbud, Judas tree
    Usual Height 20 to 35 feet, occasionally 50 feet
    Spacing 30 feet
    Sun or Shade ◑ ○
    Bloom Rosy purple (not red), rarely white, before leaves appear
    Fruit 2- to 3-inch beans, ripe in summer but brown in fall and winter
    Leaves Heart-shaped, sometimes yellow in early fall
    Trunk Usually single, up to a foot in diameter, brown, rough, branching over a person's head
    Native Range Bluffs, hammocks, fields, eastern U.S., Zones 5 to 8 (sometimes 9)
    Soil Acid, lime OK
    Drainage Moist to dry
    Root System Does not colonize
    Companion Plants Eastern persimmon, eastern red cedar, blackgum, mockernut hickory, sourwood, flowering dogwood, hophornbeam, sassafras, spicebush, wild olive
    Propagation Scarified and stratified seed
    Wildlife Flowers used by bees for honey; foliage eaten by white-tailed deer; seeds eaten by birds

In a dense forest, **redbud** is a wispy sapling. In a landscape, put it on the sunny side of a tall, deciduous tree where it will have plenty of sun to bloom and grow, but it won't get heat stressed in August. Redbud blooms very early, before the canopy tree begins to sprout new leaves. A cluster of three or more redbuds planted 20 to 25 feet apart is effective, especially if the flowers vary from deep purply pink to pale pink to lavender. Mix in yellow-blooming spicebush or white-blooming serviceberry for a real visual treat, and carpet the ground with troutlily, violets, isopyrum, or other early woodland flowers. Don't plant redbud along major roadways; it's sensitive to auto pollutants.

49. Latin Name *Chionanthus virginicus*

Common Name Fringetree, old man's tree, Grancy Graybeard

Usual Height 20 to 30 feet

Spacing 20 feet

Sun or Shade ◑ ◕ ○

Bloom White, 4- to 10-inch drooping clusters, often fragrant, before leaves appear in spring, male trees showier than females

Fruit Dark blue, 1/2 inch, fleshy but not juicy, on females, September

Leaves 4 to 8 inches, dark green, glossy, yellow to gold in fall

Trunk Single, 8 to 10 inches in diameter, reddish brown bark

Native Range Dry woods, hammocks, floodplains, savannahs, flatwoods, Southeastern U.S., Zones 6 to 9

Soil Very acid, acid, rich preferred, but poor and rocky (granite or sandstone) OK

Drainage Moist to dry

Root System Deep

Companion Plants Longleaf pine, red maple, sourwood, flowering dogwood, blackgum, mountain laurel, blueberries, possumhaw, sassafras, blackhaw viburnum

Propagation Double-stratified seed, layering, grafting, budding, softwood cuttings

Wildlife Fruits eaten by birds and mammals

Fringetree is one of the South's most beautiful ornamental trees; it has outstanding spring flowers, lustrous dark green summer leaves, and golden fall color. Both males and females are gorgeous and fragrant in flower, but the male is showier. The female has the fruits, and will attract songbirds; put the male next to patios and pathways because it isn't messy. Michael Dirr, in his *Manual,* says fringetree is resistant to urban air pollution.

50. Latin Name *Cladrastis kentukea*

Common Name Yellowwood, gopherwood

Usual Height 20 to 30 feet, rarely 60 feet

Spacing 30 to 40 feet

Sun or Shade ◑ ◕ ○

Bloom White, 12- to 14-inch clusters, fragrant, early summer, not profuse every year

Fruit Bean pods, brown in September

Leaves 5 to 11 leaflets, bright green; yellow in fall

Trunk Short, straight, up to 4 feet in diameter, smooth, gray bark

Native Range Rare, mountain coves, limestone cliffs, rich hardwood forests, Piedmont and mountains of Southeastern U.S., Zones 6 to 7 (sometimes 8), to 3500 feet elevation

Soil Limestone, but moderately acid OK, rich preferred

Drainage Moist

Root System Fibrous

Companion Plants White ash, tulip poplar, red maple, musclewood, eastern persimmon, eastern red cedar, American smoke tree, rusty blackhaw viburnum, redbud, possumhaw, flowering dogwood

Propagation Scarified or stratified seed, December root cuttings

Wildlife No information

Yellowwood's natural habitat combines limestone, sun, and moisture. It grows best near Nashville, Tennessee, and in three counties in Missouri. You can grow it elsewhere if the soil is not extremely acid. It has a reputation for having fragile limbs that don't stand up to high winds or ice storms, yet it's winter hardy to −30 degrees F. Those who have gardened with it love it and think it ought to be used more. All the handsome specimens we saw were about 30 feet tall in almost full sun, with no canopy trees overhead.

51. Latin Name *Cornus florida*
    Common Name Flowering dogwood
    Usual Height 20 to 30 feet, occasionally 50 feet
    Spacing 20 to 30 feet
    Sun or Shade ● ◐ ◑ ○
    Bloom White bracts, in spring before leaves
    Fruit $1/2$ inch, shiny red, fall and winter
    Leaves 3 to 6 inches, bright green, red in early fall
    Trunk Single- or multitrunked, up to 18 inches in diameter, bark dark, in little squares
    Native Range Dry to moist woodlands or fields, eastern North America, Zones 5 to 8
    Soil Acid to neutral, rich or poor
    Drainage Moist to dry
    Root System Deep
    Companion Plants Tulip poplar, southern sugar maple, shagbark hickory, post oak, American holly, musclewood, farkleberry, sassafras, witchhazel, viburnum, parsley hawthorn, storax
    Propagation Stratified seed, root and stem cuttings
    Wildlife Fruit eaten by bluebird, brown thrasher, cardinal, catbird, cedar waxwing, kingbird, purple finch, robin, towhee, vireo, woodpecker, and 75 other species of birds

Flowering dogwood is a year-round delight. In the spring, the white bracts seem to float in air when seen in a leafless woodland. The tree is bright green and elegant in the summer. Autumn produces bright red fruits and leaves. And winter sees it covered with pale buds. Use it just about anywhere, but don't drown it. There is some concern about its vulnerability to an anthracnose named *Discula.* This seems to occur in moist, shady, airless conditions under 95 degrees F.—such as a depression in a woods or in an overwatered, shady landscape. To play it safe where dogwoods are being attacked, consider **fringetree, hawthorn,** or **serviceberry.** All three deliver that lovely burst of white in early spring, great fall color, and songbirds.

52. Latin Name *Crataegus marshallii*
    Common Name Parsley hawthorn
    Usual Height 15 to 20 feet, rarely 35 feet
    Spacing 20 feet
    Sun or Shade ● ◐ ◑ ○
    Bloom White, sometimes with red anthers, as leaves emerge in spring
    Fruit Cherry red, $1/3$ inch, early fall
    Leaves Parsley-shaped, scarlet to wine in fall
    Trunk Usually multitrunked, up to 8 inches, smooth, scaling, lime and pale salmon
    Native Range Bottomland and floodplain woods, bluffs, Southeastern U.S., Zones 7 to 9
    Soil Acid, rich preferred
    Drainage Moist
    Root System Taproot
    Companion Plants Post oak, loblolly, shortleaf pine, flowering dogwood, sassafras, eastern persimmon, sparkleberry, storax, American beautyberry, strawberrybush
    Propagation Stratified seed
    Wildlife Fruits eaten by cedar waxwing, flicker, mockingbird, cardinal, yellow-bellied sapsucker; nectar used by hummingbirds, hairstreaks, skippers, and swallowtails; larval plant for gray hairstreak butterfly
    Related Species *C. aestivalis,* mayhaw; *C. opaca,* mayhaw; *C. viridis,* green hawthorn; many others, often hybrids and hard to identify

In full sun or bright dappled shade **parsley hawthorn** will reward you with profuse snowy blooms and scarlet fruit. In dense shade, where flowering is not so vivid, its lacy leaves and colorful trunk still make it an outstanding ornamental tree. The trunk on **green hawthorn** is also wonderful—fluted, twisting, and the color of apple-cinnamon ice cream. **Mayhaw** is not quite so ornamental, but is famous for its delicious fruit. Thornless selections of hawthorns are available in the nursery trade.

53. Latin Name *Cyrilla racemiflora*
Common Name Titi, swamp cyrilla, leatherwood
Usual Height 30 feet
Spacing 30 feet for a specimen
Sun or Shade ● ◑ ◐ ○
Bloom 4 to 6 inches, white, fragrant, early summer
Fruit Yellow to tan, ornamental in fall
Leaves 2 to 3 inches, glossy, orange and scarlet in early winter; after turning, might drop or might stay on until summer
Trunk To 14 inches, divides just above the ground, red, scaly
Native Range Acid swamps, bogs, stream banks, floodplains, along the coast from southern Virginia to East Texas, to the Caribbean and Brazil, Zones 8 to 11
Soil Very acid, acid
Drainage Wet to moist, still or running water
Root System Might colonize to form a thicket
Companion Plants Pine, tulip poplar, gordonia, red maple, sweetbay, swampbay, wax myrtle, inkberry, fetterbush, swamp azalea, decumaria
Propagation Seed or cuttings
Wildlife Nectar for bees
Related Species A dwarf form is sometimes separated into a variety or a species called *parvifolia*

Titi has a short trunk and wide-spreading branches, but it's so slow-growing, it takes years for these features to become apparent. In the meantime, you'll need to trim off suckers from time to time to direct all the energy into forming a single trunk. It blooms on the previous year's growth, so prune only right *after* flowering or you'll be cutting off the next year's blossoms. In a natural, low-upkeep landscape, titi works well planted as a thicket in wet or boggy ground, or in deep sandy soil with a high subsurface water table, where it can grow alongside flowering dogwood and mountain laurel.

54. Latin Name *Diospyros virginiana*
Common Name Eastern persimmon, common persimmon
Usual Height 15 to 25 feet when a thicket on abused land, 50 to 60 feet in post oak or other dry woodland, occasionally 100 to 130 feet in primeval forest
Spacing 30 feet for a specimen
Sun or Shade ◑ ◐ ○
Bloom Tiny, pale yellow, extremely fragrant flowers on both male and female trees, in spring when leaves half grown
Fruit Orange persimmons on female trees in fall, often hard and sour until first frost, sweetness varies from tree to tree
Leaves Glossy, golden orange to mauve in full sun in early fall
Trunk Dark brown, straight, fissured, up to 3 feet in diameter
Native Range Fields, thin woodland, Southeastern U.S., Zones 6 to 9
Soil Acid or alkaline, deep, clay, silt, clay loam
Drainage Dry, but tolerates flooding for a week
Root System Taproot, sometimes thicket forming
Companion Plants Sourwood, flowering dogwood, smooth sumac, eastern red cedar, redbud, blackgum, sassafras, fringetree, redbay
Propagation Fresh seed stratified immediately, root cuttings
Wildlife Fruit eaten by robin, opossum, raccoon, deer, bear, humans; leaves eaten by butterfly larvae; bees use flowers

Growing as a thicket on a hot, dry slope, **eastern persimmon** is ideal for erosion control. Old specimens I've seen are always straight-trunked, high branching, and free of suckers. I know this tree can be loaded with fragrant flowers in the shade, but if you also want lots of fruit and vivid fall color, place yours where it receives plenty of sun.

55. **Latin Name** *Halesia diptera*
Common Name Two-winged silverbell
Usual Height 15 to 25 feet, occasionally 55 feet
Spacing 15 feet
Sun or Shade ● ◑ ◐
Bloom White bells, 1 inch, before leaves in spring
Fruit 2 inches long, with 2 corky wings
Leaves 3 to 7 inches, dark green, thin, soft
Trunk Usually multitrunked, rarely a single trunk
up to 16 inches in diameter, brown, fissured
Native Range Hammocks, floodplains, swamp
margins, South Carolina to Arkansas and Texas,
Zones 7 to 8
Soil Acid, rich
Drainage Moist
Root System Deep
Companion Plants Swamp chestnut oak, white oak,
musclewood, cucumbertree, bigleaf magnolia,
storax, arrowwood, sweetshrub, Florida anise,
pawpaw, dwarf huckleberry
Propagation Double-stratified seed, layering, root
cuttings, greenwood cuttings in spring or fall
Wildlife Low use
Related Species *H. tetraptera* (*H. carolina*), Carolina
silverbell, Zones 6 to 8, has four-winged fruits

Two-winged silverbell is one of those trees that is
best appreciated up close; its blooms are beautifully
formed—bell-shaped, snowy white, and crisp in detail. Be
sure to plant yours under a deciduous canopy tree. Swamp
chestnut oak, white oak, beech, southern sugar maple, or
tulip poplar would be good choices. Any of these can
provide the shade that two-winged silverbell must have
in the summer. And, they are leafless in the winter,
when plenty of sunlight is needed if silverbell is going to
produce lots of spring flowers. Its kin, **Carolina silverbell**,
is very similar in its requirements. This is a larger tree with
smaller flowers and more cold-hardiness.

56. **Latin Name** *Hamamelis virginiana*
Common Name Witchhazel
Usual Height 15 to 20 feet, occasionally 45 feet
Spacing 30 to 40 feet
Sun or Shade ● ◑ ◐
Bloom Yellow, September to December, usually
after leaves fall, sharply fragrant
Fruit $1/2$ inch, brown, fall, explode to release seed
Leaves 4 to 6 inches, aromatic, yellow (sometimes
orange, purple) in fall
Trunk Crooked, usually multitrunked or low-
branching, with the main trunk up to 14 inches
in diameter, pale, smooth
Native Range Dry woods, rich woods, floodplains,
creek swamps, evergreen bogs, eastern North
America, Zones 5 to 8
Soil Acid, rich
Drainage Moist to dry
Root System Deep laterals
Companion Plants Deciduous canopy, with
strawberrybush, mapleleaf viburnum, mountain
laurel, American holly, flowering dogwood,
dwarf huckleberry, aster, goldenrod
Propagation Double-stratified seed, softwood
cuttings, layering from new wood
Wildlife Seed eaten by ruffed grouse and squirrels
Related Species *H. vernalis*, vernal witchhazel

Witchhazel is grown mostly for its winter flowers.
The photo shows the **vernal witchhazel** because I'm
partial to its coral color. Not all botanists recognize it as a
separate species from *H. virginiana*, but those who do
point to its deeper color, less treelike growth habit (it
colonizes and is shorter), and later bloom time—usually
February. Common witchhazel blooms most often in
November, when its yellow flowers blend well with
autumnal berries and late fall foliage. Cultivars of
witchhazel are selected to bloom after their own colorful
foliage has fallen, making them much showier in flower.

57. **Latin Name** *Ilex decidua*
    Common Name Possumhaw
    Usual Height 20 to 30 feet
    Spacing 20 feet for a specimen
    Sun or Shade ◑ ○
    Bloom White, tiny, in spring
    Fruit Red, orange, or yellow, early fall to spring, females only
    Leaves 2 to 3 inches, light green, not glossy
    Trunk Usually multitrunked, pale gray, smooth
    Native Range Floodplains, swamps, moist upland woods, eastern half U.S., Zones 6 to 8, except West Virginia and most of Kentucky, mostly Coastal Plain and Mississippi basin
    Soil Any except saline
    Drainage Dry, moist, or wet
    Root System Fibrous, might colonize, but rarely does so
    Companion Plants Hardwoods or pines, American holly, musclewood, hawthorns, serviceberry, sassafras, fringetree, rusty blackhaw viburnum
    Propagation Fresh seed, scarified (optional) and double-stratified seed, semihardwood cuttings
    Wildlife Fruit eaten by numerous songbirds, but only after several freeze-thaw cycles, a spring favorite of cedar waxwings
    Related Species *I. verticillata*, winterberry

If I had my way, I'd want every gardener in the South to enjoy the winter beauty of **possumhaw**. A female possumhaw is the showiest of the hollies in the winter because it doesn't have green leaves to partially hide the vivid red berries. A well-pruned specimen seems to glow on a cold winter day, even when the sky is drab and gloomy. It looks pretty terrific in a fall foliage garden, too, surrounded by oranges and golds. Plant your specimen female in full sun and give it ample room. **Winterberry** is less often a tree and requires more water.

58. **Latin Name** *Magnolia fraseri*
    Common Name Mountain magnolia, Fraser magnolia
    Usual Height 30 to 40 feet, rarely 80 feet
    Spacing 50 feet for specimen or woodland planting
    Sun or Shade ● ◐ ◑
    Bloom Creamy white to palest yellow, 8 to 10 inches across, fragrant, late spring
    Fruit Rosy red cone in fall
    Leaves Very big, 12 to 24 inches long and half as wide, with ears at the stem
    Trunk Straight, dark brown, smooth bark
    Native Range Rich woods, southern Appalachians to 4800 feet elevation, Zones 5 to 6
    Soil Acid, rich
    Drainage Moist
    Root System Shallow
    Companion Plants Hemlock, tulip poplar, basswood, cucumbertree, red oak, beech, black oak, white oak, blackgum, white ash
    Propagation Stratified seed
    Wildlife Seeds eaten by yellow-bellied sapsucker, towhee, red-eyed vireo, and eastern kingbird
    Related Species *M. macrophylla*, bigleaf magnolia; *M. ashei*, Ashe magnolia; *M. tripetala*, umbrella tree

The **mountain magnolia** and its more summer-hardy related species are commonly called the **large-leaf magnolias**. While this group of magnolias has long been ignored for landscape use, I'm happy to report the trend is changing. One reason is their huge, pale to medium green leaves, which are very striking. Even when the large-leaf magnolias are still babies, less than 10 feet tall, they provide a wonderfully bold focus, especially in a woodland setting full of more subtle shades and textures. **Umbrella tree** and **bigleaf magnolia** are native to rich woods in Zones 6 to 8. The **Ashe magnolia,** Zone 8 only, is more in the 15-to-30-foot range—a great size for small gardens.

59. **Latin Name** *Ostrya virginiana*
Common Name Hophornbeam, ironwood
Usual Height 20 to 30 feet, rarely 75 feet high
Spacing Narrow when young, 50-foot spread when mature
Sun or Shade ● ◑ ◐ ○
Bloom 2-inch catkins in spring
Fruit 1 to 3 inches, whitish, papery, hoplike, ornamental, summer
Leaves 3 to 5 inches long, yellow in early fall
Trunk Twisting, usually single and 10 inches in diameter, rarely 3 feet in diameter, cinnamon-colored shreddy bark
Native Range Hammocks, dry upland woods, eastern half of North America, Zones 4 to 8
Soil Acid, lime OK, rich preferred
Drainage Moist to dry, flooding not tolerated
Root System Taproot
Companion Plants Pine, post oak, blackgum, sassafras, redbud, musclewood
Propagation Double-stratified seed
Wildlife Seeds eaten by purple finch, downy woodpecker, mockingbird, and small mammals; flowers eaten by birds; leaves host insects valuable for nesting songbirds

Hophornbeam is grown for its ornamental summer fruits, which are white and dangling, not unlike decorations on a Christmas tree. It is adaptable to different soils, is tolerant of full sun and heavy shade, and grows to a very usable size for most home landscapes. It is closely kin to musclewood and looks similar until you examine the trunks, which are quite different. They also differ in locales of preference; musclewood can do well in wet or flooded sites, while hophornbeam wants excellent drainage.

60. **Latin Name** *Oxydendrum arboreum*
Common Name Sourwood, sorreltree
Usual Height 20 to 30 feet, occasionally 60 feet
Spacing Narrow crown, 20 feet
Sun or Shade ◑ ○
Bloom White bells on long curving spikes, fragrant, midsummer
Fruit Yellow, then tan spikes, fall
Leaves 5 to 7 inches long, very firm and glossy, pink in spring, scarlet in early fall
Trunk Straight, tall, up to 20 inches in diameter, gray, furrowed; if trunk is cut, tree will sprout from stump
Native Range Bluffs, thin upland woods, Southeastern U.S. to 5500 feet elevation, rare west of the Mississippi, Zones 6 to 8
Soil Very acid, acid, rich; deep, very acid surface soil over subsurface limestone OK
Drainage Moist to dry, does not tolerate flooding
Root System Shallow, does not colonize
Companion Plants Tulip poplar, post oak, red maple, flowering dogwood, eastern persimmon, blackgum, sassafras, mountain laurel
Propagation Fresh seed, tissue culture
Wildlife Seed eaten by songbirds, turkey, grouse, small mammals; flowers used by bees (famous honey) and butterflies; foliage browsed by deer

Of all the trees we saw in our travels throughout the Southeast, **sourwood** impressed us the most. It is nothing short of outstanding when in flower, even when seen at highway speeds. In the fall, its red foliage is always sure to elicit a reverent "Wow!" Naturally, we asked why we saw sourwood only rarely in home landscapes. Some people told us it was difficult to transplant; an equal number said it was easy. One thing I know for sure—it's easy to grow from seed, so if you can't find one at the nursery, grow your own.

61. **Latin Name** *Pinckneya bracteata (Pinckneya pubens)*
    Common Name Pinckneya, fevertree, Georgia bark
    Usual Height 15 to 20 feet, rarely 30 feet
    Spacing 15 feet
    Sun or Shade ◑ ◐ ○
    Bloom Tiny greenish flowers surrounded by 2-inch pink sepals, late May and June
    Fruit 1 inch, brown, fall
    Leaves 5 to 8 inches, soft
    Trunk Usually multitrunked, up to 10 inches in diameter, brown
    Native Range Rare, creek swamps, titi swamps, bogs, South Georgia, Florida Panhandle, south coast of South Carolina, Zone 8
    Soil Very acid, acid, sandy
    Drainage Wet
    Root System Might colonize
    Companion Plants Pine, titi, gordonia, sweetbay, redbay, wax myrtle, swamp azalea, inkberry, fetterbush, poison sumac
    Propagation Untreated seed, softwood cuttings
    Wildlife No information

It's unusual for a tree to be blooming in June, but **Pinckneya** is covered with pink at that time of year. It requires lots of moisture, as well as a fair amount of sun, so it's not always easy to find the perfect spot for it. Which might be one reason it is so rare in the wild now that fires are rare. When you do run across one, it is usually found in the shadow of a taller tree, or along the sunny edge of a swamp or bog. The wood is not very strong, and it is not long-lived. Still, it is easy to grow, and, I think, a very pretty ornamental.

62. **Latin Name** *Quercus laevis*
    Common Name Turkey oak
    Usual Height 20 to 30 feet, occasionally 60 feet
    Spacing Equivalent to height
    Sun or Shade ◑ ◐ ○
    Bloom Red flowers, 4 to 5 inches long, in spring
    Fruit Large acorns
    Leaves Chartreuse in spring, dark green and glossy in summer, red in late fall
    Trunk Less than 2 feet in diameter; sometimes shrubby; bark is black and corky
    Native Range Sandhills, oak scrub, post oak woods, Coastal Plain from southeastern Virginia to eastern Louisiana, Zones 8 to 9
    Soil Very acid, acid, sandy, poor
    Drainage Dry
    Root System Deep
    Companion Plants Longleaf pine, *Q. incana*, *Q. margaretta*, *Q. geminata*, *Q. marilandica*, southern red oak, post oak, eastern persimmon, blackgum, sparkleberry, wiregrass, bracken, reindeer moss, sandhill rosemary, trailing arbutus
    Propagation Fresh acorns in fall
    Wildlife Acorns eaten by red-cockaded woodpecker, wild turkey, bluejay

Turkey oak is the most common understory tree in a longleaf pine forest. Plant it in your landscape, and each fall you can enjoy its glossy scarlet fall color beneath the delicate canopy of longleaf pine. Compared to most oaks, it is fast-growing and short-lived. It's adapted to cope with extreme drought, and does so in several interesting ways. The large acorns store extra food and moisture, to give the seedlings a fighting chance. Also, those glossy leaves are glossy only on the topsides to reflect heat. On the undersides they are fuzzy to trap moisture. The leaves grow perpendicular to the ground to avoid the full force of the sun when it is at its highest and hottest.

63. **Latin Name** *Rhus copallina*
    Common Name Winged sumac
    Usual Height 10 to 15 feet, rarely 50 feet
    Spacing 10 to 15 feet
    Sun or Shade ◗ ○
    Bloom White, 4- to 6-inch pyramids, early summer
    Fruit Red, in 4- to 6-inch clusters on females, late summer, dry
    Leaves 8 to 12 inches long with 9 to 21 leaflets, glossy, with wings either side of the midrib, scarlet to dark red in early fall
    Trunk Multi- or singletrunked with a diameter up to 10 inches in diameter, smooth, pale gray
    Native Range Fields, roadsides, fencerows, eastern half of North America, Zones 5 to 9
    Soil Acid, sandy
    Drainage Dry
    Root System Might colonize to form a thicket
    Companion Plants Longleaf pine, shortleaf pine, post oak
    Propagation Scarified seed, semihardwood cuttings in late summer
    Wildlife Fruits eaten by mockingbird, yellow-shafted flicker, fish crow, phoebe, robin, brown thrasher, red-eyed vireo, cardinal, downy woodpecker, pine warbler; flowers visited by butterflies; bark eaten by rabbits in winter
    Related Species *R. typhina*, staghorn sumac; *R. glabra*, smooth sumac

Winged sumac is useful for new homes where the developer has pretty much denuded the property. Its leaves are extremely acid and help rebuild soil that has been stripped of its organic matter. As soon as canopy trees begin to shade it out, it dies. In an established landscape, plant it on the edge of a lawn or driveway to attract birds. **Staghorn sumac** is for Yankees and mountaineers. **Smooth sumac** is more weedy and is suitable mainly for erosion control on large-scale projects.

64. **Latin Name** *Sassafras albidum*
    Common Name Sassafras
    Usual Height 20 feet in a thicket, 40 to 90 feet as a specimen
    Spacing Half the intended height
    Sun or Shade ◗ ○
    Bloom Yellow, before leaves, male trees are showier
    Fruit Dark blue on red stalk, late summer, female trees only
    Leaves One- or two-thumbed mittens or plainly shaped, yellow, gold, and orange in early fall, aromatic
    Trunk Straight, reddish, smooth, aromatic, large trunks recorded from 1 to 5 feet in diameter
    Native Range Thin woods, old fields, eastern U.S., Zones 5 to 8 and in mountains in southern Mexico and Guatemala
    Soil Acid, coarse preferred
    Drainage Dry
    Root System Deep, often suckering
    Companion Plants Eastern persimmon, post oak, American holly, pawpaw, white ash, sourwood, flowering dogwood, musclewood, blackgum, red maple, sparkleberry, sweetleaf
    Propagation Stratified seed, root cuttings
    Wildlife Fruits a big favorite with robin, eaten in limited quantities by kingbird, crested flycatcher, eastern phoebe, catbird, brown thrasher, sapsucker, thrushes, red- and white-eyed vireos, pileated woodpecker; leaves eaten by larvae of swallowtails (and by humans as filé in gumbo; bark of roots used in tea)

Sassafras often grows in thickets, which shows off its vivid spring and fall colors to best advantage. Suggested use: plant it at the entrance to a country home or to round out the corner of a meadow. But, it can also be a well-mannered, medium to large canopy tree in a small, sunny, urban landscape.

65. Latin Name *Vaccinium arboreum*

    Common Name Sparkleberry, farkleberry

    Usual Height 20 to 30 feet, occasionally 45 feet

    Spacing 20 to 30 feet

    Sun or Shade ● ◑ ◐ ○

    Bloom White bells, ¹/₂ inch, fragrant, in spring after leaves are on

    Fruit Gritty, nonjuicy blueberries, October, lasting into winter

    Leaves ¹/₂ to 2 inches, stiff, glossy, red in early fall

    Trunk Crooked, up to 10 inches in diameter, reddish, shreddy

    Native Range Sandhills, scrub, dunes, coastal hammocks, post oak woodland, Southeastern U.S., Zones 6 to 9

    Soil Acid to slightly alkaline, saline OK

    Drainage Dry to moist, short flooding OK

    Root System Might colonize to form a thicket

    Companion Plants Post oak, live oak, longleaf pine, eastern red cedar, blackgum, eastern persimmon, sourwood, parsley hawthorn, sassafras, sweetleaf, wax myrtle, American beautyberry

    Propagation Softwood cuttings in spring, dormant hardwood cuttings

    Wildlife Fruits eaten by bluebird, catbird, yellow-breasted chat, yellow-shafted flicker, flycatcher, kingbird, oriole, phoebe, Bachman's sparrow, thrasher, hermit thrush, tufted titmouse, and mammals; larval plant for Henry's elfin butterfly, flowers provide nectar for butterflies

    Related Species *V. corymbosum,* highbush blueberry, which includes *V. ashei,* rabbitberry, and *V. elliottii,* mayberry

Sparkleberry is our only tree-sized blueberry. Its cousin, **highbush blueberry,** grows to 12 feet, is multistemmed in habit, and has delicious, highly prized fruit and late fall color.

66. Latin Name *Viburnum obovatum*

    Common Name Walter's viburnum

    Usual Height 12 to 20 feet, rarely 30 feet

    Spacing 15 feet

    Sun or Shade ◑ ◐ ○

    Bloom White, 1- to 3-inch clusters, in spring as new leaves emerge

    Fruit ¹/₄ inch, not juicy, red to black in early fall

    Leaves 1 to 2 inch, aromatic, sometimes evergreen in Zone 9

    Trunk Often multitrunked, up to 6 inches in diameter, dark rough bark

    Native Range Stream banks, floodplains, woodlands or fields, South Carolina to eastern Alabama and Florida, Zones 8 to 9

    Soil Acid, sandy or rich

    Drainage Moist to wet

    Root System Grows very slowly

    Companion Plants Sweetbay, swampbay, titi, gordonia, wax myrtle, inkberry

    Propagation Semihardwood cuttings in fall; fresh sown seed takes 2 to 3 years to germinate

    Wildlife Flowers a nectar source for butterflies; fruit eaten by birds and small mammals

    Related Species *V. rufidulum,* rusty blackhaw viburnum; *V. prunifolium,* blackhaw viburnum

Walter's viburnum is the one we found most often in Southern gardens—possibly because this small tree is better able to tolerate moist and wet landscapes. However, it's **rusty blackhaw viburnum** that is most common in the wild. It's also, I think, the prettiest, with glossy red fall leaves that look like they've been dipped in lacquer. **Blackhaw viburnum** is the most cold-tolerant of the trio. All the Southeastern viburnums are slow-growing and long-lived. They can be found in dense woods, but they flower, fruit, and color best with about 6 hours of sun each day.

6

TALL SHRUBS 5 TO 15 FEET TALL

The shrubs in this chapter rarely get over 15 feet tall, and then only by a tad. Mountain laurel and rosebay rhododendron are the tallest of this lot, sometimes reaching small-tree status—up to 40 feet—but this is so rare that it's not something you could count on happening in your landscape.

Many of these shrubs—both evergreen shrubs and flowering shrubs—sucker or colonize. This is an enormous asset when you want a mass planting, which is just a fancy name for a short thicket. Of course, you know the old saw about a watched pot never boiling; that seems to hold true for shrubs. If you want them to form an instant thicket for you, they seem to have other ideas. Or they do it at glacial speed. If this happens, just plant a mass of shrubs as if you never expected them to colonize.

The evergreen shrubs and the flowering shrubs are usually used in different ways—one as a screen, the other for permanent displays of color. But you can also com-

bine them in a sunny border around a meadow or pond, or in a shady border around a small lawn or along a neighbor's fence, where it will give you year-round pleasure. Unless you are planting a hedgerow, don't line them up. Instead, cluster them in loose curves as though they had grown up naturally.

Bottlebrush buckeye in Louise Smith's woodland garden in Birmingham, Alabama.

EVERGREEN SCREENING SHRUBS, USUALLY UNDER 15 FEET

Evergreen shrubs are the main screening plants in a small urban landscape. Agarista, inkberry, and southern bayberry should be mainstays of moist, Southern Coastal Plain gardens. They combine well with each other, and the contrast in size, color, and texture of their leaves can make even an evergreen hedge interesting. For colder climate gardens, mountain laurel and rosebay rhododendron give wonderful flowers as well as winter greenery.

The pink flower clusters of evergreen Catawba rhododendron combine beautifully with white-flowered Alabama azalea in early June at the University Botanical Gardens in Asheville, North Carolina.

67. **Latin Name** *Agarista populifolia* (previously
    Leucothoe populifolia)
    Common Name Agarista, Florida leucothoe, tall
    fetterbush
    Usual Height 8 to 12 feet
    Spacing 5 to 6 feet
    Sun or Shade ● ◑
    Bloom White bells, fragrant, late spring, on last
    year's wood
    Fruit Tan, dry, 1/4 inch
    Leaves Evergreen, 2 to 4 inches, glossy, new growth
    is coppery red
    Native Range Rare, moist hammocks, wet
    woodlands, springs, South Carolina to Florida,
    Zones 8 to 9
    Soil Acid, rich
    Drainage Very moist
    Root System Fibrous, shallow
    Companion Plants Red maple, pine, swampbay,
    sweetbay, gordonia, swamp azalea, titi, itea,
    leucothoe, wax myrtle, highbush blueberry,
    clethra, cinnamon fern, sensitive fern
    Propagation Semihardwood cuttings
    Wildlife No information

Can you get conventional gardeners and native-plant gardeners to agree on anything? You bet. It's **agarista.** They all love its glossy, evergreen foliage, its tolerance for shade, and its formal, handsome appearance. It is a somewhat stiff shrub with numerous stems that arch over gracefully. Agarista is best used as a specimen in a damp, shady corner or on the bank of a pond or stream, but I have also seen it used as a hedge.

68. **Latin Name** *Ceratiola ericoides*
    Common Name Sandhill rosemary
    Usual Height 1 1/2 to 8 feet
    Spacing 3 feet
    Sun or Shade ◑ ○
    Bloom Male flowers reddish or yellow, fall
    Fruit Tiny, red or yellow-green, on female plants
    only, winter
    Leaves Evergreen, aromatic, 1/2 inch needles
    Native Range Rare, sandhills, dunes, scrub, Coastal
    Plain from South Carolina to Mississippi, Zones
    8 to 9
    Soil Very acid, acid, sterile sand preferred
    Drainage Dry
    Root System Deep, hard to transplant
    Companion Plants Longleaf pine, turkey oak,
    winged sumac, fetterbush, lichens, evergreen
    blueberry, calamintha, yaupon holly, sweetleaf,
    bracken, wiregrass, broomsedge
    Propagation Seed, November cuttings
    Wildlife Fresh winter fruits should be valuable

If you live on deep, fast-draining sugar sand, I don't have to tell you how tough it is to keep Asian azaleas and St. Augustine lawn alive. In that case, turn to **sandhill rosemary.** This extremely attractive shrub loves that dry environment and needs very little water to look its best. In fact, if you water it the way you would conventional nursery stock, you'll do it in. That's why it's rarely found in nurseries. Specialty nurseries occasionally carry some, but you might have to grow your own. Sandhill rosemary can be used as a hedge, a screen, or a mass planting. You can periodically whack it in half to make a knee-high groundcover. It does not need fire to maintain its vigor. In fact, sandhill rosemary does not tolerate fire the way many other of the longleaf pine's companion plants can.

69. **Latin Name** *Ilex glabra*
    Common Name Inkberry, gallberry
    Usual Height 7 to 9 feet, occasionally 12 feet high
    Spacing 8 to 10 feet
    Sun or Shade ◗ ○
    Bloom White, tiny, spring
    Fruit Black (rarely white), not juicy, fall and winter, on females
    Leaves Evergreen, 1 to 2 inches, dark, glossy, foliage burn below −20 degrees F.
    Native Range Pine savannahs, flatwoods, bogs, mostly on Coastal Plains from Nova Scotia to Texas, Zones 5 to 9
    Soil Acid, sandy
    Drainage Moist, on edges of wet or over a high water table
    Root System Might colonize to form a thicket
    Companion Plants Longleaf pine, turkey oak, mountain laurel, highbush blueberry, dwarf huckleberry, redbay, ebony spleenwort, bracken fern, or swampbay, sweetbay, loblolly, titi, winterberry, wax myrtle, lyonia, clethra, itea, leucothoe
    Propagation Cleaned seed, semihardwood cuttings
    Wildlife Fruit used by at least 50 species of birds, including bluebird, brown thrasher, hermit thrush

When conditions are too wet for most non-native evergreens, rely on native **inkberry.** This useful shrub is long-lived, slow-growing, and fine-textured—all characteristics that make it desirable for formal hedges in traditional gardens. But it is also invaluable as screening and as winter bird food in more natural landscapes. When it gets lots of sun, it will become dense without shearing or pruning, as in the picture. It has a looser structure in light shade. Whatever you do, don't plant it in heavy shade; in the wild whenever the forest canopy gets multilayered and dense, inkberry dwindles away and dies.

70. **Latin Name** *Kalmia latifolia*
    Common Name Mountain laurel, calico bush
    Usual Height 10 to 15 feet, occasionally 40 feet
    Spacing 15 to 20 feet
    Sun or Shade ● ◗ ◗ ○
    Bloom 4- to 5-inch clusters of white to pink flowers, April and May, June in mountains
    Fruit Tan, dry, fall
    Leaves 3 to 4 inches, dark green, leathery, glossy
    Trunk Contorted, up to 20 inches in diameter, exfoliating with a smooth, cinnamon-colored inner bark
    Native Range Bluffs, upland woods, sandy stream terraces, New Brunswick to southeastern Louisiana, Zones 5 to 8
    Soil Very acid, acid, rich east slopes preferred
    Drainage Moist to dry
    Root System Extensive, hard to transplant, colonizes to form a thicket
    Companion Plants Beech, white oak, tulip poplar, umbrella tree, cucumbertree, storax, wild rhododendrons, wild hydrangea, strawberrybush, spicebush, leucothoe, sweetshrub, fringetree, sweetleaf, sparkleberry, pawpaw
    Propagation Difficult from seed or cuttings, tissue culture
    Wildlife Browsed by deer, poisonous to livestock

When it comes to aesthetics, **mountain laurel** has everything going for it: handsome leaves, beautiful blooms, terrific bark. It would be in every garden right now but for one problem—it is hard to propagate. The good news is that new methods may soon have this wonderful native on the market in quantity. Mountain laurel is not finicky about growing conditions as long as the soil is acid and well drained. On a slight slope with shade part of the day is ideal. But I've seen it on sunny mountainsides, in fairly dense woods, and even in longleaf pine habitats where water was not far below the surface.

71. **Latin Name** *Myrica heterophylla*
  Common Name Southern bayberry, swamp candleberry
  Usual Height 5 to 7 feet, occasionally 10 feet high
  Spacing 5 to 10 feet
  Sun or Shade ◑ ◐ ○
  Bloom Yellowish white, tiny, April
  Fruit Blue, waxy, 1/4 inch, on females only, fall and winter
  Leaves Evergreen, 3 to 5 inches, olive-green, aromatic, on black stems, will defoliate in a severe winter
  Native Range Bogs, pocosins, pine savannahs, flatwoods, New Jersey to Texas, Coastal Plain and Piedmont, Zones 7 to 8
  Soil Very acid, acid
  Drainage Wet
  Root System Will colonize to form a thicket
  Companion Plants Sweetbay, swampbay, titi
  Propagation Stratified seed, softwood or semihardwood cuttings
  Wildlife Fruits eaten by waterfowl, catbird, myrtle warbler, Carolina chickadee, tree swallow, and others
  Related Species *M. pensylvanica,* northern bayberry, Zones 6 to 8

Southern bayberry has the evergreen characteristics of wax myrtle and the larger berries, shorter height, and fatter leaves of **northern bayberry.** This is a fine low-growing shrub for all you folks who live on the kind of wetlands where crawfish roam.

72. **Latin Name** *Rhododendron maximum*
  Common Name Rosebay rhododendron, great laurel, wild rhododendron
  Usual Height 10 to 15 feet, occasionally 40 feet
  Spacing 15 feet
  Sun or Shade ● ◑ ◐
  Bloom 4- to 5-inch clusters, white, pink, rose, or lavender, June
  Fruit 1/2 inch, brown, dry, splitting open in fall
  Leaves Evergreen, 4 to 12 inches, dark green, leathery, glossy, pale iridescent underneath, curl up and drop in severe cold or in drought
  Trunk Usually multitrunked, crooked, leaning, up to 1 foot in diameter, reddish
  Native Range Hardwood forests on stream banks, ravines, slopes, or swamps, Appalachians in Georgia to Nova Scotia, Zones 5 to 6
  Soil Very acid, rich; iron-rich surface soil over limestone OK
  Drainage Moist
  Root System Shallow, colonizes to form thickets
  Companion Plants Hemlock, tulip poplar, umbrella tree, cucumbertree, musclewood, mountain laurel, leucothoe
  Propagation Seeds need constant moisture
  Wildlife Flowers used by hummingbirds and butterflies
  Related Species *R. catawbiense,* Catawba rhododendron, mountain rosebay

Rosebay rhododendron captured my heart when I saw it cascading down a densely wooded slope above a native plant garden in the Smokies. Its cousin, the **Catawba rhododendron,** is more commonly found in nurseries and is often crossed with non-native varieties. Catawba has the reputation of being more heat tolerant than rosebay, but gardeners I talked to were not finding this to be true. Both rhododendrons are beautiful plants that can make small, picturesque trees in their old age.

FLOWERING AND FRUITING SHRUBS, USUALLY UNDER 15 FEET

Flowering shrubs produce blooms on a large scale. Cluster them under canopy trees in the back yard. Cram them into a hedgerow beside your driveway. Arrange them on the edges of woodland to create a three-season, easy-care border around a church or municipal building or even an industrial complex.

And, by all means, plant them along the fence on the borders of a school yard. These attractive shrubs will provide invaluable year-round teaching opportunities, with all the activity taking place up close and personal. The children can watch winter buds swelling and flowers bursting forth, butterflies and hummingbirds sipping the nectar from blooms, and migrating birds contesting for the choicest of the fall fruits. Birds that winter over will use these shrubs for shelter, some even claiming a specific shrub as a favorite for food and lodging.

Oakleaf hydrangea, at the end of a path, makes a strong focal point in Bickie McDonnell's Memphis garden, designed by Tom Pellett. Its late spring/early summer whiteness is echoed by a limestone dry stream bed and two non-natives (white astilbe and blue-leaved hosta). Warmer accents are provided by two natives—red-flowered Indian pink and cinnamon fern.

73. **Latin Name** *Aesculus parviflora*
Common Name Bottlebrush buckeye
Usual Height 6 to 8 feet, occasionally 15 feet to 20 feet
Spacing 8 to 15 feet
Sun or Shade ● ◑ ◐
Bloom White, 6- to 24-inch spikes, early summer
Fruit Buckeyes in 1- to 2-inch tan shells, hard
Leaves Star-shaped, 5 (sometimes 7) leaflets, rarely yellow in fall
Native Range Rare, bluffs, river banks, wooded hillsides, Alabama and western Georgia, Zones 7 to 8
Soil Acid or basic, rich
Drainage Moist
Root System Colonizes, will not transplant from wild
Companion Plants Tulip tree, beech, cucumbertree, oakleaf hydrangea
Propagation Fresh seed sown immediately while still moist, root cuttings, softwood cuttings
Wildlife Flowers visited by hummingbirds

Bottlebrush buckeye doesn't look like any shrub you've ever seen. This odd-shaped shrub sounds awful when you hear it described—large and loose with vertical spikes, big flat leaves, and numerous stems springing up from the ground. In actuality, it is visually very appealing, and enormously popular with all who see it in person. (Andy apologizes; the photo doesn't do it justice.) I'd suggest using it in a shady spot by an entrance, as the focus at the end of a lawn area, or, if you have a large property, at a curve along a woodland path.

74. **Latin Name** *Callicarpa americana*
Common Name American beautyberry, French mulberry
Usual Height 4 to 6 feet, occasionally 15 feet
Spacing 6 to 8 feet, do not crowd
Sun or Shade ● ◑ ◐ ○
Bloom Tiny, white to pink, spring
Fruit Purple (white), glossy, 2-inch bunches, October to winter, not juicy
Leaves 3 to 6 inches, soft, coarse, hairy, drop early fall, rarely turning yellow
Native Range Live oak woods, post oak woods, dunes, scrub, fencerows, flatwoods, bluffs, eastern North America, Zones 6 to 11
Soil Acid, lime OK, rich or very poor OK
Drainage Dry to moist
Root System Deep
Companion Plants Live oak, post oak, pines, sparkleberry, parsley hawthorn, rusty blackhaw viburnum, flowering dogwood
Propagation Seed (stratified or wintered over in ground), softwood or hardwood cuttings
Wildlife Fruits eaten by mockingbird, purple finch (matches the color of the berries), bobwhite, catbird, robin, brown thrasher, towhee, armadillo, raccoon, and white-tailed deer

American beautyberry presents the fullest display of fruit when it gets a half day of sun. But it also does well in the light, dappled shade of a post oak/pine woodland. I've seen it in the dense shade of live oaks as the main understory shrub (growing about 8 feet apart) with spiderworts as the groundcover. A single specimen should be given lots of room to spread out its long, arching branches. Prune out dead wood only. If you drastically cut off the ends, it will look awkward instead of graceful. In a severe winter, if it freezes to the ground, you will still have fruit on new growth by fall, according to Larry Lowman, a nurseryman in Wynne, Arkansas.

75. Latin Name *Calycanthus floridus*
    Common Name Sweetshrub, Carolina allspice, strawberry shrub
    Usual Height 6 to 8 feet, occasionally 12 feet
    Spacing 4 to 12 feet
    Sun or Shade ● ◑ ◐
    Bloom Dark red, 1 to 2 inch, smells like sweet, ripe fruit, spring
    Fruit Green, then brown, 3 inches long, smells of strawberries, not edible
    Leaves 2 to 6 inches long, dark green, fuzzy, aromatic, sometimes yellow in fall
    Native Range Bluffs, floodplains, rich moist woodlands, Pennsylvania to Mississippi, Zones 6 to 8
    Soil Acid to neutral, rich
    Drainage Moist, but flooding tolerated
    Root System Shallow, might colonize to form a thicket
    Companion Plants Hemlock, sprucepine, oak, hickory, sourwood, leucothoe, rhododendrons, spicebush, hydrangeas, witchhazel, storax, pawpaw, mountain laurel
    Propagation Seed, cuttings, layering, divisions
    Wildlife No information

Neil Odenwald, an author and landscape architect in Baton Rouge, Louisiana, describes **sweetshrub** as a "bosom" plant. He explains that this is because, in earlier times, it was planted by the front door so that the lady of the house could pluck off some of the sweet blossoms to put in her bosom when going out on the town. You can enjoy this fruity fragrant shrub for its aroma most of the year; the leaves and the inedible fruit are as deliciously scented as the flowers. Sweetshrub is for touching and sniffing and seeing up close, so place it where you will pass close by frequently.

76. Latin Name *Clethra alnifolia*
    Common Name Clethra, sweet pepperbush
    Usual Height 3 to 6 feet, rarely 12 feet
    Spacing 3 to 6 feet
    Sun or Shade ● ◑ ◐ ○
    Bloom White or pink, 3- to 8-inch spikes, very fragrant, in summer on new growth
    Fruit Tiny, tan, fall, dry
    Leaves 1 to 4 inch, bronze in spring, cream to gold in early fall
    Native Range Pine savannah, flatwoods, creek and acid swamps, bogs, eastern U.S., Maine to Texas, mostly coastal, Zones 5 to 8
    Soil Very acid, acid, sand or clay OK
    Drainage Wet
    Root System Shallow, colonizes to form thickets
    Companion Plants Longleaf or loblolly pine, red maple, swampbay, sweetbay, swamp azalea, fetterbush, inkberry, itea, staggerbush
    Propagation Seed on sand, softwood cuttings, layering, division
    Wildlife Flowers visited by bees, butterflies, and hummingbirds; fruits eaten by songbirds, shorebirds, waterfowl, upland gamebirds, small mammals
    Related Species *C. acuminata,* mountain pepperbush, cinnamon clethra

Even from several feet away, you are aware of **clethra**'s outstanding fragrance—not unlike fine French perfume. But it is valued for other attributes: It blooms in summer, which is typically the off-season for shrubs. It tolerates difficult shady spots. It thrives in wet, even soggy conditions, and is stressed only if it gets too dry. And—can you believe there is more?—it has a long season of lovely fall color. In the mountains above 2500 feet, clethra is replaced by its cousin **mountain pepperbush**, a 20-foot tall shrub or tree that will not tolerate soggy conditions.

77. **Latin Name** *Croton alabamensis* var. *alabamensis*
    Common Name Alabama croton
    Usual Height 4 to 9 feet
    Spacing 3 to 6 feet
    Sun or Shade ● ◐ ◑
    Bloom Insignificant visually
    Fruit Silvery capsules, not juicy, spring
    Leaves Almost evergreen, 2 to 5 inches, aromatic, yellow-green on top, silver underneath, orange fall color or occasional orange leaves in summer
    Native Range Rare, thinly wooded river bluffs on shale or limestone, Alabama, Tennessee, Zone 7
    Soil Rich, slightly acid, lime OK
    Drainage Moist
    Root System Might colonize to form a thicket
    Companion Plants Tulip poplar, basswood, chalk maple, possumhaw, storax, scarlet buckeye
    Propagation Fresh seed in May, semihardwood cuttings
    Wildlife Seeds eaten by quail and dove

Alabama croton will instantly delight and charm you—especially with its marvelous, spicy, aromatic foliage In fact, it deserves to be in every fragrance garden. Visually, it makes a graceful, airy understory thicket or a specimen plant in moderate to heavily dappled shade. In dim light, it catches your eye with its intensely silver leaves. These leaves might stay on during a mild winter, with a few turning a pleasant, smooth, clear orange. If the leaves drop, the stems, which are silvery white, become dominant.

78. **Latin Name** *Euonymus americanus*
    Common Name Strawberrybush, hearts-a-burstin', Wahoo
    Usual Height 4 to 8 feet
    Spacing 4 to 5 feet
    Sun or Shade ● ◑
    Bloom 1/2 inch, pale lime, inconspicuous, spring
    Fruit 1 inch, strawberry red, bursts open to show scarlet seeds, early fall to winter
    Leaves 1 to 4 inches, medium green, soft, red, fuchsia, salmon, cream, or white in late fall
    Native Range Moist woodlands, hammocks, eastern U.S., Zones 6 to 9
    Soil Acid to neutral, rich
    Drainage Moist, tolerates short-term flooding
    Root System Shallow, might colonize to form a thicket
    Companion Plants Hemlock, tulip poplar, beech, white oak, sprucepine, musclewood, flowering dogwood, storax, wild hydrangea, mapleleaf viburnum, spicebush, sweetshrub, rosebay, mountain laurel, leucothoe, itea, partridgeberry
    Propagation Stratified seed, semihardwood cuttings rooted in cold frame, layering, grafting, budding
    Wildlife Seeds eaten by wild turkey, browsed by deer and rabbits

Strawberrybush is an open, airy shrub with pale green stems and it provides a lovely light touch in shady areas. We saw it in numerous gardens, evidence that it is easy to grow. It usually has red fall color, but we saw one (pictured) with white fall foliage, which we thought was outstanding with the red fruits. We have been told this is typical fall color in very heavy shade. Winged euonymus (*Euonymus alatus*) has dark red fall color and is the one you see in conventional landscapes everywhere. It is native to Asia and is too dense and heavy-looking for a native American woodland landscape.

79. **Latin Name** *Fothergilla major*
Common Name Large fothergilla, witchalder
Usual Height 2 to 5 feet, rarely to 12 feet
Spacing 3 to 5 feet
Sun or Shade ◑ ◐ ○
Bloom White, 1 to 3 inches, long fat bottlebrush spikes, fragrant, either before or with emerging leaves in spring
Fruit Tiny, brown, fall, dry
Leaves 2 to 5 inches, aromatic, dark blue-green in summer; yellow, orange, and red, sometimes all on the same leaf, in late fall
Native Range Rare, dry woods, balds, Allegheny Mountains, North Carolina to Alabama, Zones 5 to 7
Soil Acid, sandstone
Drainage Moist to dry
Root System Deep, might colonize to form a thicket
Companion Plants Tulip poplar, Carolina silverbell, cucumbertree, pawpaw, witchhazel
Propagation Double-stratified seed, cuttings, root cuttings, division; buy only nursery-propagated plants
Wildlife Seeds sometimes eaten by songbirds, game birds, small mammals; no information on nectar use of flowers
Related Species *F. gardenii,* dwarf fothergilla

There are two Southeastern fothergillas, and both are on the federal endangered list. **Large fothergilla** is for the mountains and Piedmont. **Dwarf fothergilla** is for the Coastal Plain; it can handle boggy conditions once in a while. Its height and leaves are half the size of its bigger cousin, but its flowers are just as large. It grows with the sweetbay/swampbay community, and is native only to Zone 8—although I've been told that it has been used successfully in Zone 6. Cultivars of both fothergillas are available, as is a hybrid of the two.

80. **Latin Name** *Hydrangea quercifolia*
Common Name Oakleaf hydrangea
Usual Height 6 to 8 feet, occasionally 10 feet
Spacing 6 to 8 feet
Sun or Shade ● ◐ ◑
Bloom White , 4- to 12-inch pyramidal cluster, late spring, turning rose pink, then purple
Fruit Tiny, urn-shaped, tan, dry, tinier seeds
Leaves 4 to 12 inches long, oakleaf-shaped, fuzzy when young, red, wine, and purple in late fall
Native Range Bluffs, stream banks, ravines, pine/hardwood woodlands, eastern U.S., Zones 6b to 8, mostly in limestone areas
Soil Acid, rich, deep, subsurface limestone OK
Drainage Moist to dry
Root System Might colonize to make a thicket
Companion Plants Sparkleberry, sourwood, rusty blackhaw viburnum, flowering dogwood, leucothoe, bottlebrush buckeye, smilacina
Propagation Semihardwood cuttings, root cuttings, layering
Wildlife Seeds eaten by a few songbirds, game birds, and mammals

Most gardens can accommodate only one **oakleaf hydrangea**—it's so huge and grand, it becomes the centerpiece of a late spring landscape. This shrub actually has two kinds of flowers in the same cluster: little fluffy seed-producers, and larger sterile flowers—which put on the show. They stay in color for a long time, starting off pure snowy white, then turning pink, then rose, then purple—especially in the sun. They then dry to a parchmentlike texture and stick around until the leaves turn red to purple in the fall. After the leaves have dropped, the bark claims your attention. It peels off in pale, often peaches-and-cream, papery curls. Most cultivars accentuate the sterile flowers, but when you get *all* sterile flowers, the clusters get too heavy, and the plant looks droopy and woebegone.

(Benny J. Simpson)

81. **Latin Name** *Lindera benzoin*
Common Name Spicebush
Usual Height 3 to 10 feet
Spacing 8 to 10 feet
Sun or Shade ● ◑ ◐ ○
Bloom Yellow, spicily fragrant, February, before leaves appear
Fruit $1/3$ inch, scarlet red, glossy, spicy-scented, not squishy, fall
Leaves 2 to 5 inches, lemon-scented, pale yellow as emerging, dark green, glossy in summer, yellow to gold in early fall
Trunk Multitrunked, smooth, greenish, with raised dots, bark and twigs spicily aromatic
Native Range Fields, bluffs, floodplains, hammocks, eastern North America, Zones 4 to 8
Soil Acid, coarse, sandy, rich loam preferred
Drainage Moist to dryish
Root System Deep, hard to transplant
Companion Plants Beech, swamp chestnut oak, American holly, storax, cucumbertree, mapleleaf viburnum, strawberrybush, itea, smilacina
Propagation Fresh, stratified seed, softwood cuttings, layering
Wildlife Seeds eaten by 24 species of birds, including thrushes, catbird, great crested flycatcher, red-eyed vireo, and eastern kingbird; larval plant for spicebush and tiger swallowtails

I have an immense fondness for **spicebush**. The first spring I lived in Virginia I was overcome with the most wonderful strong, spicy, sweet scent imaginable. I traced it to a lovely little tree. The stems were dotted with fluffy clumps of fragrant yellow flowers. I discovered later that the leaves, twigs, and even the fruits are aromatic also, and can be used for tea or cooking. I have been told that the cultivar currently sold in nurseries (unbelievably) does not have the delightful scent! Place spicebush in full sun to get a good crop of fruit for the birds.

82. **Latin Name** *Neviusia alabamensis*
Common Name Neviusia, snowwreath
Usual Height 3 to 6 feet, occasionally 8 feet high
Spacing 3 to 6 feet
Sun or Shade ◑ ◐ ○
Bloom White, 1 inch, yellow in bud, fluffy, faintly fragrant, early spring, on last year's wood
Fruit Small, dry
Leaves 1 to $3^{1}/_2$ inches long, soft, prominent veins underneath
Native Range Rare and endangered, thin woods, shale or limestone cliffs, isolated populations in Alabama, Georgia, Mississippi, Arkansas, and Missouri, Zones 6 to 7
Soil Acid, lime OK
Drainage Moist
Root System Shallow, fibrous, might colonize to form a thicket
Companion Plants Red maple, pawpaw, rusty blackhaw viburnum, scarlet buckeye, spicebush, itea, silverbell, storax, Atamasco lily, Solomon's seal, Louisiana phlox
Propagation Softwood cuttings, root division
Wildlife No information

I've talked to many of you who live on limestone and heard your frustration at not being able to use acid-loving shrubs such as azalea. Well, here's good news. Sweet, creamy-flowered **neviusia** blooms at the same time as azaleas, but it loves limestone. It's also versatile enough to do well in nonlimy soils. Louise Wrinkle in Birmingham, Alabama, says she has found it easy to use, and that its cascading character looks especially lovely on a moist stream bank. Its arching stems are also effective hanging over a wooden fence or a stone wall. Michael Dirr, in his *Manual*, states that neviusia has been used successfully in Zones 4 to 8.

83. Latin Name *Rhododendron austrinum*
  Common Name Yellow azalea, Florida azalea
  Usual Height 6 to 10 feet, occasionally 20 feet
  Spacing 6 to 8 feet
  Sun or Shade ● ◑ ◐ ○
  Bloom Yellow, cream, orange to coral, very sweetly
    fragrant, 3-inch clusters, early spring before or as
    leaves emerge
  Fruit 1 inch long, tan, early fall, dry
  Leaves 1 to 4 inches, soft
  Native Range Bluffs, hammocks, floodplains,
    southern Alabama, Georgia, and Florida
    Panhandle, Zone 8
  Trunk Multitrunked, 3 to 5 inches in diameter
  Soil Very acid, acid, sandy loam preferred
  Drainage Moist, tolerates seasonal flooding
  Root System Might colonize to form a thicket
  Companion Plants Sweetgum, two-winged
    silverbell, storax, Florida anise, Walter's
    viburnum, titi, itea, sensitive fern, partridgeberry
  Propagation Seed, division and layering in spring
  Wildlife Flowers used by swallowtails, gulf
    fritillaries, monarchs, hairstreaks, skippers,
    hummingbirds, and bees; nesting songbirds
  Related Species *R. flammeum*, Oconee azalea;
    R. bakeri, Baker's azalea; *R. calendulaceum*, flame
    azalea; *R. prunifolium*, plumleaf azalea

We saw **yellow azalea** in nearly every coastal and lower Piedmont native plant garden we visited. Its bloom time coincides with Piedmont azalea, and while the two look fine together, yellow azalea is loveliest when combined with itself. Then its range of pastel yellows and oranges are quite delicious together. Plant blue woodland flowers beneath for a spectacular display. The other **yellow to orange (to scarlet) azaleas** bloom in later spring or summer. They aren't as fragrant as yellow azalea, but compensate by having larger flowers. Baker's and flame azaleas have the most cold tolerance.

84. Latin Name *Rhododendron canescens*
  Common Name Piedmont azalea, southern
    pinxterflower, hoary azalea
  Usual Height 8 feet, occasionally 16 feet
  Spacing 6 to 12 feet
  Sun or Shade ◑ ◐ ○
  Bloom Pink to white, long-tubed, 3-inch clusters,
    very sweetly fragrant, early spring before leaves
  Fruit 1/2 inch long, rust red, dry
  Leaves 1 to 4 inches long, with soft white hairs
  Trunk Multitrunked, 3 to 5 inches in diameter
  Native Range Flatwoods, creek swamps, bluffs,
    hammocks, Southeastern U.S., Zones 7 to 9
  Soil Very acid, acid, rich
  Drainage Wet to moist, but never soggy all year in
    stagnant water
  Root System Shallow, might colonize
  Companion Plants Swampbay, sweetbay, willow
    oak, swamp chestnut oak, white oak, ferns,
    lizard's tail, partridgeberry, mayapple
  Propagation See *R. austrinum*
  Wildlife See *R. austrinum*
  Related Species *R. periclymenoides* (*R. nudiflorum*),
    pinxterflower; *R. alabamense*, Alabama azalea;
    R. roseum, roseshell azalea

I don't know why this shrub is called the **Piedmont azalea**; it is native to the Coastal Plain and Mississippi basin as well. We found it growing successfully in gardens all over the South, even in Memphis, Tennessee, and Asheville, North Carolina. It blooms heavily under deciduous trees or on the edge of a sunny pond. There are three other **pink to white spring-blooming native azaleas.** All hybridize with each other and with the yellow to orange azaleas to make luscious shades of warm pastels. Most of the species and many hybrids, both man-made and natural, are now available in the nursery trade. In general, the natives differ from the Asian azaleas in that they are deciduous and their colors are not as garish.

(Michael Shoup)

85. **Latin Name** *Rhododendron viscosum*
    Common Name Swamp azalea, clammy azalea
    Usual Height 5 to 7 feet, occasionally 15 feet
    Spacing 5 to 12 feet
    Sun or Shade ◑ ◐ ○
    Bloom White, sometimes flushed with pink, 2-inch clusters, sticky, musky sweet, summer
    Fruit ½ inch long, dry
    Leaves 1 to 3 inch
    Trunk Multitrunked, 3 to 5 inches in diameter
    Native Range Flatwoods, titi swamps, creek swamps, extreme eastern U.S., mostly Coastal Plain, Zones 6 to 9
    Soil Very acid, acid, rich
    Drainage Wet, but not sour and soggy
    Root System Shallow, might colonize to form a thicket
    Companion Plants Sweetgum, pond pine, red maple, sweetbay, clethra, titi, wax myrtle, fetterbush, itea, inkberry
    Propagation See *R. austrinum*
    Wildlife See *R. austrinum*
    Related Species *R. serrulatum,* swamp honeysuckle; *R. oblongifolium,* Texas azalea; and *R. coryi,* Cory azalea are recognized as separate by some scientists

You can grow the **white summer azaleas** in heavy shade, but they won't be at all happy there. Their limbs get spindly as they reach up for the sun, and they might show, at best, one or two flower clusters. Better to plant them in light shade or in full sun over a high water table or on the edge of water. In sun, this shrub is covered with fragrant blossoms for about two weeks, usually in July. I like the winter buds as well as the flowers; those on **swamp honeysuckle** are soft red with white edging. If you're on the Gulf coast, where summer heat and humidity are extreme, swamp honeysuckle will work best. **Cory azalea** is the dwarf form, getting only 2 to 3 feet tall.

86. **Latin Name** *Rosa palustris*
    Common Name Swamp rose
    Usual Height 3 to 6 feet
    Spacing 3 to 6 feet
    Sun or Shade ○
    Bloom Pink, 2 to 3 inches, midspring for about 6 weeks, fragrant
    Fruit Rosehip, red, ½ inch, fall
    Leaves 5 to 9 leaflets, sometimes prickly
    Native Range Floodplains, margins of swamps, ponds, springs, or streams, eastern North America, Zones 5 to 8
    Soil Acid to slightly alkaline
    Drainage Moist, tolerates seasonal flooding
    Root System Might colonize to form a thicket
    Companion Plants Wild swamp iris, spiderlily, thalia, pickerelweed, switchgrass
    Propagation Stratified seed, softwood or hardwood cuttings, root division, layering
    Wildlife Nesting; fruits eaten by bobwhite, Philadelphia vireo
    Related Species *R. carolina* (including *R. virginiana*), Carolina rose; *R. setigera,* prairie rose

While roses are normally very picky about good drainage, **swamp rose** is a welcome exception. As long as you don't plant it in a soggy, sour mudhole that doesn't dry out for weeks, it will do fine. The canes are arching and give the plant a nice shape with a minimum of pruning. A thornless, double-flowered selection (pictured) is available. **Carolina rose** is more fragrant, but it colonizes very aggressively. It blooms in the light shade of open woodland composed of pine, oak, and hickory. **Prairie rose** is the last to bloom of the trio. It can make a 15-by-15-foot shrub or be trained on a trellis or arbor. It is pink or white, thornless or barely thorny, and is extremely clean and well behaved. All species roses are generally healthier than hybrids and can be used on the edge of a meadow or in other wild and unwatered ways.

87. Latin Name *Stewartia malachodendron*
   Common Name Virginia stewartia, silky camellia
   Usual Height 10 to 15 feet, occasionally 20 feet
   Spacing 15 feet
   Sun or Shade ● ◑ ◐
   Bloom White, 2 to 4 inches across, with purple
      stamens, late spring
   Fruit ¹/₂ inch, woody
   Leaves 2 to 4 inches long, dark green, glossy
   Native Range Rare, moist, rich hardwood forests,
      Southeastern U.S. to East Texas, Zones 7 to 8
   Soil Very acid, rich, sandy loam preferred
   Drainage Moist to dryish
   Root System Deep, do not transplant from wild
   Companion Plants Tulip tree, umbrella tree, bigleaf
      magnolia, large fothergilla, bigleaf storax,
      fringetree, strawberrybush, bottlebrush buckeye,
      Piedmont azalea
   Propagation Fresh seed sown as soon as ripe,
      double-stratified seed, semihardwood cuttings,
      layering
   Wildlife No information
   Related Species *S. ovata,* mountain stewartia

Virginia stewartia is slow-growing and rare. It's
also unusually gorgeous, which explains why dedicated
nurserymen go to the trouble of offering it. Expect yours
to remain waist high for a number of years, which is really
OK, because it makes it easy to enjoy the flowers up close.
However, don't keep it pruned to this height; it will
ultimately become even prettier when it develops the
character of a small tree. Stewartia is famous for its cream
and brown flaking bark. **Mountain stewartia** is native to
the upper Piedmont and mountains, so it has more cold-
hardiness than Virginia stewartia. They look very similar,
except that mountain stewartia often has conventional
yellow stamens instead of the exquisite purple ones. To
make up for this lapse, it displays orange to red fall color.

88. Latin Name *Styrax americana*
   Common Name Storax, American snowbell
   Usual Height 6 to 10 feet, rarely a 15-foot tree
   Spacing 8 to 10 feet
   Sun or Shade ● ◑ ◐
   Bloom White bells, ¹/₂ inch, 5 petals per flower,
      2 to 4 flowers per cluster, late spring after leaves
      emerge, sweetly fragrant
   Fruit Small, round, dry, gray
   Leaves 2 to 3 inches
   Native Range Hammocks, flatwoods, titi swamps,
      bald cypress swamps, Southeastern U.S., Zones
      6 to 9, one population in Zone 5, mostly
      Coastal Plain and Mississippi floodplain
   Soil Very acid, acid, subsurface limestone OK
   Drainage Moist to wet
   Root System Seems not to colonize
   Companion Plants Bald cypress, sweetgum, beech,
      musclewood, American holly, fetterbush, itea,
      lizard's tail, ferns
   Propagation Fresh seed, softwood cuttings
   Wildlife No information
   Related Species *S. grandifolia,* bigleaf storax

Use **storax** in shady spots where you want lots of
midspring flowers. It usually blooms hard on the heels
of flowering dogwood. With time, storax will become a
small tree, with a smooth, dark, three-inch trunk. A
friend claims his favorite way to enjoy the flowers is to
lean back against the trunk and look straight up at the
bell-like flowers hanging beneath the fresh, new leaves.
Bigleaf storax likes better drainage and is the one
found more often in the Piedmont under deciduous
canopy trees, along with mountain laurel and wild
rhododendrons. Two Asian storaxes, Japanese snowbell
and fragrant snowbell, are commonly found in nurseries.
But, unlike the natives, they frequently suffer frost
damage, resulting in frozen tips or ugly, crispy leaves
around the flowers.

89. Latin Name *Viburnum dentatum*
    Common Name Arrowwood, southern arrowwood
    Usual Height 5 to 15 feet
    Spacing 15 feet
    Sun or Shade ● ◐ ◑ ○
    Bloom White, 2- to 4-inch clusters, late spring
    Fruit ¹/₂ inch, blue-black
    Leaves 4 to 6 inches, yellow to orange in fall
    Trunk Stems, arrow-straight, red, yellow, or gray
    Native Range Floodplains, bluffs, titi swamps, pine
        woods, eastern U.S., Zones 6 to 9, mostly
        Coastal Plain
    Soil Very acid, acid, rich
    Drainage Moist to wet
    Root System Might colonize
    Companion Plants Pine, swamp chestnut oak, red
        maple, titi, possumhaw viburnum, inkberry, itea,
        sensitive fern, royal fern
    Propagation Softwood cutting, 2 to 3 years from
        seed
    Wildlife Fruit eaten by fox, chipmunk, bluebird,
        cardinal, cedar waxwing, white-throated sparrow,
        mockingbird, robin, and some game birds; useful
        for nesting sites
    Related Species *V. nudum,* possumhaw viburnum;
        V. rafinesquianum is the northern version of
        V. dentatum, and some botanists lump the two

Oconee azalea

    Arrowwood makes a handsome specimen when its
stems are pruned up like a small multitrunked tree. It is
also a dependable hedge for screening in parking lots,
along back fences, on the edge where grass and woodland
meet, or as filler understory deep in the woods. As with
most viburnums, if you want lots of flowers and fruit and
a good show of fall color, give it at least a half day of sun.
Possumhaw viburnum is a favorite with many gardeners
because of its ornamental fruit. The berries start out an
eye-catching chartreuse in the summer. As the season
progresses, they turn white, then pink, and finally a pretty
dark blue.

7

ACCENTS AND LOW SHRUBS

While some of the plants I mention in this book can be termed old-fashioned, for example, pawpaw, sweetshrub, or Turk's cap, the accent plants I cover in this chapter are literally ancient. Needle palm, dwarf palmetto, saw palmetto, and the various yuccas all have roots back in those steamy, tropical days when dinosaurs stomped and slithered across the earth. For some reason, these plants bring out the hedonist in me, and make me think of long, lazy afternoons with nothing to do but sip iced tea and listen to arias by Puccini.

These accent shrubs normally provide greenery from 2 to 6 feet tall, but they can, and often do, get much larger. The saw palmetto, although usually under waist-high and often used as a groundcover, can sometimes reach tree size. In the wild, I always see dwarf palmetto as a low-growing groundcover, but in a garden setting it is usually a 6- to 7-foot specimen (as in the photo).

The other shrubs in this chapter are normally under 5 feet in height. Their uses range from foundation evergreens to flowers to herbs.

Moundlily yucca, beargrass, coral honeysuckle, and purple coneflower flank the garden path at Alma Plantation, owned by Iris and David Stewart, in Pointe Coupee Parish, Louisiana.

LOW EVERGREEN MASSING
SHRUBS AND ACCENTS

Except for the needle palm and the yuccas, all the evergreen shrubs in this section can make those wonderful low massings of evergreenery that are so important for foundation plantings and the newer, more sophisticated home landscapes. There is at least one for every setting, from sand dunes to mountain slopes to swamplands.

Saw palmetto makes an excellent evergreen groundcover under longleaf pines.

90. Latin Name *Conradina canescens*
   Common Name Conradina, wild rosemary
   Usual Height 1¹/₂ to 3 feet
   Spacing 3 to 5 feet
   Sun or Shade ◑ ○
   Bloom Lavender, white or purple, minty-smelling, spring
   Fruit Tiny, dry
   Leaves Evergreen, gray, needlelike, ¹/₄ to ¹/₂ inch, aromatic
   Native Range Sandhills, dunes, scrub, thin live oak woods, Alabama to western Florida, mostly near the coast, Zone 8b
   Soil Sand, beach dunes OK
   Drainage Dry
   Root System Deep
   Companion Plants Longleaf pine, live oak, turkey oak, southern magnolia, saw palmetto, dwarf palmetto
   Propagation Fresh seed, softwood or semihardwood tip cuttings
   Wildlife Flowers visited by butterflies and hummingbirds
   Related Species *C. verticillata,* Cumberland rosemary

Conradina loves sun and sandy, well-drained soil—the drier the better. It should prove to be an extremely popular groundcover shrub for those of you living in longleaf pine, scrub oak, Florida scrub, or sea coast conditions. Its gray foliage contrasts beautifully with the yellow-green of sandhill rosemary. For those living on moist soil, use the green-leaved (not gray) **Cumberland rosemary**. It, too, prefers good drainage, so use it on a sunny bank or slope. Both conradinas are charming additions to a herb or flower garden. Unlike many Mediterranean herbs, they are tolerant of high humidity. Both do well in a 12-inch terra-cotta pot; forget the saucer.

91. Latin Name *Leucothoe axillaris*
   Common Name Coastal leucothoe, doghobble
   Usual Height 2 to 4 feet, occasionally 6 feet high, can be cut back severely after blooming
   Spacing 3 to 4 feet
   Sun or Shade ● ◑ ◑
   Bloom White, or flushed with pink, 1- to 3-inch spires on previous year's growth, early spring
   Fruit Dark brown, dry, early fall
   Leaves Evergreen, 2 to 5 inches, glossy, bronze when new and in winter, on green zigzag branches
   Native Range Floodplains, creek swamps, bogs, Coastal Plain from Virginia to Louisiana, Zones 7 to 8
   Soil Acid, rich preferred
   Drainage Moist to wet
   Root System Might colonize to form a short groundcover thicket
   Companion Plants Sweetbay, swampbay, gordonia, clethra, fetterbush, itea, wax myrtle, staggerbush, highbush blueberry, wild pink azalea
   Propagation Fresh seed sown on peat moss, hardwood cuttings
   Wildlife Flowers used by bees; browsed by deer

Pronounced "loo-KO-tho-wee," this native is useful for creating masses of soft, graceful shrubbery at the feet of taller plants. It could also be used as a foundation planting. **Coastal leucothoe** withstands heat and humidity, but needs shade, dependable moisture (but not overwatering), and good air circulation to resist leaf spot. I suspect it doesn't much like automatic lawn sprinklers. We saw it in a number of gardens. In one, it effectively filled a large, rectangular planter beside a patio entrance. There, it arched gracefully over the brick edges and was kept about 2 feet high. In another garden, leucothoe made a huge bed of very attractive knee-high groundcover bordering a shady path.

92. Latin Name *Lyonia lucida*
 Common Name Fetterbush, pink fetterbush, staggerbush (staggerbush used to denote *Lyonia ferruginea* in this book)
 Usual Height 2 to 6 feet, rarely 12 feet
 Spacing 3 to 4 feet
 Sun or Shade ● ◑ ◐
 Bloom Palest shell pink (white to red), early spring before new growth
 Fruit Dark brown, dry, remains on through new flowers
 Leaves Evergreen, 1 to 3 inches long, dark, glossy
 Native Range Bogs, pine savannahs, flatwoods, acid swamps, creek swamps, Coastal Plain from southeastern Virginia to southeastern Louisiana, Cuba, Zones 8 to 10
 Soil Very acid, acid
 Drainage Moist, seasonal flooding OK, but not constant wet
 Root System Colonizes to form a groundcover
 Companion Plants Sweetbay, gordonia, titi, clethra, inkberry, itea, leucothoe, cinnamon fern, crossvine, decumaria, saw palmetto
 Propagation Fresh seed, cuttings, divisions or root cuttings
 Wildlife Flowers used by bees

Fetterbush is very showy when in flower, and makes thickets so dense that you would "stagger" trying to get through and feel "fettered"—and now you know how some plants get their common names. Fetterbush is invaluable to Coastal Plain gardeners, because it provides easy-care masses of knee- to waist-high evergreenery. Its low sweep of glossy foliage is great for separating lawn from woodland, or bordering a path, or softening the edge of a house, or . . . well, you get the idea. It does best if you get it established and then just leave it alone, except for keeping it cut back to the height you want. Fussing and watering tends to make fetterbush unhealthy.

93. Latin Name *Rhapidophyllum hystrix*
 Common Name Needle palm
 Usual Height 3 to 8 feet
 Spacing 10 to 15 feet, do not crowd it
 Sun or Shade ● ◑ ◐
 Bloom Tiny, but in a large, open cluster, palmlike, May
 Fruit Wine red, juicy, $1/2$ inch, in an open cluster
 Leaves Evergreen, dark, $2^1/2$ feet wide, 18 inches long, star-shaped with soft tips, glossy
 Trunk Up to 3 feet high and 2 feet in diameter, including the bristling 10-inch needles, black, bulbous
 Native Range Bluffs, hammocks, Coastal Plain from southeastern South Carolina to southeastern Mississippi, Zones 8 to 9
 Soil Acid, rich, subsurface limestone OK
 Drainage Moist
 Root System Shallow, fibrous
 Companion Plants Tulip poplar, American holly, southern magnolia, Ashe magnolia, red buckeye, musclewood, wild hydrangea, oakleaf hydrangea, Christmas fern
 Propagation Germinates easily from seed; do not buy a specimen collected from the wild
 Wildlife No information

Needle palm is very rare and is considered to be threatened in Florida. It's named for the needles that extrude from its trunk. It grows excruciatingly slowly and it is estimated that some of the large specimens are at least 50 years old and may be much older. To give a wonderfully tropical note to the Southern coastal garden, plant one as an accent in a courtyard. Or, plant several on a gentle or steep slope in the dappled shade of hardwoods, guarding the seedlings with chicken wire for the first three years or so. Then, I'd be patient.

94. Latin Name *Rhododendron minus* var. *minus*
   (including *R. carolinianum*)
   Common Name Dwarf rhododendron, Carolina
   laurel
   Usual Height 2 to 6 feet, occasionally 10 feet
   Spacing 3 to 6 feet
   Sun or Shade ● ◑ ◒
   Bloom Pink to rose, fragrant, in 3- to 4-inch
   clusters, early spring as new growth begins
   Fruit ¹/₂ inch, rusty brown, fall
   Leaves Evergreen, 1 to 5 inches long, dark, not
   glossy, aromatic, purplish in winter
   Native Range Stream banks, wooded slopes,
   southern Appalachians, Zones 6 to 8
   Soil Very acid, rich
   Drainage Moist
   Root System Will colonize to form a thicket
   Companion Plants Tulip poplar, white oak,
   umbrella tree, cucumbertree, bigleaf storax,
   rosebay, leucothoe, mountain laurel
   Propagation Seeds need constant moisture to
   germinate; August cuttings
   Wildlife Fruit little used, foliage browsed
   Related Species *R. m.* var. *chapmanii,* Chapman's
   rhododendron, Florida only

   Dwarf rhododendron is usually found as understory
on rocky slopes. This plant is a good choice for people
living in the mountains or the upper Piedmont. If dwarf
rhododendron is unhappy, it is prey to a multitude of
beetles and diseases. To keep it happy, tuck it under
deciduous canopy trees on a slight to steep slope in rich
organic soil that is strongly acid. It's a knockout when
massed in front of taller shrubs and trees. It seems to take
a long time for it to get much above three feet tall, and it
can be easily maintained at that height.

95. Latin Name *Sabal minor*
   Common Name Dwarf palmetto, bush palmetto
   Usual Height 3 to 6 feet, occasionally 10 feet
   Spacing 8 feet for specimen, 3 feet for groundcover
   Sun or Shade ● ◑ ◒
   Bloom White, 1- to 6-foot clusters, May or June
   Fruit Black, in 1- to 6-foot drooping clusters, fall
   Leaves Evergreen, yellow-green, 2 to 8 feet in
   diameter, fanlike, sharp-edged
   Native Range Floodplains, wet hammocks,
   northeastern North Carolina to central Florida
   to central Texas, Zones 8 to 9, chiefly on
   Coastal Plain
   Soil Acid to alkaline, rich preferred, salt spray
   tolerated
   Drainage Seasonally wet to moist
   Root System Will colonize to form a groundcover
   Companion Plants Live oak, cabbage palmetto,
   bald cypress, passionflower, curly clematis,
   Turk's cap
   Propagation Stratified seed sown in mud
   Wildlife Fruit eaten by yellow-rumped warbler,
   woodpeckers
   Related Species *Serenoa repens,* saw palmetto

   Dwarf palmetto makes a dramatic accent for that
moist spot in your garden. For a completely different
look, cut these palmettos back once a year at knee height
to make a visually exotic evergreen groundcover—yes, a
groundcover—beneath coastal live oaks or bald cypresses.
If you want a path through the palmettos, keep it wide;
the leaves are sharp! **Saw palmetto** can also be used as an
accent or a groundcover. It might reach 25 feet, but the
stem is usually horizontal, so that the plant forms a low
thicket (see photo at head of this chapter) in dry places
under longleaf pines and turkey oaks, or in Florida scrub.
Its leaves have spiny stems (toothed, like saws) and are
blue-green.

96. **Latin Name** *Vaccinium darrowii*
   Common Name Evergreen blueberry
   Usual Height ^{1}/$_2$ to 2 feet
   Spacing 1 to 3 feet
   Sun or Shade ◑ ◐ ○
   Bloom White to pink, ^{1}/$_4$ inch, clustered along branches, spring
   Fruit Blueberry, ^{1}/$_4$ inch, dark blue with a "bloom," a pale, dusty substance that rubs off
   Leaves Evergreen, ^{1}/$_4$ to 1 inch long, blue to gray-green, glossy
   Native Range Sandhills, flatwoods, coastal swales, stable dunes, Coastal Plain, Mississippi to western Florida, Zones 8 to 9
   Soil Very acid, acid, sandy preferred
   Drainage Moist to dry
   Root System Might colonize to form a groundcover
   Companion Plants Longleaf pine, titi, sweetbay, gordonia, possumhaw viburnum, inkberry, blackgum, mountain laurel, redbay
   Propagation Seed, softwood cuttings
   Wildlife Fruits eaten by bluebird, catbird, grouse, oriole, tanager, thrush, towhee, turkey, cedar waxwing, woodpeckers, great crested flycatcher
   Related Species *V. myrsinites,* evergreen blueberry

These two **evergreen blueberries** are very similar in appearance. The chief difference, as far as landscapers are concerned, is that *V. darrowii* tolerates more moisture, while *V. myrsinites* tolerates more drought. Use them wherever you need a small evergreen shrub. They can border a flower bed or substitute for a boxwood hedge in a colonial-style garden. Or, you could plant masses of them as a groundcover to eliminate expanses of lawn—both for aesthetic and environmental reasons. A groundcover of blueberries will prevent runoff, hold moisture in the soil, and provide a feast of berries for songbirds. Prune or cut back evergreen blueberries only during the winter, or you'll be destroying the fruit.

97. **Latin Name** *Yucca aloifolia*
   Common Name Spanish bayonet, aloe yucca
   Usual Height 5 to 10 feet
   Spacing 3 to 5 feet
   Sun or Shade ◐ ○
   Bloom White, sometimes purple at base on outside, 1- to 2-foot clusters on short stalk, barely emerging from the leaves, summer
   Fruit 1 to 2 inches, red to purple
   Leaves Evergreen, 8 to 24 inches long, spine at tip, sharp tiny teeth on edges
   Trunk Single, often branched, topples when it gets top-heavy
   Native Range Dunes, sandhills, coasts from North Carolina to Louisiana, Mexico and West Indies, Zones 8 to 11
   Soil Slightly acid to alkaline, brackish OK, sand, shell mounds
   Drainage Dry
   Root System Might colonize to form a thicket
   Companion Plants Southern red cedar, turkey oak, longleaf pine, live oak, cabbage palmetto
   Propagation Untreated seed, root or stem cuttings
   Wildlife Flowers fertilized by moths; larval plant for yucca giant skipper butterfly
   Related Species *Y. flaccida,* beargrass; *Y. gloriosa,* moundlily yucca

Need a strong garden accent? **Spanish bayonet** is an excellent choice. Use it singly or in a giant clump; either way, this yucca lends a tropical feel to your garden. For a tidier appearance, cut spent bloom stalks and keep the old leaves trimmed off. **Beargrass** is the smallest yucca, usually trunkless with arching leaves less than 4 feet high. It's the one we saw most commonly used. The flower stalk is slender and rises far above the leaves, sometimes to 12 feet. **Moundlily yucca** is the tallest—up to 15 feet high—and looks a lot like beargrass but with wider leaves.

LOW FLOWERING AND FRUITING SHRUBS

Each of these seven shrubs has some distinctive characteristic that makes it outstanding. Most home-owners will use these low shrubs in front of taller evergreen shrubs; there they will provide years of dependable flowers or fall color.

But, there are other uses. All are exceptionally attractive in patio pots and planters. On properties that are at least a half acre in size, these shrubs can be used in huge masses as tall groundcover.

Mapleleaf viburnum on the Fiery Gizzard nature trail in Tennessee shows off its famous pink fall color.

98. **Latin Name** *Calamintha georgiana (Satureja georgiana, Clinopodium georgianum)*
 Common Name Georgia basil, clinopodium
 Usual Height $^1/_2$ to $2^1/_2$ feet
 Spacing 2 to 3 feet
 Sun or Shade ◐ ◖ ○
 Bloom Pale pink lavender, white, summer
 Fruit Tiny, tan, dry
 Leaves $^1/_2$ to 1 inch, soft, aromatic
 Native Range Sandhills, dry woods, North Carolina
 to Louisiana, mostly Coastal Plain, Zone 8
 Soil Acid, deep sand, rocky
 Drainage Dry
 Root System Deep
 Companion Plants Longleaf pine, sweetleaf,
 conradina, sandhill rosemary
 Propagation Fresh seed, softwood or semihardwood
 tip cuttings
 Wildlife Flowers visited by hummingbirds and
 butterflies
 Related Species *Calamintha coccinea*, red basil

Most herbs grow in hot, dry, well-drained sites. It's these fiercely evaporative conditions that cause the plant to manufacture oils in an attempt to retain moisture in its leaves, and it is the oils that produce the distinctive herbal aromas and flavors. For most Southern gardeners, the chief use for both **Georgia basil** and **red basil** is in the herb garden or the flower bed. If your soil is not sandy and fast-draining, use them in a raised bed or as a pot plant on a sunny porch. If you live where these basils are native, use them in mass plantings for summer color and to feed hummingbirds.

99. **Latin Name** *Gaylussacia dumosa*
 Common Name Dwarf huckleberry
 Usual Height 4 to 20 inches tall
 Spacing 2 feet
 Sun or Shade ◐ ◖ ○
 Bloom White or pale pink, small bells, spring
 Fruit Huckleberries, black, $^1/_4$ inch, early summer
 to fall
 Leaves $^1/_2$- to 1-inch leaves, glossy, might remain
 green in winter
 Native Range Sandhills, flatwoods, dry, thin
 woods, eastern North America to the
 Mississippi, Zones 5 to 9
 Soil Very acid, acid, poor OK
 Drainage Wet in spring to dry in summer
 Root System Taproot, might colonize to form a
 groundcover
 Companion Plants Pines, post oak, turkey oak,
 inkberry, wild azaleas and wild rhododendrons,
 blueberries, sphagnum moss
 Propagation Stratified seed, cuttings
 Wildlife Fruits eaten by cedar waxwing, bobwhite,
 prairie chicken, wild turkey, mourning dove,
 grouse; flowers and young fruits eaten by larvae
 of Henry's elfin butterfly
 Related Species *G. baccata*, black huckleberry

Dwarf huckleberry makes either a fine knee-high groundcover or a low mass of shrubbery. In Zones 8b and 9, it is often evergreen, especially in protected locations. The leaves are teeny-tiny, giving dwarf huckleberry an extremely fine texture. We ran across it often in home landscapes, especially in those dry, shady spots where ferns cannot survive. It can be used as a substitute for bracken in longleaf pine landscapes, even in those maintained by fire. **Black huckleberry** (Zones 4 to 8, but more common farther north) is notable for its red to gold fall coloration.

100. Latin Name *Hydrangea arborescens*
  Common Name Wild hydrangea, sevenbark
  Usual Height 3 to 5 feet, occasionally 7 feet
  Spacing 3 feet
  Sun or Shade ● ◑ ◐
  Bloom White, 3- to 6-inch cluster, usually with fertile flowers in the middle and showy sterile flowers on the edges, on new wood, early summer, mildly fragrant
  Fruit Small, tan, ribbed and horned, tiny seeds, late fall
  Leaves 4 to 8 inch, soft green
  Native Range Rich woodlands, stream banks, bluffs, limestone or shale outcrops, eastern U.S., Zones 6 (sometimes 5b) to 8
  Soil Very acid, acid, lime OK, rich preferred
  Drainage Moist, does not tolerate flooding
  Root System Might colonize to form a thicket
  Companion Plants Tulip poplar, sourwood, musclewood, American holly, strawberrybush, mountain laurel, sweetshrub, Carolina silverbell, spicebush, leucothoe
  Propagation Stratified seed, softwood cuttings
  Wildlife Flowers visited by at least 3 kinds of bees; flowers and seeds eaten by wild turkey and white-tailed deer; roots used in medicine

Wild hydrangea is very pretty and very easy to grow. No wonder it's been a favorite with gardeners since 1736. But nowadays the cultivars on the market have so many sterile flowers and such big heads that the plants that I've seen look like petticoat frames—almost bare stalks of arching hoops with a white froth of flowery petticoat like a fringe at the bottom. Not a pretty sight. The wild version is a lot daintier with flower heads held high. Use wild hydrangea in shady spots where you want softness and summer color. For a tidier look in winter, you can cut the old stems down to about four inches; fresh new growth will appear in the spring and will be in full bloom by June.

101. Latin Name *Hypericum frondosum*
  Common Name Golden St. John's wort
  Usual Height 3 to 4 feet, rarely to 9 feet
  Spacing 3 to 4 feet
  Sun or Shade ◑ ◐
  Bloom Yellow to gold, 1 to 2 inches across, numerous, early summer
  Fruit 1/2 inch, tan, dry
  Leaves 1 to 2 inches, soft, blue-green
  Native Range Cedar glades, river bluffs, rock outcrops, rich woodlands, southern Indiana to East Texas and South Carolina, Zones 6 to 7
  Soil Acid, lime OK, rocky or sandy OK
  Drainage Moist to dry, tolerates flooding of short duration
  Root System Shallow
  Companion Plants Eastern red cedar, post oak, other oaks and hickories
  Propagation Untreated seed, cuttings
  Wildlife Seeds eaten mostly by songbirds, also upland game birds
  Related Species *H. hypericoides* (*Ascyrum hypericoides*), St. Andrew's cross

Golden St. John's wort is a handsome shrub with coppery, exfoliating bark. In June, when little else is blooming, it delivers a welcome shower of golden flowers to the shady garden. Bright dappled shade or a half day of slanting sun give the best results. If you've got denser shade or a very dry woodland setting, use **St. Andrew's cross**. It has tiny leaves and tiny cross-shaped yellow flowers that bloom in September. The flowers aren't especially showy, but there is something about the dainty way the whole plant floats that makes it especially appealing. You'll find it growing wild in dry, difficult habitats with sandhill rosemary, sparkleberry, post oak, turkey oak, and pines. It is shorter-lived than St. John's wort, but seeds out to keep a population going for you.

102. Latin Name *Itea virginica*

Common Name Itea, Virginia willow, Virginia sweetspire

Usual Height 3 to 4 feet, occasionally 6 feet, rarely 12 feet

Spacing 3 to 4 feet

Sun or Shade ● ◑ ◑

Bloom White, 4-inch spires, late spring

Fruit Tan, dry, fall

Leaves 2 to 4 inches, narrow, soft; yellow, red, or purple in late fall

Native Range Swamps, floodplains, hammocks, eastern U.S., Zones 6 to 9

Soil Very acid, acid, lime OK, rich

Drainage Moist to wet

Root System Might colonize to form a groundcover or thicket

Companion Plants Alder, bald cypress, swampbay, swamp chestnut oak, beech, clethra, swamp azalea, coastal leucothoe, wax myrtle, highbush blueberry, fetterbush, strawberrybush

Propagation Seed, cuttings

Wildlife Flowers visited by butterflies, seed eaten by birds

Itea is an extremely useful landscape plant. I've used it successfully in those deadly brick planters that builders like to stick under the eaves. Rain doesn't get in there. There's no air circulation and no drainage. Plastic plants seem to be the only hope. But, with moisture from a sprinkler system or soaker hose, itea drapes itself over the box and even blooms for you. Naturally, it is happier where its roots are free to roam a little to make a small, mass planting. Put it by a deck, on the edge of the lawn, or on the fringe of a wooded area. If you have a creek, itea provides invaluable erosion control. There, or pondside, with its feet practically in the water, it will gladly tolerate a half day of sun—even afternoon sun—and produce better fall color for it.

103. Latin Name *Malvaviscus arboreus* var. *drummondii*

Common Name Turk's cap, sleeping hibiscus, Drummond wax mallow

Usual Height 3 to 4 feet, occasionally 9 feet

Spacing 4 to 5 feet

Sun or Shade ◑ ◑

Bloom Red, 1 to 3 inches long, midsummer to midfall

Fruit 1/2-inch red berries, slightly juicy, fall

Leaves 4 to 7 inches, dormant in winter

Native Range Live oak woods, pinelands, Gulf Coastal Plain from Florida to Texas, Mexico, and Cuba, Zones 8 to 10

Soil Acid, lime OK, clay OK, poor OK, saline OK

Drainage Dry to moist

Root System Clump-forming, might colonize

Companion Plants Dwarf palmetto, saw palmetto, yucca, yaupon holly, Carolina jessamine, ebony spleenwort, bracken, spiderwort, passionflower, wild ageratum, American beautyberry

Propagation Fresh, untreated seed, softwood cuttings, root division

Wildlife Flowers visited by hummingbirds, cloudless giant sulphur, dogface butterfly, and other butterflies

I love **Turk's cap;** it blooms all summer and is a great hummingbird attractor. We found this old-fashioned, long-lived garden perennial tucked under live oaks and southern magnolias, along fences, and in dark corners of many old, undisturbed gardens of nineteenth-century Gulf coast houses. In the wild, it's found among the plants listed above. In a flower garden, use it where you want height and color in partial shade. It can take full sun, but the leaves get puckered—which I think is ugly. Turk's cap is very effective when planted in masses under a huge old live oak, even in an existing groundcover of English ivy. To keep it waist high and compact, cut it back to 4 or 5 inches after frost every year.

104. **Latin Name** *Viburnum acerifolium*
    Common Name Mapleleaf viburnum
    Usual Height 4 to 5 feet, occasionally 8 feet
    Spacing 3 to 4 feet
    Sun or Shade ● ◐ ◑
    Bloom Creamy white, 2- to 3-inch clusters, spring after leaves
    Fruit 1/3 inch, purply black, juicy, late fall
    Leaves Maple-shaped, 3 inches; pink apricot, red, or purple in late fall
    Native Range Bluffs, wooded ravines, live oak woods, eastern U.S., Zones 4 to 8, more common in Piedmont
    Soil Acid, rich, lime OK
    Drainage Moist to dry
    Root System Might colonize to form a thicket
    Companion Plants Spicebush, strawberrybush, itea, Christmas fern, green-and-gold, partridgeberry, mayapple
    Propagation Semihardwood cuttings
    Wildlife Fruit eaten by wild turkey, bluebird, cardinal, great crested flycatcher, brown thrasher, hermit thrush, cedar waxwing, pileated woodpecker, red squirrel, white-tailed deer; flowers and immature fruit eaten by larvae of Henry's elfin butterfly

Hypericum densiflorum—one of the many useful woodland hypericums.

    Mapleleaf viburnum is one of the best shrubs to use in deep, dappled shade—the kind found under a layer of canopy and then a layer of understory trees. Unlike most understory shrubs, it blooms well in the spring and colors extravagantly well in the fall without direct sunlight. With as little as one hour of sun, it produces fine fruits, making it a favorite stopping-off place for woodland birds. This attractive native shrub forms gentle thickets, but it is a bit slow to do so. You might want to plant a cluster yourself to get a good start.

8

VINES

Vines can range in size from ropes as big around as your arm to fragile little plants that produce barely six feet of skinny stem, every inch of which dies back at first frost and has to be regrown the next year.

Some vines have to be climbing upward to bloom. Others flower when they are horizontal, or even draping themselves over a wall or the rim of a planter.

The methods of climbing also differ. Virginia creeper and cross-vine can scale the side of your house with no help from you at all. You just have to cut them back periodically where they get a little too enthusiastic. Others, such as passionflower, clematis, wisteria, smilax, Carolina jessamine, and coral honeysuckle, can climb only when they are given a tree, a shrub, a structure like an arbor, or wires to cling to. They also need pruning to keep them from getting too heavy for their support system.

Don't let the delicate look of a vine fool you; you don't ever want one to grow on your roof. If the stems insinuate themselves between the shingles and then grow fat, they can exert an amazing amount of pressure, leaving

Mockingbird nest in grape arbor.

you with a potentially staggering bill for roof repairs and water damage. Trim them off in a neat line under the eaves once a year, or more often if needed.

All vines like to have their roots damp and cool, but they

bloom best up in the sun. So if you have a choice, always plant your vines on the shady north or east side of a fence or freestanding wall. They'll grow up and over toward the sun by themselves. If you're trying to get a vine established where the soil is hot and sunny, place a stepping stone or a few bricks, or even a piece of wood, over the roots to keep them cool and moist.

This is, by no means, a definitive collection of Southern vines. I feel guilty about not including even one grapevine. Trouble is, they vary so much from vine to vine, with regard to rambunctiousness, flavor, and fall color, that I've never been able to settle on just one to extol. If you have a grapevine, or access to one, by all means use it and enjoy it. Native grapes make popular food for wildlife, and, of course, marvelous jelly for humans.

There's another native vine I left out—happily. Yes, it has superb fall color, and yes, it provides superior food for wildlife. And, yes, it is very easy to grow, thriving under any conditions. But somehow I can't make myself feel at all guilty for omitting poison ivy.

The first three vines in this chapter are dependably evergreen. Coral honeysuckle is evergreen if there is no frost; in my experience, even a light touch of frost knocks off half the leaves. The other vines here are decidedly deciduous; only the Virginia creeper has really dependable and gorgeous fall color.

Crossvine, with its delicate tendril-like holdfasts, clings to a brick wall. The blooms appear in very early spring to help feed hummingbirds as they fly north to their nesting grounds. The old leaves are dark and spotted, getting ready to drop, while fresh, new, lighter green ones are already in place.

105. Latin Name *Bignonia capreolata (Anisostichus capreolata)*

Common Name Crossvine

Usual Height High-climbing

Spacing 4 feet for groundcover, 8 to 29 feet on a wall or fence

Sun or Shade ◑ ◐ ○

Bloom 2-inch trumpet, red and yellow or all red, early spring

Fruit 4- to 8-inch pod, tan, dry

Leaves Evergreen, dark, 5 to 15 leaflets, royal purple stems and veins in winter

Attachment Thready, 3-pronged holdfasts or twining

Native Range Floodplains, hammocks, fencerows, upland woods, limestone cliffs, eastern U.S., Zones 6 to 9

Soil Acid, lime OK, rich preferred

Drainage Moist to dry, brief flooding OK

Root System Deep, might colonize

Companion Plants Bald cypress, swampbay, post oak, eastern red cedar

Propagation Seed, softwood cuttings, root cuttings

Wildlife Flowers visited by hummingbirds; foliage browsed by deer in winter in Zones 7 to 9

Talk about versatility: **crossvine** can climb to the top of the highest tree or it can form an attractive groundcover. Either way, you'll have to do some pruning because it's a fast grower, sending out 10- to 20-foot shoots each year. It's ideal for a masonry wall or the side of your house, because (a) it doesn't require a trellis or support wires and (b) its holdfasts are delicate and undamaging, unlike those on English ivy or trumpet creeper. Used this way, it needs to be trimmed back from windows, doors, and eaves as needed, normally once or twice a year. Used as a groundcover—in large shady areas with few big trees and no understory shrubbery—it should be mown regularly to keep it from climbing or mounding up.

106. Latin Name *Gelsemium sempervirens*

Common Name Carolina jessamine, poor man's rope

Usual Height High-climbing

Spacing 8 feet

Sun or Shade ◑ ◐ ○

Bloom Yellow, 1- to 1½-inch trumpets, fragrant, early spring, often around Christmas also

Fruit Tiny, tan, dry

Leaves Evergreen, 2 to 3 inches long, light green, glossy

Attachment Twining

Native Range Upland woods, hedgerows, pine savannahs, hammocks, Southeastern U.S., Zones 7 to 8

Soil Very acid, acid, lime OK, rich preferred

Drainage Moist, brief flooding OK

Root System Deep, might colonize

Companion Plants White oak, black oak, post oak, live oak, pines

Propagation Seed, semihardwood or hardwood cuttings

Wildlife Flowers visited by hummingbirds and spicebush swallowtail butterfly

Related Species *G. rankinii*, swamp jessamine, Zone 8

Carolina jessamine is so useful and dependable that many adventurous gardeners get bored with it. But for black-thumb gardeners like me, dependable has it all over challenging. My Carolina jessamine drapes itself over half our balcony, and gives off a sharp, sweet fragrance. It can also be used on a fence, trellis, arbor, telephone pole, or a dead tree that you're leaving for the wildlife to inhabit. For those who tend to overwater and drown their plants, the **swamp jessamine** might do better. It doesn't have the sweet smell, but it tolerates much longer periods of sogginess. It blooms in midspring, after the Carolina jessamine is done.

107. Latin Name *Smilax smallii*
   Common Name Jacksonvine, Jacksonbrier
   Usual Height High-climbing
   Spacing Do not plant; put an existing one to use
   Sun or Shade ◗ ◑ ○
   Bloom Greenish, tiny, late spring
   Fruit Dark red to black, juicy
   Leaves Evergreen, 2 to 4 inches, glossy
   Attachment Tendrils, twining, old stems are spiny
   Native Range Floodplains, upland woods,
      hammocks, bluffs, dunes, Southeastern U.S.,
      Zones 7 to 9, mostly Coastal Plain
   Soil Acid
   Drainage Dry to moist, brief flooding OK
   Root System 1- to 2-foot tubers, will colonize
   Companion Plants Pine, post oak, hickory, live
      oak, willow oak
   Propagation Cuttings, root division
   Wildlife Fruits eaten by fish crow, mockingbird,
      catbird, robin, wild turkey, hermit thrush,
      thrasher, pileated woodpecker, and mammals;
      fruit and foliage eaten by white-tailed deer;
      thickets provide cover for birds and rabbits
   Related Species *S. auriculata*, catbrier; *S. laurifolia*,
      bamboovine

The **evergreen smilaxes**, like the deciduous ones, are found in virtually every habitat. Your task with smilax is not to coddle and nurture it, but to keep it cut back—it can make a formidable thicket. But, that's really all the attention it needs. On the aesthetic side, it sports very attractive glossy leaves. Louise Wrinkle in Birmingham, Alabama, trained one of hers on a wire over a formal fountain, while another one forms an arch over one of the doorways to her elegant home. Because the new canes of **Jacksonvine** are not spiny, they are easy to handle. As they grow, they harden into self-supporting canes. After about three years, if the canes get too big and woody, cut the vine to the ground and start over. Do this in early spring.

108. Latin Name *Clematis crispa*
   Common Name Curly clematis, blue jasmine
   Usual Height 6 to 10 feet
   Spacing 2 feet apart to cover a wall or trellis
   Sun or Shade ◗ ◑ ○
   Bloom 1 to 2 inches; blue, pink, lavender, or white;
      often two-tone, beautiful detailing, delicately
      fragrant, Easter and again in early fall,
      sometimes from spring to fall
   Fruit Tiny, dry
   Leaves 1- to 4-inch leaflets
   Attachment Twining
   Native Range Floodplains, eastern U.S., Zones 6
      to 9, mostly Coastal Plain and Mississippi
      floodplain
   Soil Acid, clay OK
   Drainage Moist to wet
   Root System Might colonize
   Companion Plants Musclewood, mayhaw,
      possumhaw, Kansas gayfeather, goldenrod, salt
      cordgrass
   Propagation Seed, softwood cuttings in summer,
      root cuttings
   Wildlife No information
   Related Species *C. viorna*, leatherflower

Curly clematis usually dies to the roots after frost and doesn't reappear until the following spring. Sometimes, if the winter is very mild, it becomes deciduous with the stems remaining alive. It is useful on a small trellis or a picket fence, and can also be used in sunny but moist planters or draped over a wall; unlike most vines, it doesn't have to climb to bloom. I would never have thought of planting it in grass, but I once saw a lovely display of two dozen plants showing an immense array of colors in a roughly mowed swale. **Leatherflower** is the better choice for the Piedmont and the mountains. It blooms late, usually in early summer, and the flowers are more closed, and range from rust to a soft purple.

109. Latin Name *Decumaria barbara*
    Common Name Decumaria, climbing hydrangea, woodvamp
    Usual Height High-climbing
    Spacing 1 per tree or each 10 feet of wall
    Sun or Shade ● ◑ ◐ ○
    Bloom White, 2 to 4 inches across, on new wood in late spring
    Fruit 1/4 inch, tan, dry, fancy, fall and winter
    Leaves 3 to 5 inches, dark green glossy, fall color is half white, half green
    Attachment Rootlets
    Native Range Hammocks, low woods, Southeastern U.S., east of Mississippi River, Zones 7 to 9
    Soil Acid, lime OK, rich preferred
    Drainage Moist, seasonal flooding OK
    Root System Does not colonize
    Companion Plants Beech, tulip tree, sprucepine, magnolias, titi, redbud, Florida anise, wax myrtle, swamp azalea
    Propagation Softwood cuttings, slow (7 to 17 years) to bloom from seed
    Wildlife No information

Decumaria is sometimes found sprawling on the ground, but it won't bloom there; it must climb to produce flowers. Most people plant it beneath a tree, allowing it to grow up the trunk. Unlike other vines that just have thick stems down low in the shade, decumaria encircles the trunk evenly in an airy fringe of greenery and flowers 1 to 2 feet out from the trunk, and up as far as you can see. We also saw one trained on a long brick wall, where it was very handsome. This vine is close kin to hydrangea, but it isn't the same as the "climbing hydrangea" sold in many nurseries and catalogs. That is a Japanese import called *H. petiolaris,* and its cultivar, with more sterile flowers, is called *H. anomola.*

110. Latin Name *Lonicera sempervirens* (including *L. s.* var. *sulphurea*)
    Common Name Coral honeysuckle
    Usual Height 15 feet
    Spacing 8 feet
    Sun or Shade ◐ ○
    Bloom 2-inch clusters of narrow, scarlet (or golden yellow) trumpets with orange tips, midspring and intermittently other times
    Fruit Red, 1/4 inch, late summer, fall
    Leaves 1 to 3 inches long, blue-green, smooth (not fuzzy like Japanese honeysuckle)
    Attachment Twining
    Native Range Floodplains, pine woods, thickets, eastern U.S., Zones 6 to 9
    Soil Acid, lime OK, rich preferred
    Drainage Moist, short flooding OK
    Root System Deep, might colonize
    Companion Plants Oaks, hickories, serviceberry, possumhaw, viburnums, fringetree, ebony spleenwort, Christmas fern, green-and-gold, partridgeberry, smilacina, spigelia
    Propagation Softwood or semihardwood cuttings in summer, layering
    Wildlife Flowers visited by hummingbirds, bees, butterflies; fruits eaten by quail, purple finch, goldfinch, hermit thrush, robin; larval plant for spring azure butterfly

If you're afraid of honeysuckle because you've experienced Japanese honeysuckle (*L. japonica*), relax. Our pretty, native **coral honeysuckle** is neither invasive nor aggressive. It can be used in any of the ways vines are usually used, but I think it is the premier choice for an arbor because it never makes a mess with drippy, juicy fruits. It is almost always blooming, and attracts hummingbirds right to where you are sitting. It provides cooling shade in the summer, but loses enough leaves to allow warming sunshine down into the sitting area in the winter.

111. Latin Name *Parthenocissus quinquefolia*
   Common Name Virginia creeper
   Usual Height High-climbing
   Spacing 3 to 5 feet for groundcover, 20 feet for wall
   Sun or Shade ● ◑ ◑ ○
   Bloom Tiny, inconspicuous, late spring
   Fruit 1/4 inch, blue, on red stems, early fall
   Leaves 5 (sometimes 3 or 7) leaflets, 2 to 8 inches long, mauve to red in early fall
   Attachment Tendrils that turn adhesive
   Native Range Upland woods, bottomlands, hedgerows, eastern North America, Zones 5 to 11
   Soil Any, saline OK
   Drainage Moist to dry
   Root System Deep, branches can root at nodes to form groundcover
   Companion Plants Pines, post oak, live oak, beech, tulip poplar, eastern red cedar, white ash
   Propagation Fresh seed, semihardwood cuttings, layering
   Wildlife Fruits eaten by chickadee, white-breasted nuthatch, mockingbird, catbird, finch, flycatcher, scarlet tanager, tree swallow, vireo, warbler, downy woodpecker, robin

Perhaps the most important thing to know about **Virginia creeper** is that it has five leaflets. That's how you can tell it from poison ivy, which has three leaflets but otherwise looks very similar. The stems' aerial rootlets have disks that fasten onto wood or masonry. This vine is lushly green all spring and summer, brilliantly red in fall, and covered with black berries for songbirds during fall and winter. But it's a vigorous climber, so keep it trimmed away from windows and roofs. Another important use is as groundcover, especially in post oak woods. There, upkeep consists of pulling it off the tree trunks once a year. In this shady environment, its fall color is mauve and pink instead of red.

112. Latin Name *Passiflora incarnata*
   Common Name Passionflower, maypop
   Usual Height 6 feet, occasionally 15 feet
   Spacing 3 feet
   Sun or Shade ◑ ◑ ○
   Bloom Lavender (white), 3 inches across, summer
   Fruit Pale yellow, 2 inches long, edible, early fall
   Leaves 3 to 6 inches long, three-lobed, soft, green until first hard frost
   Attachment Tendrils
   Native Range Fields, pine woods, thin live oak woods, thin scrub, fencerows, Southeastern U.S. and Bermuda, Zones 7 to 10
   Soil Any except saline, rich preferred
   Drainage Moist to dry
   Root System Deep, might colonize to form a groundcover
   Companion Plants Live oak, palmetto, loblolly, sweetgum, eastern red cedar
   Propagation Seed, cuttings
   Wildlife Flowers visited by Gulf fritillary butterfly; larval plant for zebra longwing, Julia, Gulf fritillary, and variegated fritillary butterflies

Passionflower has large lavender flowers that are arranged in unbelievably intricate and fantastical layers. This is one of those vines that gets a fresh start each year, so it never gets too big or ungainly. It has tendrils for climbing, but it is often found sprawling along the ground, where it seems to bloom just as—well, passionately—as if it were on a fence. For several years now, a friend has used passionflower as a groundcover underneath a live oak. His only maintenance is, from time to time, to discourage it from climbing up the tree. I let mine clamber up a small tree in the courtyard outside my office window; I love to watch the Gulf fritillary life-cycle take place as orange caterpillars turn into orange butterflies.

113. **Latin Name** *Wisteria frutescens* (includes
   W. macrostachya)
   Common Name American wisteria, Kentucky
      wisteria
   Usual Height Low-climbing
   Spacing 6 to 8 feet
   Sun or Shade ● ◑ ◐ ○
   Bloom Lavender blue (white), 4- to 6-inch clusters,
      late spring, on new wood, after leaves emerge,
      fragrant
   Fruit 2- to 4-inch pod, tan, not velvety
   Leaves 5 to 19 leaflets, dark green, glossy
   Attachment Twining
   Native Range Floodplains, gum swamps, upland
      thickets, stream banks, eastern U.S., Zones 5 to 8
   Soil Slightly acid to neutral, rich preferred
   Drainage Moist, tolerant of seasonal flooding
   Root System Deep, might colonize, stems might
      root at nodes
   Companion Plants Sweetbay, river birch, alder,
      possumhaw, blackgum, inkberry, viburnums
   Propagation Cuttings (takes too many years to
      bloom from seed)
   Wildlife Larval plant for Zarucco duskywing and
      long-tailed skipper butterflies

American wisteria has the potential to be far superior
to the commonly used Asian species. First, its leaves are
prettier—a dark, shiny green. It's also much better
behaved. All that is needed is for a few innovative
nurseries to select the most outstanding specimens and
make them available to the public. Qualities to choose for
are rich color, outstanding fragrance, and highly glossy
leaves. A white selection, 'Nivea,' has already been made.
American wisteria blooms after the leaves come out
instead of on bare wood. Use it on an arbor, pergola,
garden house, fence, or lattice.

Lonicera sempervirens var. sulphurea—
the yellow form of coral honeysuckle.

9

SHADY GROUNDCOVERS

The Southeastern United States is blessed with a rich array of low-growing evergreen and flowering groundcovers—only a small sampling of which could be included in this book. Most of those I did include where ones we'd seen thriving—not merely surviving—in at least three gardens. This told me that (1) they were available from at least some nurseries, (2) they could be transplanted and established successfully, and (3) they were not terribly hard to grow in a home landscape.

But you'll notice as you read about these groundcovers that most are rare and endangered in the wild, especially the evergreens. When you go to buy them at a nursery, you'll discover that they are not easy to find and, if you should come across them, chances are they won't be available in large quantities. Why? Because there hasn't been a great demand for them by the gardening public. The typical home gardener has never even heard of them. Or, if they have heard of them and have tried to grow them, they probably got discouraged. Most modern home landscapes are too harsh for these groundcovers.

First, you have to understand that most groundcovers and woodland flowers are native only to stable hardwood forests where conditions are predictable. In the spring, while the deciduous trees are still leafless, these natives get ample sunlight to warm up the soil and help them bloom. Later, in the summer, the fully leafed-out trees provide filtered shade to keep these natives from becoming sunburned.

The soil is even more important. If you've ever walked through a hardwood forest, you must have noticed that wonderful bounciness underfoot. That's because the soil is rich in leaf mold, well aerated by earthworms, and covered with a loose mulch of decomposing leaves. On a typical forest floor, there are three years of leaves visible at all times. The top 1 to 2 inches is recognizably leaves. Beneath that is an inch of half-decomposed leaves, and then an inch or so of compost. Below all that, the compost is mixed with the soil. If the soil is basically sandy or sterile, all the nutrients, except for some minerals, come from the composted leaves. This mulch is doing all the work of enabling the soil to capture rain-fall, retard evaporation, and modulate temperatures.

Now, let's look at the typical urban or suburban landscape—especially yours. You, or the folks who owned the house before you, have probably been compacting the soil for years simply by walking on it and watering it. You've probably been using herbicides, synthetic fertilizers, and pesticides, which, among other things, have killed or seriously wounded your earthworms and other necessary soil organisms. And, I'll bet, you rake and bag your leaves in the fall, so there's no leaf mulch.

You no doubt have lots of pines because they are fast-growing and evergreen. But, being evergreen, they don't let light and warmth in during March and April the way deciduous trees do. If you have hardwood trees, you have pruned them up high to get as much sun on your lawn as possible. And, very likely, you don't have a single understory tree to help make up the shade.

This hard, sterile, overcontrolled environment is *not* what a woodland groundcover wants. Neither are other modern land uses, such as parking lots, school yards, shopping centers, or pine

Newly planted commercial landscape at Martin Marietta Aggregates in Raleigh, North Carolina, imitates a forest floor. Design by LA Carole Cameron and native plant expert Margaret Reid using rescued woodland groundcover and flowers.

plantations. So, it's obvious why native groundcovers are becoming scarce—they are losing their habitats.

Providing a safe haven in your landscape for threatened groundcovers can be a noble act. But please use good sense. If you know of plants that are destined to be bulldozed, then by all means rescue them, and give them a home if you can. And if your home environment is not suitable, call your local arboretum or nature preserve, or a friend whose landscape *is* suitable. There, the groundcovers will thrive and multiply.

If you'd like to use a native groundcover but have a lawn now, can you convert? Yes, but it will take two to five years. This is what must happen:

1. The trees on or bordering your property will have to grow to a size that will provide sufficient shade. If you don't have hardwood trees, plant some. No need to poison your lawn; when shade develops, it will kill off the grass. To speed things along, you can spread about 4 inches of pine needles, shredded bark, or compost on top of the grass.

2. Allow your soil to reconstitute itself. Stop using pesticides, herbicides, synthetic fertilizers, and anything else that kills off microorganisms in the soil. Stop raking and bagging leaves and grass cuttings. Let them decompose to renew and aerate the soil. In other words, be lazy. Your soil will thank you.

3. When your conditions are right, do *not* go into the wilds and dig up groundcovers. Remember, they are endangered. Find the ones you want in local nurseries. They are becoming more available all the time. Or, get some healthy groundcovers from the landscape of a friend or relative.

If you own a wooded property and already have native groundcovers, protect them and help them multiply. If deer, rabbits, or other critters are nibbling at them and your supply is small, protect them with a chicken-wire barrier until you have a population large enough to share with the wildlife.

EVERGREEN SHADY GROUNDCOVERS

Evergreen groundcovers are mostly suitable for small areas, as they are currently rare and in short supply. Cherish them in a home garden. Protect them in the wild.

The ones that are easiest for the average gardener are pussytoes, running cedar, partridgeberry, butterweed, lyreleaf sage, and moss.

*This moss lawn (*Thuidium delicatulm*) was once a grass lawn for children to play on. After they grew up, Louise Smith quit fighting the moss, and let it take over. The result is this lovely, smooth patch of velvet. Maintenance consists of mowing in spring and fall to cut down the delicate flowers that germinate in the moss.*

114. Latin Name *Antennaria plantaginifolia*
    Common Name Pussytoes, plantainleaf, everlasting,
      mouse ear, ladies' tobacco
    Usual Height 2-inch mat when not in flower
    Spacing 1 foot apart for quick cover
    Sun or Shade ◗ ◖
    Bloom White, ¼-inch clusters, fuzzy like pussy
      toes, female flowers flushed with pink, on slender
      stalks, early spring
    Fruit Small, ripe soon after flowering
    Leaves Evergreen, 2 inches long, silvery beneath
    Native Range Dry woodlands, eastern North
      America, Zones 4 to 8
    Soil Acid, poor, sandy or rocky preferred
    Drainage Dry
    Root System Shallow, colonizes by runners to form
      a groundcover
    Companion Plants Dry pines, beech, white oak,
      post oak, umbrella tree, fringetree, serviceberry,
      mountain laurel, ebony spleenwort, bracken,
      galax, whorled loosestrife
    Propagation Division
    Wildlife Foliage browsed by deer in winter

Since most groundcovers require steady moisture to
stay dense, **pussytoes** fills a much needed niche; it does
very well in lightly shaded, dry landscapes. It's also quite
attractive, although the whitish, fuzzy flowers, each the
size of a kitty's toe, are not what I would call knockouts.
I'd cut them off as soon as they are through blooming.
There is no need to let them go to seed, as the seeds
are not known to be useful to wildlife, and the plant
propagates itself mostly by spreading out from the roots.
This gives you a smooth flow of soft silver-green leaves for
all but two weeks out of the year.

115. Latin Name *Galax urceolata* (formerly *G. aphylla*)
    Common Name Galax, beetleweed, coltsfoot,
      wand flower
    Usual Height 3- to 6-inch mat when not in flower
    Spacing Rare, so 6 inches apart in a tiny area to get
      it started
    Sun or Shade ● ◗
    Bloom White, 2- to 5-inch spikes on 1- to 2-foot
      leafless stems, late spring or early summer
    Fruit Dustlike tiny seeds, early fall
    Leaves Evergreen, round or heart-shaped, 2 to 6
      inches wide, bright green, glossy, leathery, wine
      red in fall and winter
    Native Range Rocky woodlands, Southeastern
      U.S., Zones 6 to 7, Alabama to Maryland
    Soil Very acid, rich, loose, sandy preferred, mulch
      required
    Drainage Moist to dry
    Root System Colonizes by red rhizomes to form a
      groundcover
    Companion Plants Rhododendrons, azaleas,
      mountain laurel, vernal iris
    Propagation Fresh seed in coldframe, summer
      cuttings, spring divisions
    Wildlife Winter browse for white-tailed deer

Once upon a time, **galax** was very plentiful in the
wild, covering large areas with its fresh, glossy leaves.
Today it is rare, so please don't gather yours from the
wild. I know of no reputable nursery that propagates
galax. Whenever I saw it in a garden, I was told that it
had been rescued from the path of a bulldozer. Don't try
galax unless you can give it a good home. It needs rich
acid loam—the kind where wild rhododendrons and
mountain laurel grow with ease. In the right conditions,
galax should spread quickly and make a fine groundcover,
but in the typically impoverished soil of the average home
landscape, its progress will be very slow.

116. **Latin Name** *Hexastylis arifolia (Asarum arifolium)*
Common Name Heartleaf, evergreen wild ginger
Usual Height 2 to 4 inches, not matlike
Spacing 2 to 4 feet apart, they don't like to be crowded
Sun or Shade ● ◑
Bloom Half-hidden, purply brown, spring
Fruit Fleshy, soon after flowering
Leaves Evergreen, very glossy, triangular, 5 to 8 inches long, whitish green with dark green along the veins
Native Range Pine woods, hardwoods, swamp forests, Southeastern U.S., Zones 6 to 8
Soil Very acid, acid, rich, pH 5 to 6 preferred
Drainage Moist to dry
Root System Slow-growing to form 18-inch clumps, ginger-smelling
Companion Plants Southern magnolia, sprucepine, wild azaleas and rhododendrons, sourwood, mountain laurel, Christmas fern, broad beechfern, troutlily, fly poison, Solomon's seal, smilacina, Jack-in-the-pulpit, dwarf iris, foamflower, hepatica, black cohosh, partridgeberry
Propagation Fall division, slow from seed
Wildlife Winter browse
Related Species *H. shuttleworthii*, Shuttleworth's ginger

If you want a thick carpet of groundcover, don't set your heart on **heartleaf**. However, it *is* perfect for small, jewel-like gardens. Its elegant, completely evergreen leaves are so glossy, and bear such unusual markings, that they are as attention-getting as colorful flowers. Plant scattered clumps of heartleaf for winter color, and interplant with woodland flowers and small, polite ferns that won't overrun it. **Shuttleworth's ginger** is very similar, except that *its* leaves are colored just the opposite—dark green with light green veins. As for that dense, green carpet . . . go with deciduous wild ginger, *Asarum canadense.*

117. **Latin Name** *Lycopodium flabelliforme (L. digitatum)*
Common Name Running cedar, ground pine
Usual Height 5 to 10 inches, usually a 6-inch cover
Spacing 3 to 6 feet
Sun or Shade ● ◑ ◑
Bloom Pale yellow spikes on forked stems, summer
Fruit Spores, no seeds
Leaves Evergreen, dark green, cedarlike
Native Range Dry woods, well-drained pinelands, eastern North America, Zones 4 to 7
Soil Acid, rich or poor OK
Drainage Dry to slightly moist
Root System Shallow, spreading by stems barely aboveground
Companion Plants Upland pines, post oak, Christmas fern, ebony spleenwort, mayapple, pussytoes, foamflower, spiderwort, fire pink
Propagation From spores or stem cuttings
Wildlife Winter browse

Look at **running cedar** and you'd think it was kin to pine, cedar, or some other conifer. It's actually a clubmoss and related to ferns. It lost so much habitat and was so often gathered for Christmas decorations that for many years it was rare. But as old fields are returning to woodlands, it is starting to make a comeback. Many groundcovers, like galax, prefer old, well-established hardwood forest conditions. But running cedar isn't that picky, making it a good choice for ordinary gardeners to experiment with. It may be hard to get established, but once it is firmly rooted, it can spread over large areas fairly quickly.

118. **Latin Name** *Mitchella repens*
     Common Name Partridgeberry, twinberry, running box
     Usual Height 1- to 2-inch mat
     Spacing 1 foot apart for quick cover
     Sun or Shade ● ◐ ◑ ○
     Bloom White, $^1/_2$ inch, in pairs, late spring to fall, fragrant
     Fruit Red (white), round, $^1/_2$ inch, dry, in pairs, fall and winter
     Leaves Evergreen, round, $^1/_2$ inch, dark glossy, in pairs
     Native Range Rich hardwood forests, pine-oak-hickory woods, stream banks, hammocks, eastern North America, Zones 4 to 8
     Soil Acid, rich
     Drainage Moist
     Root System Shallow, stems root when they touch the ground
     Companion Plants Hemlock, pine, tulip poplar, post oak, mountain laurel, leucothoe, decumaria, foamflower, green-and-gold, smilacina, vernal iris, spigelia, heartleaf
     Propagation Stratified seed, cuttings, layering, division
     Wildlife Fruits eaten by ruffed grouse, bobwhite, wild turkey, skunk, and white-footed mouse

Partridgeberry is one of the most adaptable and easy-to-grow groundcovers for the home gardener in the Southeast. I've seen acres of it in the woods, proving that in rich, dappled shade, it doesn't need supplemental water to form a dense cover. If you do have a bout of drought and it wants water, don't worry—it will tell you in no uncertain terms, wilting dramatically. You'll generally have a couple of days to react before parts of it begin to die.

119. **Latin Name** *Polytrichum commune*
     Common Name Haircap moss, pigeonwheat moss
     Usual Height 4- to 6-inch carpet
     Spacing Can get 100 feet across
     Sun or Shade ● ◐ ◑
     Bloom None
     Fruit Spores, not seeds
     Leaves Evergreen, $^1/_2$ inch long, yellow-green
     Native Range Moist woodland, stream banks, all over the world
     Soil Very acid, acid, poor preferred
     Drainage Moist to wet
     Root System Threadlike roots called rhizoids
     Companion Plants Pines, hardwoods, ferns, woodland flowers
     Propagation Spores
     Wildlife Sometimes used in building nests
     Related Species *Thuidium delicatulum*, fern moss

There are, on average, 100 different kinds of moss in each county in the South, with **haircap moss** being an especially common one. The moss lawn shown at the beginning of this chapter is composed of **fern moss**. You usually don't have to go to a lot of trouble to acquire moss; if you have shade and moisture, it will magically appear. A daily one-minute misting with the hose on a stone terrace, a stone wall, or a bare, shady piece of ground can often encourage a bumper crop. If you have the right conditions, and moss doesn't appear for you, try this recipe, courtesy of my friend Lorine Gibson. Collect some moss from your neighborhood and mix it in a blender with buttermilk. A bit of manure is optional. Rub this moss batter onto bare ground or into the cracks and fissures of your rocks and walkways where it tends to be damp. Then, mist frequently until your moss is off to a good start.

120. Latin Name *Salvia lyrata*
Common Name Lyreleaf sage
Usual Height 2- to 4-inch mat, 1- to 2-foot flowers
Spacing 1 foot apart for quick cover
Sun or Shade ● ◑ ◐ ○
Bloom Pale blue to white, early spring
Fruit Small, tan, dry, shortly after blooming
Leaves Evergreen, 4 to 8 inches long, dark green in sun, some turn maroon when stressed, aromatic
Native Range Roadsides, meadows, thin woodlands, stable dunes, eastern half U.S., Zones 6 to 9
Soil Acid, poor, lime OK, clay OK
Drainage Dry to seasonally wet
Root System Clump-forming, self-sows vigorously
Companion Plants White ash, live oak, post oak, butterweed, yellowtop, eared coreopsis, lanceleaf coreopsis, black-eyed Susan, purple coneflower
Propagation Seed, division
Wildlife Flowers a favorite with hummingbirds and butterflies

Lyreleaf sage is a cinch to grow, making it a great plant for beginners or laissez-faire gardeners. It is especially useful for those on clay or on dry soils overlying limestone, where so many plants are difficult. It can form a groundcover in a dry, bare, shady spot. When in bloom, the flowers blend together visually to make a pale blue haze that seems to float off the ground. Mow lyreleaf sage after it has set seed, and mow it anytime afterwards up until March. It can also be used in a sunny lawn for spring color, as it can tolerate a small amount of foot traffic. The rosettes and grass can coexist peacefully.

121. Latin Name *Senecio aureus*
Common Name Butterweed, golden groundsel, golden ragwort
Usual Height 2- to 4-inch mat, 2 to 3 feet when in bloom
Spacing 18 inches apart
Sun or Shade ● ◑ ◐ ○
Bloom Yellow, drooping petals, 1 inch across, very numerous, early spring to summer
Fruit White, fluffy, late spring
Leaves Evergreen, heart-shaped, 1 to 4 inches long, green above, purple underneath
Native Range Bogs, meadows, pastures, wet woods, floodplains, eastern North America, Zones 3 to 9
Soil Acid, rich preferred
Drainage Moist to dryish, seasonal flooding OK
Root System Colonizes to form a groundcover
Companion Plants Alder, sweetgum, eastern persimmon, white ash, river birch, musclewood, shagbark hickory, willow oak, partridgeberry, wild violets, lyreleaf sage
Propagation Seed, divisions in spring
Wildlife Flowers important to bees
Related Species *S. obovatus*, squawweed; *S. glabellus*, yellowtop

This little flower illustrates how, often, loveliness and usefulness can go unnoticed. Senecios are normally considered to be weeds. You've probably pulled out or poisoned many of them in your life. Yet, **butterweed** can be an evergreen groundcover with flowers that rival any popular garden flower. **Squawweed** is a good alternative for those of you living in limestone areas. **Yellowtop**, although an annual, seeds itself so thickly on wet sites in the Deep South that it forms a winter groundcover from October until February. Then, for nearly three months, it flowers so profusely that it makes a field of gold in either shade or sun. Scythe or mow it down after it has sown its seeds for next year.

122. **Latin Name** *Smilax pumila*
Common Name Dwarf smilax, wild sarsaparilla
Usual Height 6 inches, can get to 18 inches by climbing with tendrils
Spacing 1 foot apart for quick cover
Sun or Shade ◑ ◐
Bloom Yellowish green, summer
Fruit Red to orange, glossy, in 1- to 2-inch clusters, winter to spring
Leaves Evergreen, 2 to 4 inches long, reddish in winter, first fuzzy, then glossy, always fuzzy and pale underneath
Native Range Maritime woods, live oak woods, flatwoods, sandhills, bluffs, hammocks, pine woods, Coastal Plain, South Carolina to Texas, Zones 8 to 9
Soil Sandy, poor
Drainage Dry
Root System Deep, wide-spreading
Companion Plants Live oak, cabbage palmetto, longleaf pine, post oak, sprucepine, pawpaw, American beautyberry, Turk's cap
Propagation Softwood cuttings
Wildlife Fruits eaten by many birds and mammals

Dwarf smilax is an excellent groundcover for those of you who live in the kind of dry, difficult sandy soil that supports live oaks, post oaks, and longleaf pines. It has a big enough leaf and sufficient height to be a suitable groundcover on large sites. It's also pretty enough to be in a small, refined courtyard area where you see it up close all the time. Unlike most smilaxes, dwarf smilax is essentially thornless.

Shuttleworth's ginger

DECIDUOUS SHADY GROUNDCOVERS

Deciduous groundcovers can sometimes be evergreen in a mild winter, but you can't count on their staying that way. They will, however, be a dependable ground-cover for you from spring to frost. In the winter, don't plant pansies on top of them; let their roots stay unharmed under a comforter of leaves.

Wherry foamflower has been planted closely together to make a flowering groundcover under the red-flowered scarlet buckeye at Piccadilly Farm in Bishop, Georgia.

123. **Latin Name** *Asarum canadense*
    Common Name Wild ginger
    Usual Height 3- to 5-inch carpet
    Spacing Spreads about 1 foot a year
    Sun or Shade ● ◑
    Bloom Strange, half-hidden, purply brown, spring
    Fruit Large, fleshy, late spring
    Leaves 3 to 6 inches across, medium green, heart-shaped, fuzzy, appear in early spring and remain until a hard frost
    Native Range Rich woods, eastern half North America, Zones 3 to 7
    Soil Acid, lime OK, pH 6 to 7 preferred, rich
    Drainage Moist
    Root System Will colonize to form a groundcover, ginger-smelling
    Companion Plants Beech and other hardwoods, smilacina, Solomon's seal, partridgeberry, hexastylis, Christmas fern, Jack-in-the-pulpit, troutlily
    Propagation Slow from seed, summer cuttings, root divisions in fall
    Wildlife No information
    Related Species *Hexastylis* is used to designate the evergreen gingers

Wild ginger is the easiest of the gingers to grow. We saw it frequently in Piedmont and mountain gardens, where its vigor was obvious; it had always grown faster and covered more territory than the other woodland groundcovers. Its valentine-shaped leaves make a rich texture that works well for large areas. Yet its low height is smooth enough to provide a stage for ferns or taller woodland flowers, such as Jack-in-the-pulpit. For some reason, probably summer heat, wild ginger seems to be neither native nor adaptable to Zone 8, which covers most of the Coastal Plain.

124. **Latin Name** *Chrysogonum virginianum* var. *australe*
    Common Name Southern green-and-gold
    Usual Height 2- to 6-inch mat
    Spacing 1 foot apart for quick cover
    Sun or Shade ◑ ◑
    Bloom Dark yellow, 1 inch across, early spring
    Fruit Dark seeds, late spring
    Leaves 1 to 3 inches long, soft, rounded
    Native Range Dry woodlands, pinewoods, eastern U.S., Zones 7 to 8
    Soil Slightly acid, rich preferred, sandy or rocky OK
    Drainage Dry to moist, not tolerant of flooding
    Root System Stems root to form a groundcover
    Companion Plants Tulip poplar, post oak, ebony spleenwort, Christmas fern, partridgeberry, smilacina, spigelia
    Propagation Division, layering
    Wildlife No information
    Related Species *C. v.* var. *virginianum*, northern green-and-gold, Zones 6 to 7

Green-and-gold is becoming extremely popular, and not just among Notre Dame alumni. No wonder; it's very pretty, and thrives best on neglect. In too much shade, it starts straining toward the sun. With too much water, it gets sick. Bright dappled shade or a half day of sun on well-drained ground seems to be just right. The southern variety is best for a groundcover, and is the one we saw over and over in gardens we visited. The **northern green-and-gold** is clump-forming and gets taller—about 16 inches high. It also grows under hardwoods, and is often found with Solomon's seal, smilacina, Jack-in-the-pulpit, foamflower, Christmas fern, New York fern, and northern maidenhair fern.

125. **Latin Name** *Hepatica americana*
   Common Name Round-lobed hepatica, liverleaf
   Usual Height 3- to 4-inch mat when not in flower
   Spacing 9 to 12 inches
   Sun or Shade ● ◐
   Bloom White, pink, pale blue, lavender, 1/2 to 1 inch across, on fuzzy, 4- to 6-inch stems, midspring with winter-red leaves
   Fruit Small, ripe soon after flowering
   Leaves Sometimes evergreen, 1 to 3 inches wide, three-lobed, glossy, wine-red in fall (and winter)
   Native Range Rich wooded slopes, bluffs, stream banks, eastern North America, Zones 5 to 8
   Soil Very acid, acid, subsurface limestone OK, rich
   Drainage Moist to dry
   Root System Might colonize a little
   Companion Plants Hardwoods, maidenhair fern, fly poison, Solomon's seal, smilacina, dwarf iris, heartleaf, black cohosh, foamflower
   Propagation Fresh seed sown in fall produces best result, slow from divisions, can be rescued any time with a good rootball
   Wildlife Winter browse
   Related Species *H. acutiloba,* sharp-lobed hepatica, mountain hepatica

Hepatica is one of the earliest plants to bloom in the spring. After flowering and setting seed, the previous year's reddish leaves disappear. The plant rests for a week or so before new, green, shiny leaves develop. Use hepatica as a groundcover only in a very small space, because its texture is too fine to sustain visual interest over a larger area. Extend your population by always letting it go to seed. But be patient; the seedlings will display only two leaves the first year. Some gardeners believe that **round-lobed hepatica** prefers very acid soil and **sharp-lobed hepatica** prefers slightly acid to neutral soil. I don't know about that, but it does seem sure that round-lobed hepatica is more heat tolerant.

126. **Latin Name** *Pachysandra procumbens*
   Common Name Allegheny spurge
   Usual Height 4 to 9 inches
   Spacing 1 to 2 feet for quick cover
   Sun or Shade ● ◐ ◐
   Bloom White to pink, 2- to 4-inch spikes, fragrant, early spring, before new leaves
   Fruit Dry capsule with 6 seeds
   Leaves Evergreen (with protection) until after the plant flowers in the spring, 2 to 4 inches long, dark green mottled with pale green, on pale coral stems
   Native Range Rare, rich woods, calcareous bluffs and ravines, northwestern South Carolina, northwestern Florida to southeastern Louisiana, Mississippi, and central Kentucky, Zones 6 to 8
   Soil Slightly acid, lime OK, rich
   Drainage Moist
   Root System Colonizes by rhizomes to form a groundcover
   Companion Plants Needle palm, red buckeye, Carolina silverbell, storax, itea, mayapple, Solomon's seal, royal fern, spigelia, bloodroot, blue phlox
   Propagation Softwood cuttings, division in fall
   Wildlife No information

Gardeners who have used **Allegheny spurge**, our native pachysandra, claim that it is both prettier and healthier than the better-known Japanese version (*P. terminalis*). Ours is completely evergreen in Zone 8, but in severe winters farther north it might go deciduous if it isn't protected from the wind. It seems to adapt to any acid soil, although in the wild Allegheny spurge is found only in rich soils over limestone. Because it has so few native habitats left, it is rare everywhere it occurs and is considered endangered in Florida. Be sure to buy yours from a nursery that propagates its material and does not dig from the wild.

127. **Latin Name** *Tiarella cordifolia* var. *collina* (formerly *wherryi*)

   Common Name Foamflower

   Usual Height 6 inches, 12 to 20 inches in flower

   Spacing 9 inches

   Sun or Shade ● ◑ ◐ ○

   Bloom White, 1- to 6-inch spike, midspring

   Fruit Tiny, dry

   Leaves Evergreen (if protected), 2 to 4 inches long and wide, fuzzy, with purple markings, wine-red in winter

   Native Range Rich woods, eastern North America, Zones 5 to 7

   Soil Very acid to acid, rich, moist cracks in granite cliffs

   Drainage Moist, not tolerant of flooding

   Root System Crowns

   Companion Plants Beech, Fraser's magnolia, southern lady fern, Christmas fern, bellwort, troutlily, fly poison, Solomon's seal, smilacina, dwarf iris, Jack-in-the-pulpit, heartleaf, black cohosh, mayapple, hepatica partridgeberry, green-and-gold

   Propagation Seed, division

   Wildlife No information

   Related Species *Tiarella cordifolia* var. *cordifolia*, mountain foamflower

The basic and widespread **mountain foamflower** forms an attractive and natural groundcover, but it likes things relatively cool, so it is confined to the mountains. The one we saw in gardens, and the one that is available in the nursery trade, is **Wherry's foamflower,** a native variety that handles heat much better, even in Zone 8. This one is not a natural groundcover, so to use it that way, plant yours close together. Or, since it is so well behaved and the blooms are pretty enough to stand on their own, use it in your shady flower garden.

128. **Latin Name** *Uvularia sessilifolia*

   Common Name Spreading bellwort, strawlily

   Usual Height 6 to 8 inches, rarely 12 inches tall

   Spacing 1 foot apart for quick cover

   Sun or Shade ● ◑ ◐ ○

   Bloom Pale yellow, narrow bells, under the leaves, midspring

   Fruit Three-cornered, 1 inch, green in summer, ripe early fall

   Leaves Light, yellow-green

   Native Range Hardwood slopes, bluffs, coves, eastern North America, Zones 4 to 8, Piedmont and mountains to Florida Panhandle

   Soil Acid, rich

   Drainage Moist, does not tolerate flooding

   Root System Colonizes to form a groundcover

   Companion Plants Under hardwoods with ferns and woodland flowers

   Propagation Seed, division

   Wildlife No information

   Related Species *U. perfoliata*, merrybells

Bellworts are lovely and popular woodland plants. Two of them—**spreading bellwort** and **merrybells**—colonize to form groundcovers. Use them in shady gardens where there is rich soil, good drainage, and lots of composting leaf mulch. The April flowers are lovely, slender bells that require up-close viewing to be appreciated. The rest of the year, until frost, you have a groundcover, as shown in the picture. Let the flowers go to seed the first few years, until you have an area covered as densely as you desire. Merrybells and the giant bellwort, *U. grandiflora* (a flower, not a groundcover), are unusual because both the blooms and the seeds are borne on a short stem that comes out of the center of the leaf.

10

FERNS

Where you find woodland flowers and groundcovers, you are also very likely to find ferns; they like the same environment, that is, shade, dependable moisture year round, and a rich, loose, friable soil that is acid to neutral in pH. Ferns do their growing during spring and fall; during summer, they just try to outlast the heat.

When ferns are happy, they get aggressive, making them ideal as groundcovers. Some ferns are clump-forming, so they can be used as accents in flower beds or among other forms of groundcover.

Ferns look like they belong in some prehistoric landscape. In fact, that's where these ancient plants started out eons ago. Some parts of a fern are, well, odd-looking. Which is not to say they aren't attractive in a wonderfully primeval way.

Come spring, the first sign you see of ferns are **fiddleheads.** These are the fern's leaves, but at this stage they are so tightly furled and rolled up that they look like fuzzy shepherd's crooks. Fiddleheads are often pink, yellow-green, or silver, and are as ornamental as those early woodland flowers that appear at the same time. It usually takes the fern's leaves about six weeks to unfurl and develop, giving later-blooming woodland flowers time to show off before the ferns reach full size and dominate the scene.

Ferns have two kinds of leaves: **sterile leaves,** which are ordinary leaves, and **fertile leaves,** which bear **spores,** what ferns have instead of seeds. The spores are as teensy as dust. The only way they're visible is in little groups called **fruit dots,** which are arranged in patterns on the back side of the fertile leaves or clustered in three-dimensional packages called **spore cases.** Spores do not turn directly into ferns. First they become an intermediate plant called a **gametophyte,** which in turn produces a **sporophyte,** which finally becomes a fern. This process is a little like how frogs develop, from eggs to tadpoles to croakers.

Most ferns you buy at the nursery didn't go through this exotic process; they were propagated by root division. Those with a **crown,** the hard mass at the top of the roots, are best divided in spring with a sharp knife. Ferns with colonizing roots can be chopped up just about any time.

This is fine for growing individual ferns. But if you need a large quantity for a landscape, you need to grow them from spores. These easy directions are from a lecture given by Roger Boyles at the 1992 Cullowhee Native Plant Conference:

Pick one fern leaf covered with fruit dots or, in the case of sensitive fern, one stalk full of spore cases. Place in a paper sack (not plastic) and put it in the refrigerator for two or three days. As the leaf withers, it will release the dustlike spores. Now, half-fill 10 mason jars with soil, and sterilize both soil and jars in your canner. Next, plant the spores very sparingly, spritz the top with sterilized water, and cover the tops with plastic wrap. Place the jars under a fluorescent light for 12 hours a day for 23 to 37 days until you have a green mist in the jars. Spritz again and cover for another two weeks. Then divide the gametophytes with tweezers and place them farther apart on more sterile soil. Six weeks later, they will be sporophytes and ready to be transplanted again, this time to rich, organic soil. By the end of one year, you should have many tiny ferns in 4-inch pots ready to be transplanted one last time into your fern garden.

The three *Dryopteris* ferns and Christmas fern are evergreen. The others are more interesting and versatile, ranging from ultradry to ultrawet. They can be used as groundcovers, as accents in shady flower gardens, in either sunny or shady water gardens, in hanging baskets, tucked into stone walls, or naturalized in the correct habitat and allowed to do as they please.

Broad beechfern and three other kinds of ferns are visible in this picture of the Mountain Garden at the North Carolina Botanical Garden in Chapel Hill.

129. Latin Name *Dryopteris marginalis*
Common Name Marginal fern, marginal shieldfern, marginal woodfern
Usual Height 20 inches, rarely 3 feet high
Spacing 2 feet
Sun or Shade ● ◑
Fiddleheads Golden brown, furry, spring
Fruit Spores, clustered in visible fruit dots along margins of the leaflets, dark brown, late summer
Leaves Evergreen, upright, dark, leathery
Native Range Moist woods and clearings, banks, ravines, eastern North America, Zones 5 to 7
Soil Acid, lime OK, rich and rocky preferred
Drainage Moist
Root System 1- to 4-inch-high crown with shallow radiating roots, clump-forming, not a colonizer
Companion Plants Tulip poplar, beech, other hardwoods, Christmas fern, ebony spleenwort, southern lady fern, merrybells, troutlily, fly poison, Solomon's seal, smilacina, dwarf iris
Propagation Spores, crown divisions in spring
Wildlife Shelter for toads and lizards
Related Species *D. celsa,* log fern, Zones 6 to 7; *D. ludoviciana,* Florida shield fern, Zones 8 to 9

The *Dryopteris* family is mostly evergreen and is extremely popular with landscapers. The three mentioned here are the ones I found being grown and used in the South. **Marginal fern,** like Christmas fern, is very polite; it makes a larger clump each year, but it never goes galloping all over your garden. Of course, if you want a groundcover, then you *do* want one that gallops—and that would be **log fern,** so named because it often grows on fallen logs. Both of these ferns are somewhat heat sensitive. For those of you on the Coastal Plain who have to endure really hot summers and heavy, wet soil, try **Florida shield fern,** another groundcover fern. Although native to Zone 8, this fern is reported to be hardy in Zones 6 to 10. Both groundcover ferns might get to be 4 feet tall.

130. Latin Name *Polystichum acrostichoides*
Common Name Christmas fern
Usual Height 18 to 24 inches, rarely to 3 feet
Spacing 2 feet
Sun or Shade ● ◑
Fiddleheads Silvery, early spring
Fruit Spores in masses of fruit dots, summer
Leaves Evergreen, narrow, dark, upright
Native Range Rocky woods, stream banks, hammocks in swamps, eastern North America, Zones 5 to 10
Soil Acid, lime OK, rich, rocky or sandy preferred
Drainage Moist
Root System Shallow, clump-forming, no crown
Companion Plants Hemlock, sprucepine, tulip poplar, beech, post oak, foamflower, smilacina, partridgeberry, heartleaf, green-and-gold, broad beechfern, southern lady fern, ebony spleenwort
Propagation Spores, root divisions
Wildlife Used by ruffed grouse

Christmas fern is evergreen, smallish, and well behaved, making it the premier fern for Southern gardens. It got its name because it is green at Christmas time. We saw it everywhere, used as edging, planted close together as groundcover, and, most effectively, as accents in shady flower gardens. Usually knee high and planted in clumps of two or three, it gives continuity there without being overpowering. My least favorite use is as a groundcover. Planted en masse, Christmas fern still tends to look like a collection of individuals, not the smooth carpet intended. I've been told that if it gets too much sun, it will look short and pale; it should be an unusually dark shade of green.

131. **Latin Name** *Adiantum pedatum*
   Common Name Northern maidenhair fern
   Usual Height 1 to 2 feet
   Spacing 2 feet for quick cover, 4 feet for clump
   Sun or Shade ●
   Fiddleheads Wine-red, early spring
   Fruit Spores
   Leaves Lacy, on whorled black stems
   Native Range Rich woods, North America, Zones 4 to 8
   Soil Acid, lime OK, rich
   Drainage Moist, cannot dry out, but cannot be wet
   Root System Shallow, black, wiry, colonizing to form a groundcover
   Companion Plants Maples, tulip poplar, most ferns and woodland flowers
   Propagation Spores, division of roots easy in fiddlehead stage
   Wildlife Shelter for toads and lizards
   Related Species *A. capillus-veneris,* southern maidenhair fern, North America and Europe, Zones 7 to 11

Maidenhair fern, with its black stems and rue-shaped leaflets, is distinctive and elegant. It isn't hard to grow as long as its needs are met. It likes to be evenly moist all year—not drippy wet and, most definitely, not dry. It doesn't bounce back at all well after being subjected to even a brief dry spell. It is not a plant for naturalizing, unless you have a cool, moist woods, a seep, a rocky spring, or some other very special site. Plant it close to your house where you will remember to water it. And, because of its exacting requirements, it's best not to depend on it to fill too large an area. The **northern maidenhair fern** takes more cold and a more acid soil. The **southern maidenhair fern** tolerates more alkalinity, even growing in limestone walls, and more heat and humidity.

132. **Latin Name** *Asplenium platyneuron*
   Common Name Ebony spleenwort
   Usual Height 12 to 18 inches
   Spacing 1 foot
   Sun or Shade ● ◐ ◑
   Fiddleheads Especially small, early spring
   Fruit Spores, fruit dots like ribs along the spine of the vein
   Leaves Fertile leaves upright, narrow, dark green; sterile leaves prostrate at base, smaller, paler, might be evergreen
   Native Range Well-drained woods, moist fields, floodplains, eastern North America to Rocky Mountains, Zones 5 to 9
   Soil Acid or alkaline, sandy, rocky poor soils OK
   Drainage Moist to dry, not tolerant of flooding at all
   Root System Clump-forming, with spreading, wiry, black rootlets
   Companion Plants Tulip poplar, post oak, shortleaf pine, dwarf huckleberry, Christmas fern, troutlily, mayapple, pussytoes, galax, green-and-gold, partridgeberry
   Propagation Spores, division
   Wildlife No information

Ebony spleenwort is small, well mannered, and ideal for areas that are too dry for most other ferns, except bracken. If you use it as a groundcover, plan on watering it regularly all summer to keep it thick. But don't expect it to make a smooth cover. Like Christmas fern, it is too individualistic to make a dense, even blanket. It takes a lot more sun than most ferns, and can even be used as an accent in a half-sunny flower garden. Plant it between boulders or in the cracks of an unmortared stone wall; its light, airy appearance looks graceful there, where other ferns would look too bulky.

133. Latin Name *Athyrium filix-femina* var. *asplenioides*
   Common Name Southern lady fern
   Usual Height 18 to 36 inches
   Spacing 4 feet apart for quick cover
   Sun or Shade ◑ ◐
   Fiddleheads Usually lime-green, spring, and then summer and fall
   Fruit Spores, curving fruit dots
   Leaves Lacy, large, broad, light green
   Native Range Moist semishade, bluffs, river banks, eastern U.S., Zones 6 to 8
   Soil Acid to neutral, rich
   Drainage Moist, tolerates seasonal flooding
   Root System Colonizes aggressively
   Companion Plants Hemlock, southern magnolia, swamp chestnut oak, sprucepine, American holly, possumhaw viburnum, sensitive fern, Christmas fern, broad beechfern, northern maidenhair fern, marginal fern, most early woodland flowers
   Propagation Root division
   Wildlife Shelter for woodhouse toad, anoles

Southern lady fern is just what most folks imagine when they hear the word "fern." It is waist high, lacy, delicate-looking, and easy to grow. Even black-thumbs have no trouble, as long as they remember to water it (not drown it) whenever it starts getting a little dry in the summer. Unlike maidenhair fern, it is very forgiving; if the foliage starts turning brown and crispy, water it and it will spring back with fresh new fronds. While some gardeners consider it a nuisance because it's aggressive and can overwhelm more timid ferns and woodland flowers, it's a good choice for those who have the room to let it go and don't want to spend a lot of time and effort in the garden.

134. Latin Name *Onoclea sensibilis*
   Common Name Sensitive fern, bead fern
   Usual Height 1 to 2 feet, occasionally 3 feet
   Spacing 1 to 2 feet for quick cover
   Sun or Shade ● ◑ ◐
   Fiddleheads Pale red, early spring
   Fruit Spores, in beads on fertile stalks, early summer
   Leaves Sterile, broad, simple, light green
   Native Range Woodlands, hammocks, stream banks, floodplains, eastern North America, Zones 4 to 8
   Soil Acid, rich
   Drainage Wet to moist
   Root System Colonizes, shallow brown, thick
   Companion Plants Loblolly pine, swamp chestnut oak, sweetbay, wax myrtle, musclewood, clethra, fetterbush, swamp azalea, crossvine, decumaria, cinnamon fern, netted chain fern, lizard's tail
   Propagation Root division
   Wildlife Shelter for salamanders, frogs

Sensitive fern usually grows knee high and makes a fine groundcover in wet places. It can even be aggressive in locations most other plants wouldn't even consider. It grows in very soggy sites, as long as it gets oxygen; sour clay and stagnant water are too extreme. In the wild, it is usually seen with cinnamon fern. The two look great together. Cinnamon fern provides a tall, lacy counterpoint to low, smooth sensitive fern. Lizard's tail is also usually present, providing flowers in early summer. The beaded stalks of sensitive fern are decorative in the winter garden, but I prefer to cut them and use them in dried arrangements indoors. For an even shorter ferny groundcover in these same conditions, see netted chain fern.

135. Latin Name *Osmunda cinnamomea*
Common Name Cinnamon fern
Usual Height 2 to 3 feet, rarely 6 feet in Southeast
Spacing 3 feet
Sun or Shade ● ◑ ◐ ○
Fiddleheads Silvery, wooly, turning to cinnamon brown, early spring
Fruit Cinnamon-colored spore cases on fertile stalks, late spring
Leaves Sterile, lacy, broad, bright green, wooly in early spring, yellow fall color
Native Range Swamps, ponds, stream banks, eastern North and Central America, Zones 4 to 11
Soil Acid, rich
Drainage Wet to moist, tolerates shallow water all year
Root System Bristly crown of osmunda fiber, shallow black roots, clump-forming in Southeast
Companion Plants Red maple, redbay, itea, highbush blueberry, sensitive fern, netted chain fern, royal fern, lizard's tail, goldenclub
Propagation Fresh green spores, crown division
Wildlife Spring wool on leaves used for nests

You'll want to use **cinnamon fern** as an accent plant rather than as a groundcover. Team it up with sensitive fern, netted chain fern, and lizard's tail along a creek bank, on the shady side of your house where drainage is seasonally poor, or in a rich, moist bed in your garden. Cinnamon fern is found in full sun, but only when it is sitting in shallow, barely moving water. There, it can be combined with tuckahoe, pickerelweed, and other water plants. Unless you have a natural bog, spring, or dependable seep on your property, plan to use it only in the shade.

136. Latin Name *Osmunda regalis*
Common Name Royal fern
Usual Height 2 to 3 feet, rarely 6 feet in Southeast
Spacing 3 to 4 feet
Sun or Shade ● ◑ ◐ ○
Fiddleheads Wine-red, smooth, stout, early spring
Fruit Golden clusters of spore cases on fertile stalks, midsummer
Leaves Sterile, large, simple, pale green
Native Range Bogs, wet meadows, western hemisphere and Europe, Zones 5 to 11
Soil Acid, limestone OK, rich preferred
Drainage Wet to moist, tolerates shallow water all year
Root System Elevated 1- to 6-inch crown of osmunda fiber, deep, black roots, clump-forming in Southeast
Companion Plants Most woodlands, most ferns and woodland flowers
Propagation Spores, division of crown
Wildlife No information

Although **royal fern** is tolerant of a wide range of conditions, I've seen it most often in lightly shaded moist—not wet—sites. It seems to be able to thrive with less consistent water than cinnamon fern. Royal fern is an accent fern, tall and stately, and its relatively simple leaves make it stand out in contrast to more lacy ferns. Use it in shady flower gardens where you want height, in coastal gardens that have a tropical flavor, and in mountain gardens where you want a softening touch.

137. **Latin Name** *Pteridium aquilinum*
Common Name Bracken
Usual Height 1 to 4 feet in Southeast
Spacing 2 to 3 feet apart for quick cover
Sun or Shade ● ◑ ◐
Fiddleheads Three-clawed, silvery, furry, early spring
Fruit Spores in fruit dots on margins of leaflets
Leaves Three-parted, large, broad, airy, light green, bronze in fall
Native Range Dry woods, burned areas, thickets, almost worldwide
Soil Acid, poor, sterile sand preferred
Drainage Dry to moist, does not tolerate flooding
Root System Very deep, colonizes aggressively if not kept dry
Companion Plants Longleaf pine, turkey oak, post oak, sparkleberry, sassafras, wiregrass, little bluestem, sandhill rosemary, conradina
Propagation Root division
Wildlife Shelter for many small animals

Bracken is your fern of last resort. Extremely aggressive, it's often called the weed of the fern family and shouldn't be used where any other ferns can grow—it would soon take over the place. But it is absolutely invaluable in dry, thin woodland, where it is your only choice for an extensive, ferny, drought-tolerant groundcover. Its roots have been reported to go as deep as 10 feet in search of water. If there is no rain for several weeks in the summer, it will go dormant. It is only after three months of drought that parts of it will start to die. In a landscape, you can mow the edges to give it shape, the same way you would do contour mowing in a meadow, or for mayapple. Each year, cut it back after the fall color has faded, so that the new spring growth will not be intermixed with dead leaves. It also tolerates being burned.

138. **Latin Name** *Thelypteris noveboracensis*
Common Name New York fern
Usual Height 12 to 18 inches, occasionally 2 feet
Spacing 1 foot apart for quick cover in the Southeast
Sun or Shade ● ◑ ◐
Fiddleheads Light green, early spring
Fruit Spores, in round or kidney-shaped fruit dots
Leaves Chartreuse, lacy
Native Range Moist woods, hammocks, eastern North America, Zones 5 to 7
Soil Acid, rich, rocky crevices OK
Drainage Moist
Root System Shallow, black, wiry, colonizes more slowly in the South
Companion Plants Hemlock, maples, beech, rosebay rhododendron, red maple, fringetree, Solomon's seal, Jack-in-the-pulpit, smilacina, Christmas fern, broad beechfern, northern maidenhair fern
Propagation Spores, root division
Wildlife Shelter for garden toads
Related Species *T. hexagonoptera,* broad beechfern, Zones 5 to 8; *T. kunthii,* normal shield fern, Zones 8b to 11

Many species of *Thelypteris* make fine garden ferns. **New York fern,** in spite of its name, is a good choice for Southern gardens, being less aggressive here than it is in colder climates. It is valuable primarily for its bright yellow-green color, which makes a pleasant groundcover. The **broad beechfern** has distinctive triangular leaves, is a little taller and a little more heat tolerant than New York fern, and is darker green in color. The two are often found growing together under hardwoods with a variety of woodland flowers. **Normal shield fern** tolerates alkaline clay and is a very dependable fern for the Deep South.

139. **Latin Name** *Woodwardia areolata* (formerly
    Lorinseria areolata)
  Common Name Netted chain fern
  Usual Height 12 inches, occasionally 30 inches
  Spacing 18 inches apart for quick cover
  Sun or Shade ● ◗ ◑
  Fiddleheads Bronze, early spring
  Fruit Spores in chained fruit dots on fertile leaves
  Leaves Sterile, glossy green, thin, wavy
  Native Range Swamps, wet woods, floodplains,
    lime sinks, eastern North America, Zones 5 to 9
  Soil Very acid, rich, over lime OK, brackish OK
  Drainage Moist to wet
  Root System Shallow, brown, slender, colonizing
  Companion Plants Bald cypress, red maple, redbay,
    sweetbay, itea, highbush blueberry, cinnamon
    fern, sensitive fern, lizard's tail
  Propagation Spores, root division
  Wildlife Shelter for frogs, toads, and newts

*Naturally ferny limestone seep at home of
Matthew Dew in Lake City, Tennessee.*

Netted chain fern looks a lot like sensitive fern,
the chief difference being that it grows closer to the
ground. But, they are not related. In the wild, I see
netted chain fern most often in fairly dark woods
that are so wet they are squishy underfoot. It also
grows in the sandhills and in post oak woods where
the water table intersects the surface, making a
pocosin or bog. The leaves are simple, giving a feeling of calm and continuity so important to a groundcover. It would be my first choice for a mass planting
under titi, sweetbay, or wax myrtle. On the edge of a
shady pond, use it with lizard's tail, cinnamon fern,
and tuckahoe.

11

WOODLAND FLOWERS

Woodland flowers, along with groundcovers, ferns, and leaf mulch, are the normal cover for the forest floor in the Southeastern deciduous woodlands. In winter and spring, the forest floor receives dappled sunlight, but in summer and fall, the light is very dim. For that reason, most woodland flowers bloom in very early spring while branches are still bare or just beginning to flower or leaf out. These flowers occur commonly in hardwood forests; when you find them in pine/oak forests, they are usually under the oaks, not the pines.

While some of these flowers maintain green leaves all year, most of them put all their energy into spring blooming and stay dormant the rest of the year. These flowers are called **spring ephemerals** because they stay around such a short time. Treat them as you would daffodils or other long-lived spring bulbs. Allow the foliage to die back on its own before cutting it back. This feeds the roots so they are ready to go again the next year. Some of the foliage is so delicate that it dies back without your ever noticing, especially if ferns and summer woodland flowers are planted adjacent to quickly fill in the spaces vacated by the ephemerals.

Not all the spring flower foliage dies in the spring. Some looks good until seed is set in late summer or fall. Some stays green until frost. And some have tall leafy stems that die back at frost, but then grow **basal rosettes,** sunbursts of fresh greenery that hug the ground or arrange themselves above the leaf mulch to get sun all winter. (All that information is in the profiles under the heading on leaves.)

Spring ephemerals bloom before the trees are covered with leaves.

Some woodland flowers are bulbs, or have a special shallow type of flattened bulb called a **corm.** Most, however, have **rhizomes,** thickened horizontal roots like iris roots. Some of these colonize to make extensive masses. Others colonize very slowly to make clumps that get a little bit bigger every year. Then, there are some woodland flowers—normally the shorter-lived perennials—that **self-sow,** or reseed themselves, to expand their territory. Spotted phacelia is the only flower in this chapter that is not a perennial.

Woodland flowers can be used in shady flower gardens just the way you'd use most other flowers. Or, they can be planted in drifts under trees and allowed to wander wherever they wish. Margaret Reid, a skilled native-plant gardener in Raleigh, North Carolina, has developed what she calls the "playhouse" technique for planting a woodland garden. She doesn't try to do too much—no more than 6 feet by 6 feet—at any one time. This tiny area becomes her playhouse and in it she develops a composition with rocks, logs, bird bath, ferns, flowers, and groundcovers that reminds her of some particularly beautiful spot she has seen in the woods. For a year she weeds, waters, and perfects it. Then, the next year, she starts another playhouse. After many years, this technique has resulted in an exquisite shady dell on one side of her house.

Only a few nurseries bother to carry woodland flowers, because most are slow-growing. Many of them take two to three years to reach blooming size. For a nursery to be able to offer them to you, a lot of time, energy, dedication, and money has to be invested. So be appreciative when you come across them, and understand why these beautiful flowers cost more than run-of-the-mill flora.

Also, be sure they've been **nursery propagated.** And be aware that this does *not* mean the same as "nursery grown," a tag some unscrupulous nurseries use to fudge the fact that the plants were "grown" only a month or so in the nursery after being dug from the wild. "Nursery propagated" means that the plants were grown from seed or cuttings, or that the nursery maintains stock plants and divides them each year, and leaves the ones in the wild alone.

Finally, bloodroot, trilliums, lady slippers, and violets are not included in this book, even though they are very well known. They are rarely propagated by nurseries because they are the most difficult and slowest-growing of all.

In summer, ferns and shade-loving flowers replace the spring ephemerals.

SPRING-BLOOMING WOODLAND FLOWERS

Spring-blooming woodland flowers grow mostly under deciduous trees, so they have the benefit of spring sunlight penetrating the bare branches and reaching the forest floor. Because they have no competition for the available sunlight, they generally grow quite short, usually below knee high.

Blue phlox, alumroot, foamflower, moss, and ferns have been allowed to find a home on these shady stone steps in Louise Smith's garden in Birmingham, Alabama.

140. **Latin Name** *Aquilegia canadensis*
   Common Name Wild red columbine
   Usual Height 20 to 30 inches, shorter in the
      mountains
   Spacing 2 feet
   Sun or Shade ● ◑ ◖
   Bloom Red and yellow, 2 inches long, nodding,
      early spring and whenever the weather is cool
   Fruit Tan, dry, self-sows easily, 2 weeks after bloom
   Leaves Often evergreen, dainty, floating effect
   Native Range Calcareous woods, most of North
      America, Zones 3 to 8
   Soil Acid, lime OK, rocky, sandy, not too rich
   Drainage Dry to moist, not tolerant of flooding
   Root System Deep, thick rootstocks, does not
      colonize
   Companion Plants Flowering dogwood,
      strawberrybush, sweetshrub, partridgeberry,
      foamflower, smilacina, Christmas fern,
      bloodroot, violets, toothwort, celandine poppy,
      Atamasco lily, black cohosh, Small's penstemon,
      broadleafed goldenrod, Short's aster
   Propagation Seed (sown uncovered)
   Wildlife Flowers visited by hummingbirds, bees,
      and butterflies; seeds eaten by finches, buntings

Ironically, the better you treat **wild red columbine,**
the shorter its lifespan. In a well-tended garden, with rich,
overly moist soil, it will grow too fast and expire in a year
or less. It reseeds, so it's easy to keep a broad patch of it
going. You can transplant seedlings in the fall and put
them where you want them. On the other hand, it is
naturally long-lived in not-too-dense dryish woodland, on
the edge of moist woodland, or in limestone walls. I've
had one specimen in a terra-cotta pot with no saucer for
about ten years. Wild red columbine is essentially
evergreen (it goes dormant at 110 degrees F. or −10 F.,
but puts out new leaves immediately after the crisis) and
blooms twice in the spring and once in the fall.

141. **Latin Name** *Arisaema triphyllum*
   Common Name Jack-in-the-pulpit, Indian turnip
   Usual Height 12 to 18 inches, occasionally 3 feet
   Spacing 18 inches
   Sun or Shade ● ◑
   Bloom Pale green, purple markings, 1 to 3 inches,
      late spring
   Fruit Red berries clustered on the stalk, showy,
      mid- to late summer
   Leaves 1 or 2, 12 to 16 inches across, 3 (to 5)
      leaflets, held like an umbrella over the flower,
      dormant late summer to spring
   Native Range Rich bluffs, floodplains, hammocks,
      eastern North America, Zones 4 to 8
   Soil Acid, rich
   Drainage Moist to wet
   Root System Corm, up to 2 inches thick
   Companion Plants Tulip poplar, magnolias,
      storax, heartleaf, foamflower, partridgeberry,
      ferns, green dragon, smilacina
   Propagation Fresh or stratified seed
   Wildlife Fruit and leaves eaten by wild turkey and
      wood thrush; all parts caustic to most animals
   Related Species *A. dracontium,* green dragon

Everywhere we saw **Jack-in-the-pulpit,** it had seeded
out and spread far from its original site in the garden.
But, nobody considered this a problem; this is one
popular flower. For one thing, its colorful fruits provide
welcome color in the middle of a stifling summer. It does
have a somewhat sinister-looking blue, fleshy stalk and
large leaves, but these just give it a tropical feeling. It
mixes well with large-leafed magnolias and assorted ferns.
Surrounded by more sedate woodland flowers, it makes a
dramatic accent. **Green dragon** is almost equally well
liked. It has 7 to 15 leaflets, slender green flowers in late
spring or early summer, and orange berries. The two are
often found growing together, but if you live over
limestone, you might have better luck with green dragon.

(George Pyne)

142. Latin Name *Dentaria laciniata* (*Cardamine laciniata, C. concatenata*)
Common Name Cutleaf toothwort, pepperroot
Usual Height 6 to 8 inches, rarely 15 inches high
Spacing 6- to 10-inch clumps
Sun or Shade ●
Bloom White, 4-petaled, often flushed with pink or lavender, $3/4$ inch, in a loose cluster, early spring
Fruit 1 inch long, dry, slender, late spring
Leaves 3 leaves, on the stem under the flowers, deeply cut and toothed; spring only
Native Range Floodplains, rich woods, stream banks, limestone outcrops, Southeastern U.S., Zones 6 to 8, rare in Coastal Plain
Soil Acid, rich, lime OK
Drainage Moist, seasonal flooding OK
Root System Shallow, long, thin rhizome, colonizes very slowly
Companion Plants Hardwoods, hepatica, bloodroot, merrybells, troutlily, trillium, green dragon, Jack-in-the pulpit, ferns, Allegheny spurge
Propagation Fresh seed, root division
Wildlife Eaten by white-footed mouse
Related Species *D. heterophylla*, toothwort, pepperroot; *D. diphylla*, two-leaved toothwort

Cutleaf toothwort is a spring ephemeral, which is to say, it is delicate and dainty and visible only during that season. It blooms very early when none of the trees have started to leaf out. Each clump is quite vivid and is used effectively when tucked into various spots throughout a shady spring garden. Green dragon and ferns are good candidates to fill its place during the rest of the year. Allegheny spurge is a thin enough groundcover in the spring for toothwort to find room to grow right up through it and bloom. *Dentaria heterophylla* has similar spring flowers, but forms large attractive patches of green leaves in the winter. It, too, vanishes by late spring. Two-leaved **toothwort** is usually the earliest to bloom.

143. Latin Name *Dicentra eximia*
Common Name Wild bleeding heart
Usual Height 9 to 12 inches, rarely 2 feet
Spacing 12- to 18-inch clumps
Sun or Shade ●
Bloom White to pale pink, dark pink or purple, $1/2$ inch, spurred, clustered, early spring to frost
Fruit 1 inch long, peapod-shaped, dry, late summer, self-sows
Leaves Sometimes evergreen, 2 to 10 inches long and wide, very fancy and ferny
Native Range Rich, mountain woods from North Carolina to New York, Zone 6, rare
Soil Acid, rich, rocky
Drainage Moist
Root System Rhizome, colonizes very slowly
Companion Plants Beech, umbrella tree, Solomon's seal, smilacina, violets, foamflower, Jack-in-the-pulpit, green-and-gold, Christmas fern, New York fern, northern maidenhair fern
Propagation Fresh seed, stratified seed
Wildlife No information
Related Species *D. canadensis*, squirrel corn; *D. cucullaria*, Dutchman's breeches

Wild bleeding heart is one of those plants that gardeners dream of. It is small, neat, evergreen, and long-blooming—about 8 months. Though native only in the mountains, it can easily handle the heat of the Piedmont, provided you plant it under a shade tree where the soil is rich and moist. Plant several individual plant clumps where you'd like them to naturalize, then let them seed out and go where they want to. **Squirrel corn** and **Dutchman's breeches** are spring ephemerals. Both can naturalize to cover large patches of forest floor in a deciduous woodland in the upper Piedmont or in the mountains, and both can grow in rich soils over limestone.

144. **Latin Name** *Erythronium albidum*
Common Name White troutlily, dogtooth violet, adder's tongue
Usual Height 6 inches, occasionally 10 inches
Spacing 8 inches apart in a drift
Sun or Shade ● ◗
Bloom White, 1 inch, solitary, nodding, very early spring
Fruit Dry, late spring
Leaves Two, green, mottled with purple, 4 to 8 inches long, glossy, from February to May
Native Range Woods and prairies, Maryland to Kansas to the Gulf states, Zones 6 to 8
Soil Acid, rich, lime OK
Drainage Moist to dry
Root System Corm, the size of a dog's tooth, produces offsets
Companion Plants Under hardwoods, blooms with violets, hepatica, interplanted with later woodland flowers and ferns
Propagation Offsets from corms, untreated seed sown in fall produces flowers the third or fourth spring
Wildlife Browsed by deer
Related Species *E. americanum*, yellow troutlily

Troutlilies are among the very earliest of the woodland flowers to bloom. They are also called dogtooth violets, although they are not violets. Plant the corms (flattened bulbs) about 3 inches deep in loose leaf mold and humus. You won't find them easily in nurseries, and when you do you won't find a lot available. So get what you can, plant them, and then let them seed out to form the large colony you envisioned. Troutlilies are a must for woodland landscapes where, if given half a chance, they can cover acres. The **white troutlily** has the showiest bloom, while the **yellow troutlily** is the most widespread in the eastern United States.

145. **Latin Name** *Geranium maculatum*
Common Name Wild geranium, cranesbill
Usual Height 1 to 2 feet
Spacing 2 feet in drifts
Sun or Shade ● ◗
Bloom Pink, white, lavender, 1 to 1 1/2 inches across, in large, showy clusters, early spring
Fruit 1-inch "cranesbill," dry, late spring
Leaves Almost evergreen, changing in September, fancy
Native Range Rich woods, meadows, eastern half U.S., Zones 5 to 8
Soil Acid, rich
Drainage Moist
Root System Thick rhizomes, colonizes
Companion Plants Hardwoods, broad beechfern, trillium, hepatica, closed gentian
Propagation Seeds, root division
Wildlife Seeds eaten by mourning dove, bobwhite, and white-tailed deer

If you're a novice gardener, **wild geranium** is one of the best woodland flowers to start out with. It's easy to grow, and not at all delicate, rare, or hard to find. In a relatively short time, it can cover a large area. Plant three or five up-slope from where you want to have the big show. The roots will spread and the seeds will scatter downhill, and in just a few years you will have an impressive display. It's also effective with mosses and ferns on the banks of a small stream or in a tiny, shady flower bed. Just because it's easy, don't get the idea that this is some low-class plant. It behaves itself nicely, not getting weedy or pushy around its neighbors in the garden.

146. Latin Name *Heuchera americana*
   Common Name Alumroot
   Usual Height 18 inches, rarely 3 feet
   Spacing 2 feet
   Sun or Shade ● ◑
   Bloom Pale greeny yellow or purple, tiny, lacy
      cluster on stalk, early spring
   Fruit Dark red seeds, late spring
   Leaves Almost evergreen, 4 to 6 inches, maple-
      shaped, fuzzy, red, yellow-green, and purple
      in fall
   Native Range Rich or rocky woods, eastern North
      America, Zones 5 to 8
   Soil Acid, lime OK, rich, rocky
   Drainage Moist to dry
   Root System Crown
   Companion Plants Whorled loosestrife, galax,
      troutlily, wild red columbine
   Propagation Seeds sown in spring, division of
      crown spring or fall
   Wildlife No information
   Related Species *H. villosa,* hairy alumroot,
      mountain alumroot

The appeal of **alumroot**'s flowers is very subjective;
some gardeners don't think much of them, while I, for
one, find their subtle mistiness very attractive. Everybody
likes the leaves, however. They're large, distinctive, and
very colorful in the autumn. Because alumroot is almost
evergreen, it is sometimes used as a groundcover. However, I like it best as a solitary plant nestled into rocks or
growing out of an unmortared rock wall—granite, sandstone, or limestone—it makes no difference. I'm told that
it makes an excellent pot plant. **Hairy alumroot** is very
similar.

147. Latin Name *Iris cristata*
   Common Name Dwarf iris, crested iris
   Usual Height 6 inches
   Spacing 1 foot, 10 feet apart for naturalizing in the
      woods
   Sun or Shade ● ◑
   Bloom Pale blue to deep blue (rarely white in the
      wild), 2½ inches across, early spring
   Fruit Tan, dry, midsummer
   Leaves 4-inch iris leaves, sometimes 8 inches,
      dormant from fall to April
   Native Range Rich woods, Southeastern U.S.,
      Zones 5 to 7
   Soil Acid, rich
   Drainage Moist
   Root System Narrow rhizome, colonizes
   Companion Plants Hardwoods, rhododendrons,
      magnolias, Christmas fern, ebony spleenwort,
      marginal fern, Jack-in-the-pulpit, Solomon's seal,
      smilacina, trillium, fly poison, merrybells
   Propagation Division of clumps, seed
   Wildlife Flowers used by hummingbirds and bees
   Related Species *I. verna,* vernal iris, Zones 6 to 8,
      fragrant

The flowers of **dwarf iris** are surprisingly huge in
relation to the overall plant, and all bloom at once. It is
easy to grow and very popular. We saw both blue- and
white-flowered forms in nearly every Piedmont garden we
visited. **Vernal iris** blooms early on a two-inch stalk and is
intensely fragrant. It prefers very acid soil and is found
under pine trees with galax and wild azaleas, or in dryish
woods under post oaks. Its foliage grows after it blooms
and is taller and narrower than the foliage of dwarf iris.
The Coastal Plain variety, *I. verna* var. *verna,* sometimes
looks grassy. The mountain variety, *I. verna* var. *smalliana,*
looks more like the dwarf iris. Both vernal irises have been
reported to be evergreen in some locations.

(George Pyne)

148. **Latin Name** *Isopyrum biternatum*

   Common Name Isopyrum, false rue anemone
   Usual Height 5 to 6 inches, rarely 20 inches
   Spacing 5- to 6-foot clumps
   Sun or Shade ●
   Bloom White, $^3/_4$ inch across, usually in large clusters, long bloom period in early spring and sometimes all winter
   Fruit $^1/_4$ inch, dry, late spring
   Leaves Rue-shaped leaflets, late fall to spring, dormant in summer
   Native Range Rich woods, limestone ledges, eastern North America, Zones 5 to 8
   Soil Acid, lime OK, rich preferred
   Drainage Moist, tolerates seasonal flooding
   Root System Slender, fibrous, colonizes
   Companion Plants Hardwoods, toothwort, troutlily, dwarf iris, mayapple, wild ginger, green-and-gold, fragrant phlox, blue phlox, northern maidenhair fern
   Propagation Seed, root division
   Wildlife Bees visit flowers

Isopyrum, pronounced "eye-so-PYE-rum," quickly forms large patches of lemony-green foliage that are visually delightful all through the winter. When late March or earliest April rolls around, it blooms extravagantly for a whole month—an unusually long time. The little white flowers are so delicate that they ruffle in the breeze. By May, the leaves and flowers begin to fade. Jenny Andrews of Cheekwood Gardens in Nashville recommends planting maidenhair fern on one edge of each patch. The lacy green fronds of the fern then take over for summer and fall without hurting the isopyrum.

149. **Latin Name** *Phacelia bipinnatifida*

   Common Name Spotted phacelia, loose-flowered phacelia
   Usual Height 1 to 2 feet
   Spacing 2 feet
   Sun or Shade ● ◖
   Bloom Violet-blue, $^1/_2$ inch, cupped, in loose clusters, early to midspring
   Fruit Dry, June
   Leaves Biennial, fuzzy, 2 to 3 inches, dies back and new plants start in midsummer, some foliage always present
   Native Range Rich woods, Blue Ridge and west, Zones 5 to 8
   Soil Acid, rich, rocky, lime OK
   Drainage Moist
   Root System No special structure because short-lived
   Companion Plants Pines, hardwoods, leaf mulch
   Propagation Fresh seed, self-sows
   Wildlife No information

Spotted phacelia is a biennial, which means it is leafy for a year and a half, then it blooms the second spring, and dies after setting seed. When you maintain a patch of spotted phacelia, you'll always have leafy plants present (although not in the abundance necessary for a groundcover) and only about half the plants will bloom each spring. Also, your patch will travel around a bit. But that's okay, because spotted phacelia will never bore you. In a woodland area, especially on a rich slope, it will treat you to different layouts every year. If you are maintaining phacelia in a well-ordered, shady flower bed, transplant the seedlings each fall to the exact spot you want them. Lazy gardeners and beginning gardeners will love this woodland flower—it's easy.

150. **Latin Name** *Phlox divaricata*
 Common Name Blue phlox, blue woodland phlox, Louisiana phlox
 Usual Height 8 to 18 inches
 Spacing 12 to 18 inches
 Sun or Shade ● ◑ ◐
 Bloom Blue to lavender, white, 3/4 inch, early spring
 Fruit Dry, late spring
 Leaves 1 inch long, narrow, present only in spring, or thin in winter and dormant in summer, or evergreen groundcover—big genetic differences
 Native Range Rich hardwood forests, bluffs, calcareous hammocks, eastern North America, Zones 4 to 8
 Soil Acid, rich, lime OK, clay OK
 Drainage Moist
 Root System Colonizes
 Companion Plants Pines and hardwoods, Atamasco lily, Solomon's seal, Allegheny spurge, spigelia, wild red columbine, scarlet sage, asters, ferns
 Propagation Fresh seed, root division in fall or winter, layering, cuttings
 Wildlife Flowers visited by swallowtails, gray hairstreak, western pygmy blue butterflies; roots eaten by voles and rabbits

 Blue phlox is an extremely popular garden flower. It blooms at the same time as wild azaleas, Atamasco lily, celandine poppy, and wild geranium. Most of the blue phlox available in Southern nurseries goes dormant after flowering. If you have a carpet of it, interplant it with aster or goldenrod, and mow everything at a 4-inch setting in June. In your shady garden, keep it in small clumps so that as it disappears or gets thin, ferns, gentian, bowman's root, or other summer flowers that are planted around it can fill in for it.

151. **Latin Name** *Podophyllum peltatum*
 Common Name Mayapple
 Usual Height 12 to 18 inches
 Spacing 2 feet apart in a drift
 Sun or Shade ● ◑
 Bloom One, white, sometimes flushed with pink, 2 inches, waxy
 Fruit 1 to 2 inch, lemon-shaped, juicy, greenish or pale yellow
 Leaves Two, 9 to 12 inches, held over the flower like twin umbrellas, appear early spring and disappear by June
 Native Range Rich woods, moist meadows, calcareous hammocks, bluffs, eastern North America, Zones 4 to 8
 Soil Very acid to acid, rich preferred
 Drainage Moist to dry
 Root System Colonizes
 Companion Plants Post oak, maple, and other hardwoods, leaf mulch, lawn
 Propagation Seed (blooms third year), root division while dormant
 Wildlife No information

 Mayapple is another easy plant that's ideal for beginning gardeners. But it's not for a well-planned, shady flower garden. It likes to form large colonies, and it doesn't give other spring woodland flowers much of a chance. I know one gardener who, for years, has maintained a thriving colony as part of his lawn. Each spring, he does contour mowing to make a tiny patch of lawn surrounded by mayapples, which make a beautiful groundcover that extends into his evergreen shrub beds and summer flower gardens on one side and into woodland on the other. Then, after the mayapple leaves turn yellow and shrivel—usually by the end of June—he mows them and has lawn to the borders of his beds.

152. **Latin Name** *Polygonatum biflorum*
Common Name Solomon's seal
Usual Height 2 feet, rarely over 3 feet
Spacing 2 to 3 feet
Sun or Shade ●
Bloom Pale green to white bells, $^1/_2$ inch long, hanging in pairs under the leaves, midspring
Fruit Blue, fleshy, $^1/_4$ to $^1/_2$ inch, hanging in pairs, late summer
Leaves Yellow-green, smooth, 2 to 8 inches long, on long, arching stems, go dormant after fruit ripens until spring
Native Range Rich woods, bluffs, calcareous hammocks, eastern North America, Zones 4 to 8
Soil Acid, rich
Drainage Moist
Root System Rhizome, but not colonizing
Companion Plants Beech, tulip poplar, most woodland flowers and ferns
Propagation Root cuttings
Wildlife Roots eaten by mammals, fruits occasionally eaten by birds

Solomon's seal makes a dramatic accent in the shady woodland garden. It is grown chiefly for the arching stems and the bright yellow-green leaves, in other words, for its texture. It blends in nicely with almost all of the choicest woodland flowers and ferns, and stays green into August in Zone 8 and into the fall farther north. A 4- to 5-foot tall variety called great Solomon's seal is popular with many gardeners. Nurseries usually market it under the label of *P. commutatum* or *P. canalicutum,* names usually recognized only as varieties of *P. biflorum.*

153. **Latin Name** *Silene virginica*
Common Name Fire pink, scarlet catchfly
Usual Height 1 foot, rarely 2 feet, because stems recline as they get long
Spacing 18 inches
Sun or Shade ● ◑ ◑
Bloom Red, $1^1/_2$ inch across, midspring (to midsummer)
Fruit $^1/_2$ inch long, narrow, tan, dry, summer
Leaves Basal rosette, reddish green in winter
Native Range Thin woods, slopes, eastern North America, Zones 4 to 8
Soil Acid, poor preferred, rocky OK
Drainage Moist to dry
Root System Taproot, does not colonize, short-lived
Companion Plants Post oak, black oak, green-and-gold, spigelia, vernal iris, eared coreopsis, ebony spleenwort, Christmas fern
Propagation Seed, cuttings
Wildlife Flowers visited by hummingbirds and butterflies; seeds eaten by junco, pine siskin, sparrows, water pipit, horned lark
Related Species *S. polypetala,* fringed pink

Fire pink likes a little more sun than most of the woodland plants, but the only place where it can do without any shade at all is up in the mountains where it doesn't get so hot and evaporation is not so intense. Fire pink usually blooms in April, along with blue phlox, wild geranium, foamflower, wild bleeding heart, and celandine poppy. Its relative **fringed pink** can take more heat. It has large, showy, pink flowers in April, and when it's not in bloom it colonizes to form an attractive groundcover.

154. Latin Name *Smilacina racemosa*
    Common Name Smilacina, false Solomon's seal, false spikenard, Solomon's plume
    Usual Height 14 inches, occasionally 3 feet
    Spacing 2 to 3 feet apart, stalks will end up 9 to 12 inches apart
    Sun or Shade ● ◐ ◑
    Bloom White, tiny, 1- to 4-inch cluster, mid- to late spring
    Fruit Red to maroon, speckled while ripening, 1- to 4-inch cluster, mid- to late summer
    Leaves 3 to 6 inches long on arching stalk, dormant in winter
    Native Range Rich woods, bluffs, Canada and eastern half of U.S., Zones 4 to 8
    Soil Very acid to acid, rich
    Drainage Moist
    Root System Rhizome, colonizes
    Companion Plants Under hardwoods with most ferns and woodland flowers
    Propagation Seed, root division
    Wildlife Fruits occasionally eaten by birds, foliage browsed by deer

Smilacina's common names make me angry. Calling it "false" this or that makes this lovely native sound so . . . well, deceptive and second rate, like a poor imitation. It's nothing of the sort! Smilacina has leaves that look similar to those of Solomon's seal, and it is also a member of the lily family—but it has much showier flowers and fruits. It's a very handsome woodland flower that is easy to grow and is a good size for the garden. It blooms later in the spring than most of the woodland flowers, so it is great to plant under mountain laurel or arrowwood along with eared coreopsis. It's a superior shade-garden plant, so you can use it there or naturalized in a woodland area.

155. Latin Name *Stylophorum diphyllum*
    Common Name Celandine poppy, yellow wood poppy
    Usual Height 1 foot, occasionally 2 feet
    Spacing 18 to 24 inches
    Sun or Shade ● ◑
    Bloom Yellow to orange, 4 petals, 1 to 2 inches across, several to a cluster, early spring, occasionally to fall
    Fruit 1 inch, fat, bristly, nodding, dry
    Leaves 4 to 10 inches, lacy, dormant from summer (fall) to February
    Native Range Rich woods, eastern half of North America, spotty distribution, rare, Zones 4 to 7
    Soil Acid, rich, lime OK
    Drainage Moist
    Root System Clump-forming, short-lived
    Companion Plants White oak, beech, bloodroot, Jack-in-the-pulpit, New York fern, broad beechfern, spotted phacelia, wild geranium
    Propagation Fresh seed, self-sows
    Wildlife No information

Despite the fact that **celandine poppy** is very easy to grow, it is a rarity, both in the wild and in home gardens. A shame, because it is so vivid in appearance that it makes more delicate and subtle woodland flowers seem almost invisible. That's why you'll want to team it up with other flowers that are showy enough to hold their own: spotted phacelia, wild geranium, Atamasco lily, dwarf iris, and fire pink. For ideas on how to put all these flowers together effectively, refer to the plan entitled **Spectacular April Shade Garden.**

156. Latin Name *Tradescantia virginiana*
  Common Name Virginia spiderwort
  Usual Height 2 feet
  Spacing 2 feet
  Sun or Shade ● ◐ ◑ ○
  Bloom Blue to lavender (white), 1 to 2 inches
    across, loose cluster, early spring to summer,
    mornings only
  Fruit Small, dry, soon after blooming
  Leaves Grasslike, evergreen, unless they die back
    briefly in August
  Native Range Thin woods, roadsides, stable dunes,
    eastern North America, Zones 5 to 8
  Soil Acid, lime OK, rich OK
  Drainage Dry to moist
  Root System Clump-forming
  Companion Plants Black oak, post oak, live oak,
    American beautyberry, lyreleaf sage, smilacina,
    fire pink, sundrops, spigelia
  Propagation Seed, division of clumps
  Wildlife No information
  Related Species All the spiderworts make good
    garden plants

There are lots of very attractive spiderworts to choose from—pink ones, fuchsia ones, very short ones, and some with fat, fuzzy leaves. I've seen spiderworts growing in profusion under the deep shade of live oaks, on a sandy bank that gets scorching afternoon sun, in moist, peaty soil near a seep with mayapples and maidenhair fern . . . clearly, a very adaptable genus. Spiderworts are also long-lived. If they do seed out, they are easy to remove if you don't want more. Use them in the shady or sunny flower garden, or in masses as a transition from a sunny area to woodland shade. **Virginia spiderwort** is the one most commonly found in nurseries. It's easy to grow nearly everywhere, even far outside its native range.

157. Latin Name *Zephyranthes atamasco*
  Common Name Atamasco lily
  Usual Height 8 to 15 inches
  Spacing 12 to 18 inches
  Sun or Shade ● ◐ ◑
  Bloom White (pink), 3- to 4-inch trumpet, early
    spring to June
  Fruit Black seeds, soon after blooming
  Leaves Grasslike, 4 to 8 inches tall, dormant after
    setting seed
  Native Range River swamps, bluffs, limestone
    outcrops, roadsides, Virginia to Mississippi,
    Zones 7 to 8
  Soil Acid, lime OK, rich
  Drainage Moist, tolerates seasonal flooding
  Root System Bulb, clump-forming
  Companion Plants Tulip poplar, sprucepine,
    eastern red cedar, royal fern, spigelia, crinum
    lily, blue phlox, wild red columbine
  Propagation Seed, division of clumps
  Wildlife No information
  Related Species All the zephyranthes make
    handsome garden plants

Every time I see **Atamasco lily,** I am bowled over by its flashy good looks. I still relish the memory of one gorgeous drift wedged into the crack of a huge boulder at the Birmingham Botanical Garden. Atamasco lily is a small, neat plant, but it has huge flowers that bloom in great numbers. It definitely does not take a back seat to the likes of celandine poppy, blue phlox, and other gaudy native flowers. Use it in a shady flower garden, or let it naturalize in a moist to wet woodland that is not too dense. To get maximum color, give it an hour or so of direct sunlight, or several hours of bright, dappled sun.

SUMMER- AND FALL-BLOOMING WOODLAND FLOWERS

Summer- and fall-blooming woodland flowers often reach waist high. It is sometimes quite dark on the woodland floor in the summer, when every leaf in the canopy and understory overhead is already turned to catch each available ray of sun. If your wood-land is thin, open, or short, more light will get in, and your plants will have more blooms. If your shade is dense, place these plants within ten feet of the patio or driveway—or whatever constitutes your clearing in the woods.

Spigelia provides a spot of May color in Lolly Jackson's wooded front yard in Houston, Texas. Two-leaved toothwort (Dentaria diphylla) bloomed earlier with wild ginger; Georgia basil will flower later. Broad beechfern, normal shield fern, and Christmas fern mingle with the woodland flowers. This garden was designed by Will Fleming.

158. Latin Name *Amianthium muscaetoxicum (Zigadenus muscaetoxicus)*
Common Name Fly poison
Usual Height 1 to 2 feet, rarely 5 feet
Spacing 2 feet
Sun or Shade ◑ ◐
Bloom White, turning greenish, 2- to 6-inch cluster, blooms from bottom up, midspring to early summer
Fruit Small, bright orange, late summer to early fall
Leaves Appear in March, grasslike, narrow (lily family), shorter than the flower stems, go dormant after fruit is ripe
Native Range Rich woodland edges, sandhills, flatwoods, bluffs, meadows, savannahs, eastern U.S., Zones 6 to 8
Soil Very acid, acid, rich or poor
Drainage Moist, tolerates seasonal flooding
Root System Bulb
Companion Plants Longleaf pine, willow oak, grasses, blueberries, mountain laurel, smilacina, Solomon's seal, dwarf iris, Jack-in-the-pulpit, black cohosh
Propagation Seed
Wildlife Really is poisonous to flies

Sometimes common names can be so off-putting. Tell your friends that you have **fly poison** in your garden, and the last thing they're likely to think of is a pretty white flower. The waxy blooms glisten with a clear, sticky substance. Naturally, I assumed that this secretion enticed flies to their doom, but I can't find any written verification for this. Fly poison is well behaved in a flower garden that is either moist and sunny or lightly shaded. It is also effective when planted in drifts in low groundcover under a big old tree. We saw the best flowering where it received at least one or two hours of direct sunlight.

159. Latin Name *Aruncus dioicus*
Common Name Goat's beard, bride's feathers
Usual Height 3 to 6 feet
Spacing 4 to 6 feet
Sun or Shade ● ◐
Bloom White, 6- to 24-inch cluster, male plants showier, late spring or early summer
Fruit Seed, dry, ripe one month after flowering, female plants
Leaves 8- to 20-inch leaves, 2- to 5-inch leaflets, dormant in winter
Native Range Rich woods, eastern half U.S., Zones 5 to 7, Piedmont and mountains, northern Europe
Soil Acid, rich
Drainage Moist, tolerates seasonal flooding
Root System Woody crown, clump-forming
Companion Plants Hemlock, basswood, wild ginger, hepatica, toothwort, smilacina, Jack-in-the-pulpit, black cohosh
Propagation Seed, division
Wildlife Larval plant for dusky blue butterfly

You can find **goat's beard** blooming deep in the woods, its white flowers leaping out at you from a backdrop of dark green summer leaves. It blends well with black cohosh, another tall woodland flower that sports white summer blooms. Together they represent "theme and variation," which always make for good design—or good music for that matter. Given more sun and ample water, such as by a pond, goat's beard can get massive and bushy, displaying giant plumes of white. Because goat's beard is big, it is more visible from a distance than loosestrife or gentian. If you have a large property and a shady slope that can be viewed from more than 50 feet away, masses of it coming down the slope can be as visually exciting in summer as wild azalea is in spring.

160. Latin Name *Aster shortii*
    Common Name Short's aster
    Usual Height 1 to 3 feet
    Spacing 2 to 4 feet
    Sun or Shade ● ◐
    Bloom Light purple, 1 inch, profuse, early fall
    Fruit Dry, small, mid- to late fall
    Leaves 2 to 6 inches, basal rosette in winter
    Native Range Rocky woods, thin woods, woodland edges, Southeastern U.S., Zones 6 to 8
    Soil Acid, rich, rocky, lime OK
    Drainage Moist
    Root System Clump-forming, short-lived
    Companion Plants White ash, maple, blue phlox, Solomon's seal, spigelia, spiderwort, wild red columbine, Allegheny spurge, butterweed
    Propagation Seed, division, self-sows
    Wildlife Flowers visited by hummingbirds, butterflies, bees; seeds eaten by cardinal, finch, grosbeak, sparrows, thrasher, towhee, chickadee, nuthatch, titmouse, wild turkey

I first saw **Short's aster** used in the wildflower garden at Cheekwood, in Nashville, and I was instantly captivated. White ash was just beginning to turn overhead, and most of the woodland flowers (except for broadleaf goldenrod) were through blooming. But Jenny Andrews, the curator, ingeniously allowed this aster to spread itself thinly throughout the garden, creating a soft purple haze beneath the reds and golds of autumn. As with all asters, the centers of the flowers start out yellow, but after pollination they turn dark red, which makes the lavender-blue of Short's aster look especially rich.

161. Latin Name *Blephilia hirsuta*
    Common Name Woodmint
    Usual Height 1 to 4 feet
    Spacing 1 foot apart or scattered in a woodland
    Sun or Shade ● ◐
    Bloom Lavender to purple, 1 inch, 2 to 6 weeks in summer
    Fruit Flower heads turn taupe-colored, dry, shiny seed, early fall
    Leaves Evergreen rosettes, but small in summer
    Native Range Moist woods, eastern North America, Zones 4 to 8
    Soil Acid, rich, lime OK
    Drainage Moist to dry, tolerates seasonal flooding
    Root System Colonizes
    Companion Plants White ash, wild red columbine, Solomon's seal, smilacina, toothwort, spigelia
    Propagation Division
    Wildlife No information
    Related Species *B. ciliata,* sunny woodmint

The **woodmint** we photographed at Cheekwood was less than 18 inches tall, although this native perennial is listed as getting up to 4 feet tall. The rosettes had clustered themselves about 6 inches apart, making an almost evergreen groundcover, which is reason enough to use it. But its long summer bloom period is its chief asset. **Sunny woodmint** is similar, but it grows in dry, open woods or in meadows. Even though both woodmints are in the mint family, their leaves and flowers are not minty enough to qualify for herb status.

162. **Latin Name** *Cimicifuga racemosa*
   Common Name Black cohosh, black snakeroot, fairy candles
   Usual Height 3 to 8 feet
   Spacing 3 feet
   Sun or Shade ●
   Bloom White, one or more 6- to 24-inch "candles," blooming from the bottom up, early to midsummer
   Fruit Dry, tan, winged, ripe shortly after blooming
   Leaves Large, coarsely lacy, below the flowers, dormant after seeds ripen until spring
   Native Range Rich woods, eastern U.S., Zones 5 to 7, Coastal Plain up to 4000 feet in the mountains
   Soil Acid, rich, acid over lime OK
   Drainage Moist
   Root System Clump-forming, woody crown
   Companion Plants Tulip poplar, few shrubs, wild ginger, ferns, merrybells, troutlily, fly poison, Dutchman's breeches, Solomon's seal, smilacina, dwarf iris, Jack-in-the-pulpit, heartleaf, mayapple, foamflower, fire pink, spiderwort
   Propagation Seed, root division
   Wildlife Larval plant for spring azure butterfly
   Related Species *C. americana* is less heat hardy

Black cohosh is a handsome plant that is a must for woodland gardens in those parts of the South where it is summer-hardy. Plant it deep in a woodland, or on the edge where it will get just an hour or two of direct morning sun. In a shady flower bed, plant it where you want height and width. It blooms for two to three weeks, beginning in late May in the Coastal Plains and in late June in the mountains. Native Americans considered this plant to be an excellent bug repellent, as well as an antidote to snakebite.

163. **Latin Name** *Gentiana andrewsii*
   Common Name Bottle gentian, closed gentian
   Usual Height 1 to 2 feet
   Spacing 2 feet
   Sun or Shade ● ◑
   Bloom Purple blue to white, 1¹/₂ inches long, late summer
   Fruit Tan, dry, containing many fine seeds, early fall
   Leaves 1 to 6 inches long, spring to frost
   Native Range Wet fields and woods, eastern North America, Zones 3 to 7
   Soil Acid, rich, lime OK
   Drainage Moist to wet
   Root System Woody crown, clump-forming
   Companion Plants Cardinal flower, inland sea oats, wild geranium, hepatica
   Propagation Root division
   Wildlife Flowers visited by bumblebees

All gentians are strikingly unusual and highly desirable flowers; too bad they're difficult to grow. The **bottle gentian** is the only one we saw being used, and then only in a few gardens. But from those few, it looks as though it can be grown successfully everywhere in the South, even on the Coastal Plain. Although it is hard to get started, once it's established it will stick around for quite a while. Just make sure the soil is always moist (not necessarily wet) and not too acidic. The only other problem we saw was that it always seems to have stems that are too weak to hold themselves upright. So, let it lean on sturdier plants, or just let it sprawl around.

164. Latin Name *Lysimachia ciliata*
  Common Name Fringed loosestrife
  Usual Height 18 to 30 inches
  Spacing 2 feet
  Sun or Shade ● ◑
  Bloom Yellow, 1 inch, summer
  Fruit Dry capsule of seeds, ripe 2 months after blooming
  Leaves 2 to 6 inches long, dormant in winter
  Native Range Moist woods, floodplains, shady stream banks, North America east of the Rocky Mountains, Zones 4 to 8
  Soil Acid, rich
  Drainage Wet to moist, tolerates seasonal flooding
  Root System Colonizes
  Companion Plants Royal fern, cinnamon fern, New York fern, sensitive fern, cardinal flower, inland sea oats
  Propagation Cuttings, root division
  Wildlife No information
  Related Species *L. quadrifolia,* whorled loosestrife

Fringed loosestrife can be a knee-high groundcover or, in slightly drier conditions, a slowly spreading clump. The prettiest planting we saw was in a fern garden in North Carolina, just where the Coastal Plain and Piedmont meet. Fringed loosestrife is similar in height and density to the ferns, so it blended in well and provided a welcome and subtle change of texture. Its scattered, bright yellow flowers were a bonus.

165. Latin Name *Poteranthus trifoliatus* (formerly *Gillenia trifoliata*)
  Common Name Bowman's root, Indian physic
  Usual Height 1 to 4 feet
  Spacing 2 to 3 feet
  Sun or Shade ● ◑
  Bloom White (pink), 1 inch, loose clusters, early summer
  Fruit Dry, fuzzy, early fall
  Leaves 1 1/2- to 3-inch oval leaves in threes, dormant in winter
  Native Range Rich woods, wooded slopes, eastern North America, up to 4500 feet, Zones 5 to 7
  Soil Acid, rich, rocky, acid over lime OK
  Drainage Moist to dry
  Root System Woody crown
  Companion Plants White oak, sourwood, serviceberry, fringetree, pussytoes, galax, whorled loosestrife, bracken fern, ebony spleenwort
  Propagation Seed, division, self-sows
  Wildlife No information
  Related species *P. stipulatus,* American ipecac

For a plant with small, distantly spaced flowers and light, open foliage on sparse slender stems, **bowman's root** is surprisingly showy. The overall effect is, in fact, dramatic because the flowers are such a crisp, pure white. In a shady setting, it really jumps out. Bowman's root blooms on the same schedule as Small's penstemon, goat's beard, black cohosh, and oakleaf hydrangea—all good candidates for a white theme garden. (See the plan entitled **June Wedding.**) **American ipecac,** native from Mississippi to Maryland, has fancier leaves and is more heat tolerant. Although still a woodland plant, it is more likely to be found in disturbed habitats where it can get more sun.

166. Latin Name *Scutellaria incana*
    Common Name Downy skullcap
    Usual Height 18 to 40 inches
    Spacing 2 feet
    Sun or Shade ● ◑ ◐ ○
    Bloom Blue to purple, in 6-inch spikes, summer
    Fruit Dark, dry, early fall
    Leaves 2 to 5 inches long, soft, basal rosette in winter
    Native Range Sandhills, dry bluffs, pine woods, eastern U.S. to Kansas, Zones 6 to 8
    Soil Acid, rich
    Drainage Dry to moist
    Root System Clump-forming
    Companion Plants Post oak, tulip poplar, partridgeberry, green-and-gold, spigelia, foamflower, alumroot
    Propagation Seed, cuttings
    Wildlife Browsed by deer
    Related Species *S. integrifolia,* tall skullcap; and *S. elliptica,* hairy skullcap, are spring skullcaps used in Southeast gardens

We saw a lot of skullcap in a lot of gardens, but by far the most handsome was **downy skullcap.** You don't see a lot of it in the wild, even where it is indigenous. Still, it seems to be the skullcap with the greatest ability to fit in well just about anywhere. Another advantage is that it blooms later than the other garden skullcaps—and steady, dependable summer color in a shady garden is valuable indeed. Use it where you need height in the shady flower garden, or use it in drifts in a woodland garden. It has the same density and height as many ferns, but it is more drought-tolerant than all but bracken.

167. Latin Name *Solidago flexicaulis*
    Common Name Broadleaf goldenrod
    Usual Height 2 feet, occasionally 4 feet
    Spacing 2 to 3 feet
    Sun or Shade ● ◑ ◐ ○
    Bloom Yellow, scattered, late summer to frost
    Fruit Fluffy, white, shortly after blooming
    Leaves 3 to 8 inches, soft, die back after setting seed, winter rosette appears in January, starts growing tall in July
    Native Range Rich woods, cool slopes, eastern U.S, Zones 6 to 7, mostly in mountains
    Soil Acid, rich, lime OK
    Drainage Moist
    Root System Clump-forming, might colonize
    Companion Plants Tulip poplar, troutlily, mayapple, Solomon's seal, smilacina, summer phlox, Short's aster
    Propagation Fresh seed, root division
    Wildlife Flowers visited by butterflies; seeds eaten by swamp sparrow, pine siskin, and meadow mouse
    Related Species *S. caesia,* bluestem goldenrod; *S. sphacelata,* golden fleece

Broadleaf goldenrod is the sleeper of the shady garden. All through the winter it appears as a green rosette hugging the ground. It continues to be a low-profile inhabitant of the garden while, all about it, the spring woodland flowers burst forth. But in midsummer, it starts to grow and makes a neat leafy mound. Then, as October approaches, it starts to bloom, its lovely yellow flowers lasting until first frost. **Bluestem goldenrod** and **golden fleece** are also well behaved and shade-tolerant, the latter tolerating drier, rockier conditions and more sun than the first two.

168. **Latin Name** *Spigelia marilandica*
Common Name Spigelia, Indian pink, pinkroot
Usual Height 2 feet
Spacing 2 feet
Sun or Shade ● ◑
Bloom Red trumpets with yellow mouths, 1 to 2 inches long, late spring or early summer, 2 to 6 weeks
Fruit Small, dry, midsummer
Leaves 2 to 4 inches, dark glossy, mounded foliage, dormant in fall and winter
Native Range Rich woods, bluffs, calcareous hammocks, Southeastern U.S., Zones 6 to 9
Soil Acid, rich preferred, sandy, lime OK
Drainage Moist
Root System Clump-forming
Companion Plants Post oak, tulip poplar, Christmas fern, ebony spleenwort, partridge-berry, green-and-gold, smilacina, blue phlox
Propagation Untreated seed kept dry over winter and sown in spring
Wildlife Flowers used by hummingbirds

Spigelia makes a nicely rounded knee-high clump in the garden. When it's in bloom, it can be quite eye-catching and very photogenic. It mixes nicely with ferns and low groundcovers. Flowers that should bloom at the same time are oakleaf hydrangea, sundrops, downy phlox, and wild penstemons. If your spigelia is a little late, then it can have butterflyweed, stokesia, black-eyed Susans, and summer phlox as garden companions.

June shade garden of Edith Eddleman, Durham, North Carolina.

12

GARDEN FLOWERS

The shady flower garden—the focus of the last few chapters—is really the recreation of a natural woodland floor, a copy of a native southeastern habitat. It is so beautiful that it cannot be improved on by us.

In contrast, a **sunny flower garden** is a human contrivance—a human conceit—that depends entirely on our own labor and ingenuity. Mother Nature never designed a formal, weeded, carefully arranged flower garden.

Many home gardeners assume that any flower not sold in a nursery must be a low-class weed. Native wildflowers, they believe, have no place in their "civilized" gardens. This misconception has, for far too long, deprived us of much beauty. The fact is, those common garden flowers (shasta daisies, hybrid day lilies, dianthus, etc.) were once wildflowers themselves, and have become "acceptable" only after generations of selections.

But this selection process has made these flowers more demanding of us; they must be pampered. If you have gobs of spare time and love to spend it this way, fine. But for the rest of us, introducing native flowers into gardens can give us all the exciting color and diversity we want, at a fraction of the work.

True, some tending will be necessary—invading weeds plucked, rambunctious plants tamed, and room made from time to time for favorites that are themselves not very pushy.

However, the more native flowers you use, the easier your job will be. They need little or no help from you. And, when you aren't constantly replacing plants and having to overwater, overfertilize, and doctor unhappy flowers, you can concentrate on your design.

But don't forget that native plants grow in many diverse habitats. Group your plants according to their individual tastes in soil and moisture. If one plant is native to boggy areas, don't place it next to a plant that is native to well-drained, sandy soils with high acidity. One of them will be very unhappy.

Design your garden to accommodate several habitats. Assign those plants that need more water to the lower places. On the more elevated areas, use plants that need good drainage. Aerate the soil and dig in sand and mulch if the soil is too compacted.

To make this easier for you, in the plant profiles, after **Companion Plants**, I've listed flowers that like the same conditions. They're often found growing with the featured plant in the wild, so chances are excellent that they'll get along in your garden. I've also limited the list to those of equal vigor that would be complementary with regard to growth rate and color scheme. The first ones are those that are likely to bloom in the spring and early summer. After the slash mark (/) are those that bloom in the late summer or fall.

The chief pleasure of a flower garden is its color, with the best blooms occurring in full sun. But many of you don't get full sun; you may get only a half day in the morning or afternoon. If you put a sun-loving flower in too much shade, it will usually seek out the sun. It may get the "leans," become too tall and flop over, or travel to a more agreeable spot.

To know if a plant travels or stays put, you need to know about the **Root System**. An annual has a thin, small root system, because it doesn't plan to be around very

This classic double border, designed and maintained by Kitty and Neil Taylor in Collierville, Tennessee, is made possible by using flowers that are either native or naturalized in the Memphis area. Andy took this picture from under the grape arbor on the last day of May. At the opposite end of the garden is a stone patio nestled under a huge old post oak.

long; it flowers, sets seed, and then dies. But most flowers in your garden will be perennials, meaning that they will live for at least two years (some make it for 50 years or more). Perennials need big, strong root systems to help them withstand freezes, droughts, and the encroachments of other plants.

Some perennials have **bulbs;** they tend to stay put and not expand. Bulbs usually make baby bulbs (bulblets) that are attached to the mama bulb. To get them to spread, wait until they're dormant, dig them up, gently detach the new bulbs, and place them where you want them.

Most perennials have **rhizomes,** short fat roots that grow horizontally. These are the **travelers.** If you've ever seen an iris root, you've seen a rhizome. Some plants never stray off. These are called **clump-formers.** Every year,

the clump gets bigger and bigger until the center becomes hollow. At that point, gardeners do something called "lift-and-divide." They dig up the whole clump and replant the youngest, most vigorous roots from the edges back into the center of the space where the clump came from.

The best time to plant a flower garden is in the fall. New plants have a chance to grow roots, and seeds can sprout without getting burned up by the summer sun.

In the winter, the flower garden appears to be sleeping, although many of the flowers show **winter rosettes**—sunbursts of green leaves from just a couple of inches wide to over a foot across. A rosette often vanishes in the spring or summer when the flower grows tall and blooms. The leaves are on the stem, instead. As the flowers set seed and the stem

leaves start to look ragged, a new rosette forms. At this point, cutting off the old stem won't harm the plant. If a rosette has not appeared, don't eliminate the bottom two green leaves.

Mulch your garden in the winter to protect the roots from winter freezes. I simply rake on a blanket of leaves. Be sure not to cover over the rosettes. Old leaf mulch starts decomposing with the warmth of spring, and by the time the flowers begin to bloom, it should have all but disappeared. When this happens, I lay down another inch of compost to protect the roots from the summer sun.

In this chapter, I've grouped the flowers according to **most likely bloom time.** This should make figuring out color schemes much easier.

SPRING-BLOOMING GARDEN FLOWERS

The sunny flower garden doesn't get geared up until end of May and into June. Sometimes these spring flowers continue to bloom to midsummer and even into fall. But if they do, the blooms are sporadic. Most gardeners cut these flowers back to rosettes after blooming, unless they want ripe seed, or the seed head is ornamental.

A view of the east side of the Taylor double border shows Carolina bushpea, sundrops, downy phlox and a pink Carolina phlox mixed in with an assortment of old roses, naturalized plants, and a few well-adapted cultivars. A week later, a white Carolina phlox and Mississippi penstemon will be blooming along with blue Stokes aster, and the bushpea and roses will serve as green backdrop.

169. **Latin Name** *Amsonia ciliata*
Common Name Texas bluestar
Usual Height 1 to 2 feet
Spacing 1 to 2 feet
Sun or Shade ◐ ○
Bloom Pale blue, ¹/₂ inch, star-shaped, in clusters, early spring
Fruit Dry, narrow, fall
Leaves Very narrow, dormant in winter
Native Range Sandhills, post oak woods, scrub, Southeastern U.S., Zones 7 to 8 and to Zone 6 in Missouri
Soil Acid, lime OK, poor OK, sand preferred
Drainage Dry
Root System Clump-forming
Companion Plants Blue false indigo, lanceleaf coreopsis, purple coneflower, downy phlox/ sundrops, wiregrass, broomsedge, little bluestem, splitbeard bluestem, pink muhly
Propagation Fresh seed, root division, cuttings
Wildlife No information
Related Species *A. tabernaemontana*, woodland bluestar; *A. illustris*, swamp bluestar; *A. ludoviciana*, sandhill bluestar; *A. rigida*, marsh bluestar

Texas bluestar is my favorite among this quartet of bluestars, and not just because I live in Texas. It's a small plant, neat and tidy, with its flowers held high above the foliage. It loves full sun, but will bloom as long as it gets four hours of direct sunlight. Its only other requirement is excellent drainage. It can take the drought of the sandhills, as does my second favorite, **sandhill bluestar**. This one is quite rare in the wild, but is available to buy. It is 2 to 3 feet tall, thin, and a deep steely blue. **Woodland bluestar** is the most widespread in the Southeast, because it takes the most shade, but its flowers are partially hidden by its uppermost leaves. **Swamp bluestar** is best for clay with only a half day of sun.

170. **Latin Name** *Anemone virginiana*
Common Name Thimbleweed
Usual Height 18 to 36 inches
Spacing 1 to 2 feet
Sun or Shade ◐ ○
Bloom White, 1¹/₂ inches across, late spring to early summer
Fruit 1-inch capsule, fluffy seed—very ornamental
Leaves 3 inches long, divided into leaflets, winter rosette
Native Range Rich woods, post oak woods, pineland, woodland edges, eastern half U.S., Zones 3 to 7, Canada
Soil Acid, rich, lime OK
Drainage Moist to dry
Root System Woody crown, clump-forming
Companion Plants Butterflyweed, pale coneflower, beebalm, downy phlox/summer phlox, silkgrass, aromatic aster, little bluestem
Propagation Seed
Wildlife No information

Even though **thimbleweed**'s flowers are spaced somewhat far apart, it still manages to stand out in a flower garden—its white makes a stronger impression than yellow, pink, or blue. For that reason, I don't recommend bunching it up in one place; it is so vibrant it can throw everything out of balance. On the other hand, interspersed with other whites—white forms of summer phlox, coneflower, and Mississippi penstemon—it can produce a marvelously showy effect. Don't cut back its flowers after blooming; you'll want to enjoy its equally ornamental, fluffy white seed heads. Flowers and seed heads combine to give you about two months of color.

171. Latin Name *Asclepias tuberosa*
    Common Name Butterflyweed
    Usual Height 18 to 30 inches
    Spacing 2 to 3 feet
    Sun or Shade ◑ ○
    Bloom Orange (yellow to red), in flat-topped clusters, late spring to early summer
    Fruit 3- to 5-inch pod
    Leaves Narrow, dormant in winter
    Native Range Sandhills, flatwoods, post oak woods, meadows, pinelands, eastern two-thirds North America, Zones 4 to 9
    Soil Acid, lime OK, poor or rich OK
    Drainage Dry, moist OK, does not tolerate wet for even a short time
    Root System Very deep taproot, clump-forming
    Companion Plants Thimbleweed, downy phlox, white baptisia/silkgrass, little bluestem, broomsedge
    Propagation Fresh seed, root cuttings
    Wildlife Flowers a source of nectar for tiger, spicebush, eastern black, and pipevine swallowtails, cloudless giant sulphur
    Related Species *A. incarnata*, swamp milkweed, Zones 7 to 8; *A. lanceolata*, red milkweed, coastal, New Jersey to Texas

Butterflyweed has a lot going for it; it's long-lived, very well mannered, it attracts butterflies like crazy and it's extremely showy. You can get it to bloom twice, thereby attracting even more butterflies, by cutting off the old flower heads and not letting them go to seed. **Swamp milkweed** grows to 5 feet—a good thing, because its pink- to rose-colored flowers bloom in late summer along with other tall fall flowers, such as joepyeweed, salt marshmallow, cardinal flower, and swamp sunflower. **Red milkweed** is really more of a dark orange and, although narrow, can be showy in a cluster. It grows in both fresh and brackish wet soils along the coast with salt marshmallow.

172. Latin Name *Baptisia alba* (includes *B. leucantha*, *B. pendula*, and *B. lactea*; old *B. alba* is now *B. albescens*)
    Common Name White baptisia, white wild indigo
    Usual Height 2 to 3 feet, rarely 6 feet
    Spacing 2 feet
    Sun or Shade ○
    Bloom White, 1-inch pea-flowers in 6- to 9-inch spikes, midspring in Deep South, early summer farther north
    Fruit $1/2$ to 1 inch, black or green, nodding, ripe 4 to 6 weeks after blooming
    Leaves Three leaflets, top half of stems under flowers, bright green or pale blue, turn black in fall, dormant in winter
    Native Range Sandhills, post oak woods, flatwoods, eastern half North America, Zones 5 to 9
    Soil Acid, sand preferred, poor OK, clay OK
    Drainage Moist, tolerates seasonal flooding
    Root System Deep, clump-forming, long-lived
    Companion Plants Spiderwort, Texas or sandhill bluestar, lanceleaf coreopsis, downy phlox/ mountain mint, silkgrass, little bluestem, wiregrass, splitbeard bluestem, pink muhly
    Propagation Scarified seed, root division, cuttings
    Wildlife No information
    Related Species *B. australis*, blue false indigo

The most striking thing about **white baptisia** is the dark blue-gray stems and other trim that set off its white flowers. This gives the plant an unusual, even sophisticated appearance. To best show off the stems while white baptisia is in bloom, silhouette it against a wall. In a perennial bed, plant low-growing downy phlox or pink coreopsis at its feet. **Blue false indigo** is larger—3 to 5 feet tall and 3 feet wide—and has blue flowers and blue foliage. Its requirements are similar to those of white baptisia, except that it will tolerate lime.

173. Latin Name *Coreopsis auriculata*
　Common Name Eared coreopsis, dwarf tickseed
　Usual Height 2- to 4-inch mat of leaves, 6 inches to 2 feet in bloom
　Spacing 1 foot
　Sun or Shade ◗ ○
　Bloom Yellow to gold, 1 to 2 inches across, early to midspring
　Fruit Dry, ripe shortly after blooming
　Leaves Almost evergreen rosettes, might go dormant in summer
　Native Range Rich woods and openings, eastern red cedar habitats, Southeastern U.S., east of the Mississippi, Zones 6 to 8
　Soil Acid, rich, lime OK
　Drainage Moist
　Root System Stolons, colonizes
　Companion Plants Wild red columbine, Small's penstemon, Stokes aster, spigelia/Short's aster
　Propagation Seed, root division
　Wildlife Flowers visited by butterflies; seed eaten by songbirds
　Related Species *C. lanceolata,* lanceleaf coreopsis; *C. grandiflora,* common coreopsis

When we talked about coreopsis to Southern gardeners, most of them favored this one. **Eared coreopsis** is short and dainty, and the ones we saw were invariably in a shade garden. But the flowers seemed to be straining toward the sun so hard that their stems were almost horizontal. The ones we encountered in full sun looked a lot happier. Given lots of sun, eared coreopsis is likely to bloom in early spring, rather than midspring. If you allow the shade of neighboring tall flowers to protect eared coreopsis rosettes during the summer, it might bloom for you again in the fall. **Lanceleaf coreopsis** and **common coreopsis** are more aggressive, but useful for black-thumb gardeners or those who live on dry or clay soil.

174. Latin Name *Echinacea pallida*
　Common Name Pale coneflower
　Usual Height 3 feet
　Spacing 2 feet
　Sun or Shade ○
　Bloom Narrow, drooping petals are pale pink to rose, 3 to 5 inches across, globular centers are green, red, purple, or brown, late spring to early summer
　Fruit Centers turn dark and fill with prickly seed
　Leaves Rosette, almost evergreen, renews in fall
　Native Range Thin woods, rocky glades, prairies, eastern U.S., Zones 5 to 9, rare east of Mississippi River
　Soil Acid, lime OK, rich preferred
　Drainage Moist to dry
　Root System Thick, fleshy, clump-forming
　Companion Plants Beebalm, Small's penstemon, giant rudbeckia/cutleaf rudbeckia, summer phlox, Indiangrass, switchgrass
　Propagation Seed sown in fall or spring, division
　Wildlife Flowers visited by bees
　Related Species *E. paradoxa,* yellow coneflower; *E. purpurea,* purple coneflower

We took this picture of **pale coneflower**, with its hula skirt of petals, in May in Knoxville, Tennessee. Small's penstemon was still in its glory, and butterflyweed was just thinking of starting. Pale coneflower is likely to bloom into early summer. If you think all coneflowers are a shade of pink or purple, meet **yellow coneflower,** seen in the background. It usually starts flowering a tiny bit earlier than pale coneflower, and then their bloom times overlap. The petals of both droop, but yellow coneflower's short leaves are more upright and grasslike. **Purple coneflower** is the one most gardeners are familiar with. It also has a white form on the market. It begins to bloom in midspring in Texas, but I am told it is definitely a summer bloomer for you folks in the Southeast.

175. **Latin Name** *Iris fulva*
Common Name Copper iris
Usual Height 18 inches to 5 feet
Spacing 12 to 18 inches
Sun or Shade ◐ ○
Bloom 2 to 3 inches, brick-red to orange, rarely yellow, early spring with wild azaleas
Fruit 2- to 3-inch dry capsule
Leaves 2 to 3 feet, swordlike, evergreen in shallow water or a flower bed, dormant in summer and early fall in a swamp that goes dry
Native Range Pine savannahs, bald cypress swamps, Mississippi River basin and along coast to Georgia, Zones 6 to 9
Soil Acid, rich, lime OK
Drainage Moist, seasonally flooded
Root System Usual iris rhizome, colonizes
Companion Plants Yellow azalea, other swamp irises, spiderlily, yellowtop, spiderwort/eleocharis, whitetop sedge
Propagation Seed, root division
Wildlife Flowers used by hummingbirds and bees
Related Species *I. virginica*, *I. brevicaulis*, *I. giganticaerulea*, *I. hexagona*, *I. nelsonii*, swamp iris

Copper iris is popular with many Southern gardeners because of its vivid coppery red color and its small, crisp, elegant appearance. It grows naturally in swamps and bogs that are wet in winter and spring, but dry out during the summer—yet it's perfectly happy in a flower bed. Where it doesn't get overly wet or dry, it tends to be evergreen. In Louisiana, copper iris and all the other Southern swamp irises meet. The resulting natural hybrids inspired those gorgeous cultivars known as Louisiana iris.

176. **Latin Name** *Monarda didyma*
Common Name Oswego tea, beebalm, red bergamot
Usual Height 2 to 4 feet, occasionally 6 feet
Spacing 3 feet
Sun or Shade ◑ ◐ ○
Bloom Red, 2- to 4-inch cluster, late spring to early summer in most Southeast gardens, midsummer to fall in its native habitat
Fruit Brown, dry, aromatic, ripe 2 months after blooming
Leaves 3 to 6 inches long, smooth, aromatic, winter rosette
Native Range Rich woods, stream banks, meadows, mountains in Georgia to 6500 feet to Maine and Michigan, Zones 5 to 7
Soil Acid, rich
Drainage Moist
Root System Rhizomes, might colonize, lift and divide every 3 years
Companion Plants Wild hydrangea/lobelias, joepyeweed, spiked gayfeather, cutleaf rudbeckia
Propagation Root division, seed
Wildlife Flowers visited by butterflies, hummingbirds, and bees

Oswego tea has been a favorite garden flower in the South for several generations, and not just because of its brilliant red blooms. It is a delightful herb, too. It's a member of the mint family (check out the square stems) and all parts of the plant are aromatic. I've been told that Oswego tea is sometimes used as the flavoring for Earl Grey tea, and it can certainly be brewed up to make a fine drink by itself. The crushed leaves are supposed to alleviate bee stings. I came close to leaving this wonderful plant out of the book because it has always had a problem with powdery mildew. But Gene Cline, a grower in Georgia, is marketing a selection called 'Jacob Cline,' which seems to be mildew-proof.

177. Latin Name *Monarda fistulosa*
    Common Name Beebalm, wild bergamot
    Usual Height 2 to 4 feet, occasionally 6 feet
    Spacing 3 feet
    Sun or Shade ○
    Bloom Pink, white to purple, 2- to 4-inch heads, minty aromatic, late spring to early summer or early to midsummer
    Fruit Brown, dry, aromatic, seeds ripe 2 months after blooming
    Leaves 2 to 4 inches long, fuzzy, pale, strongly mint-flavored
    Native Range Meadows, post oak woodlands, North America east of the Rockies, Zones 4 to 8
    Soil Acid, lime OK, rich preferred, but poor sand OK, clay OK
    Drainage Moist to dry, tolerates short spells of winter wet
    Root System Rhizomes, might colonize, lift and divide every 3 years
    Companion Plants Pale coneflower, giant rudbeckia, white baptisia, mountain mint/prairie gayfeather, aromatic aster, little bluestem, Indiangrass
    Propagation Root division, seed, cuttings
    Wildlife Flowers visited by hummingbirds, bees, pipevine swallowtail and other butterflies; foliage browsed by deer

Beebalm is a superb garden flower, well adapted all over the South. It is long-lived and easy-going, thriving under almost any conditions—even extreme heat. Some of you may have had mildew on your beebalm; the selection pictured, 'Claire Grace,' from Southern Perennials and Herbs in Tylertown, Mississippi, is touted as having more mildew resistance and exceptional purple color. Most beebalms are pink or lavender. Like Oswego tea, beebalm makes a tasty herbal tea and flavoring and is reputed to draw out the poison from a bee sting.

178. Latin Name *Oenothera tetragona* (*O. fruticosa* subsp. *glauca*)
    Common Name Sundrops
    Usual Height 1 to 2 feet, rarely 5¹/₂ feet
    Spacing 2 feet
    Sun or Shade ◑ ◕ ○
    Bloom Yellow, 2 inches across, daytime, midspring to early summer
    Fruit ¹/₂ inch long, dry, summer
    Leaves 1 to 5 inches long, toothed, dark green, bronze fall color, winter rosette is often reddish
    Native Range Sunny rocky places or thin woods, North America east of the Mississippi River basin, Zones 5 to 8
    Soil Acid, rich, clay OK, sandy, rocky OK
    Drainage Moist to dry
    Root System Colonizes by stolons or runners
    Companion Plants Butterflyweed, Mississippi penstemon, Texas bluestar, spiderwort/orange rudbeckia, mountain mint, switchgrass, Indiangrass
    Propagation Seed, root division
    Wildlife Flowers used by hummingbirds
    Related Species *O. fruticosa*, sundrops

Wait long enough and everything comes back into style; this time it's old-fashioned **sundrops.** It was one of the pass-alongs—those marvelous and rewarding perennials that are easy for everyone to grow and so got passed from one garden to another. Sundrops is usually 2 feet tall in the garden. The one in the photo is a seven-year-old clump. The flowers stay open all day and close up at dusk. The other **sundrops** (*O. fruticosa*) looks very similar and has almost the same range, but has a much longer bloom time. It differs, they say, in that it is tolerant of lime and brackish soil, and gets less upset by wet soil—at least in the winter. The two are often found together in gardens and seem to have hybridized.

179. **Latin Name** *Penstemon digitalis* complex
Common Name Mississippi penstemon, smooth white beardtongue
Usual Height 18 inches, rarely 3 feet
Spacing 2 feet
Sun or Shade ◑ ○
Bloom White, with purple guidelines for bees, 1-inch trumpets, clustered, late spring to early summer, about 4 weeks
Fruit Tan, dry, ripe a month after blooming
Leaves Winter rosette
Native Range Meadows, thin woodlands, ditches, eastern half of North America, Zones 4 to 9; probably native only to the Mississippi River basin and naturalized elsewhere (Pennell)
Soil Acid, lime OK, rich, sand or clay loam
Drainage Moist to dry, tolerates seasonal flooding
Root System Woody crown, taproot, clump-forming
Companion Plants Beebalm/obedient plant, hibiscus, boltonia, Indiangrass, switchgrass
Propagation Seed, cuttings, division
Wildlife Bumblebees

Do you live in the Coastal Plains or along the Mississippi River, where clay loam and poor drainage make it difficult to grow many flowers? Well, that's where we found **Mississippi penstemon** blooming profusely—and not in raised beds, either. One memorable sight was masses of it in front of blooming agarista. As more and more of you learn about this beauty, it is bound to become a staple in many Southern gardens. To assure a permanent supply, keep the ripe seed. Cut off the bloom stalks as they turn brown; they aren't at all decorative. The rosettes will be low and green throughout the summer, and will renew themselves in the fall. If a rosette disappears, plant fresh seed in that same spot.

180. **Latin Name** *Penstemon smallii*
Common Name Small's penstemon
Usual Height 18 to 30 inches
Spacing 2 feet
Sun or Shade ◑ ◑ ○
Bloom Lavender, 1$^1/_2$ inches long, clustered, late spring to early summer, about 4 weeks
Fruit Tan, dry, a month after flowering
Leaves 2 to 6 inches, toothed, 6- to 14-inch winter rosette
Native Range Edges of woodland, cliffs, mountains of North Carolina, South Carolina, Georgia, and Tennessee, Zones 6 to 7
Soil Very acid to acid, rich, sandy or rocky OK
Drainage Moist, intolerant of wet
Root System Taproot, short-lived perennial
Companion Plants Carolina bushpea, blue false indigo, bowman's root, spiderwort, fire pink/Oswego tea, cutleaf rudbeckia, little bluestem
Propagation Seed, cuttings, division
Wildlife No information
Related Species *P. laevigatus,* hairy beardtongue

Small's penstemon looks similar to Mississippi penstemon and we saw it used frequently in gardens, especially in the mountains and Piedmont. The picture shows it with inland sea oats under a sugar maple at Native Gardens in Greenback, Tennessee. Edith Eddleman, in Durham, North Carolina, likes to use Small's penstemon with sundrops and spiderwort in the sun, and with heartleaf and lady fern in the shade. It is a short-lived perennial, so save seed and replant it every two or three years.

181. **Latin Name** *Phlox pilosa*
Common Name Downy phlox, prairie phlox
Usual Height 8 to 20 inches
Spacing 1 foot
Sun or Shade ◑ ◐ ○
Bloom Pink to purple (white), 3- to 4-inch clusters, early spring to early summer, about 4 weeks, fragrant
Fruit Dry, ripe a month after blooming
Leaves 2 to 3 inches long, very narrow, downy, dormant after blooming
Native Range Sandhill, post oak woods, clearings, roadsides, eastern half of U.S., Zones 4 to 8, rare in mountains
Soil Acid, rich or poor, sand preferred, lime OK, clay OK
Drainage Dry, tolerates brief winter flooding
Root System Clump-forming, some colonize
Companion Plants Mississippi penstemon, Texas and sandhill bluestar, blue false indigo, white baptisia, lanceleaf coreopsis, butterflyweed, beebalm, sundrops/major coreopsis, rudbeckias, aromatic aster, wiregrass, little bluestem, broomsedge
Propagation Root division, root cuttings, stem cuttings, seed
Wildlife Nectar plant for butterflies

Downy phlox might make a tidy, low-growing clump, or it might sprawl and colonize and make a lovely, low drift of color. Either way, it will be a delight in your flower bed. Its leaves appear in early spring, and before you know it, it is a froth of blooms, which lasts for about a month. Then, it dies back and remains dormant until the next spring. Because it is low-growing, and because its roots don't interfere with the health of any other flower, I let mine (a traveler) go wherever it wants to. When sun strikes the flowers, they release a sweet spring fragrance that you can pick up ten to fifteen feet away.

182. **Latin Name** *Stokesia laevis*
Common Name Stokes aster
Usual Height 12 to 18 inches, rarely 30 inches
Spacing 2 feet
Sun or Shade ◑ ◐ ○
Bloom Blue, lavender to white, 2 to 4 inches across, late spring to early summer, occasionally early fall, closes at dusk
Fruit Seed ripe 2 months after flowering
Leaves Almost evergreen, 1- to 2-foot rosettes
Native Range Pine savannah, flatwoods, Coastal Plain east of the Mississippi River, Zone 8
Soil Very acid to acid, sandy, rich
Drainage Moist
Root System Colonizes to form a groundcover of rosettes, lift and divide every 3 to 4 years
Companion Plants Pitcherplant, curly clematis, fragrant phlox, spiderlily, swamp iris, lanceleaf coreopsis, spikerush/pine lily, redroot, pineland hibiscus, tall skullcap, fall obedient plant, wild ageratum, cardinal flower, swamp sunflower, whitetop sedge, sugarcane plumegrass, pink muhly
Propagation Seed, root division, root cuttings, self-sows
Wildlife Flowers visited by butterflies

Growing **Stokes aster** is a snap. Despite its native range, it seems to be winter hardy to Zone 5. It blooms best in full sun in a flower garden where you can team it up with purple coneflower, butterflyweed, lanceleaf coreopsis, and other easy and popular perennials. In the wild, it is usually in a spot where it gets a half day of shade, or is near water, or in a longleaf pine savannah that stays soggy half the year. You'll find it there with the companion plants listed above. Stokes aster blooms big in late spring, and then continues to bloom into summer—but only if you cut off the flower heads before they go to seed. It rests during the hottest part of the summer.

183. **Latin Name** *Thermopsis villosa* (*T. caroliniana*)
     Common Name Carolina bushpea
     Usual Height 3 to 5 feet
     Spacing 3 feet
     Sun or Shade ○
     Bloom Yellow to pale cream pea-flowers, on 4- to
         12-inch (sometimes 18-inch) spikes, late spring
         to early summer
     Fruit 1- to 2-inch peapod, velvety, pressed to the
         flower stalk, late summer
     Leaves 3 leaflets, 2 to 4 inches long, dormant in
         winter
     Native Range Clearings, southern Appalachians,
         Zones 5 to 7
     Soil Acid, rich
     Drainage Moist
     Root System Woody rootstock, clump-forming
     Companion Plants Oswego tea, butterflyweed,
         Small's penstemon, bowman's root, spiderwort/
         lobelia, cutleaf rudbeckia, southern lady fern
     Propagation Seed, division of root stock with a
         hatchet
     Wildlife No information

Home garden of Triny Cline in Canton, Georgia, has masses of Stokes aster between the drive and a pond.

    Carolina bushpea grows naturally in forest clearings in the mountains. If you don't happen to live there, no problem. It accommodates itself to gardens all over the South, even in the Coastal Plain. It just needs watering in the summer. Its height makes it a dominant member of the garden; only blue false indigo is as tall this early in the year. Complementary plants are white baptisia, sundrops, and suitable blue flowers. Orange-flowered butterflyweed makes a wonderful counterpoint. Give Carolina bushpea ample room; it doesn't look its best when it's crowded. And be patient; it's a slow starter and might take 2 to 3 years to get established. It's well worth the wait.

SUMMER-BLOOMING GARDEN FLOWERS

Midsummer, the period from mid June to early August, is the most important time for the flower garden. This is when it is most likely to lag because of intense heat. For the most part, the midsummer bloomers are tall, and can shade their own roots adequately. This is the time of year when you should be able to sit back and just enjoy your garden, watch the butterflies and hummingbirds, and, in the evening, stroll around and inhale its floral scents.

This midsummer flower and herb garden in hot, humid Tylertown, Mississippi, was designed by Barbara and Mike Bridges to both test and demonstrate the Southern perennials and herbs they sell in their wholesale nursery. In this picture you can see redroot, 'Claire Grace' beebalm, major coreopsis, an unnamed beebalm, black-eyed Susan, and a yellow cone-flower (Ratibida pinnata), as well as non-native vitex and patrinia.

184. Latin Name *Coreopsis rosea*
Common Name Pink coreopsis, pink tickweed
Usual Height 1 foot, occasionally 3 feet
Spacing 1 to 2 feet
Sun or Shade ◐ ○
Bloom Pink (white), 1 inch across, yellow centers, late summer
Fruit Dry, tiny, ripe soon after blooming
Leaves Thready, 1 to 2 inches long, light green, chief attraction
Native Range Grassy swamps, damp, peaty soils, East Coast, Zones 6 to 8
Soil Very acid to acid, sand preferred
Drainage Moist to wet
Root System Rhizome, colonizes
Companion Plants Seashore mallow, hibiscus, cardinal flower, swamp sunflower, boltonia, joepyeweed, switchgrass, spikerush
Propagation Root division, seed
Wildlife Seed eaten by songbirds
Related Species *C. nudata,* swamp coreopsis

Pink coreopsis is grown for its foliage, which resembles, for most of the growing season, a delicate green mist about 9 inches tall. The tiny pink daisies, although attractive, appear only in scattered numbers and are not the reason you'd add this flower to your landscape. Place pink coreopsis up front in your garden, or around a taller flower that is leafless at its base, such as hibiscus or boltonia. **Swamp coreopsis** has 2-inch pink flowers and ferny leaves and takes very wet conditions. It gets 4 feet tall and blooms in the spring. It is not winter hardy north of Zone 8.

185. Latin Name *Coreopsis verticillata*
Common Name Threadleaf coreopsis
Usual Height 1 to 2 feet
Spacing 2 feet
Sun or Shade ◐ ○
Bloom Yellow, 1 to 1½ inches across, yellow centers, early summer
Fruit Dry, black, ripe soon after blooming
Leaves 2 inches long, divided into thready segments
Native Range Dry pines or post oak woods, Maryland to South Carolina to West Virginia, Zones 6 to 7
Soil Acid, poor OK, sandy preferred
Drainage Dry
Root System Rhizome, colonizes slowly, lift and divide every 3 to 4 years
Companion Plants Black-eyed Susan/silkgrass, both mountain mints, splitbeard bluestem, pink muhly
Propagation Seed, root division
Wildlife Seed eaten by songbirds
Related Species *C. major,* major coreopsis

Threadleaf coreopsis was a popular perennial in the early part of the century. Then, for some reason, it fell out of favor. Today, it's making a welcome comeback. Many nurseries carry threadleaf coreopsis, and most carry 'Moonbeam' coreopsis, which is probably a hybrid of threadleaf and some other undetermined flower. Threadleaf coreopsis has dark yellow blooms for the first half of the summer, then provides soft, ferny foliage until frost. For midsummer yellow flowers, go with **major coreopsis.** It gets 2 to 3 feet tall and the flowers can be as large as 3 inches across. It is native in sandhills and on sunny, rocky mountain slopes in Zones 6 to 8.

186. **Latin Name** *Crinum americanum*
  Common Name American crinum lily, southern swamp lily
  Usual Height 2 to 3 feet
  Spacing 2 to 4 feet
  Sun or Shade ● ◑ ◐ ○
  Bloom White, sometimes flushed with pink, red stamens, 3 to 4 inches across, in clusters of 4, May to November, very fragrant
  Fruit Capsules burst to release large green seeds
  Leaves 3 to 4 feet long, strap-shaped, firm, glossy, dormant a short time in winter after a hard freeze
  Native Range Cabbage palmetto swamps, marshes, coastal hammocks, Southeastern Gulf coast, Zones 8 to 9
  Soil Acid, lime OK, rich preferred
  Drainage Wet to moist
  Root System 1- to 4-inch bulb, colonizes
  Companion Plants Spiderlily, copper and other swamp iris, lizard's tails, tuckahoe, cardinal flower
  Propagation Separation of bulblets
  Wildlife No information
  Related Species *Hymenocallis* spp., spiderlily

Nearly everyone is familiar with the old-fashioned crinum lilies. They come from South Africa and Asia, and you see them in dry, abandoned ground around old homesites. They bear romantic names, such as "milk-and-wine." Our native **crinum lily** is much prettier. Its glossy erect leaves and its upright and extremely fragrant flowers are two features that make it superior to those droopy foreign varieties. Although found naturally in or at the edge of swamps, crinum lily feels right at home in a flower garden—either sunny or shady—as long as it gets a little summer watering. **Spiderlily** (223) is very similar, but it blooms in the spring and must have sun.

187. **Latin Name** *Eryngium yuccifolium*
  Common Name Eryngo, rattlesnake master, button snakeroot
  Usual Height 3 to 4 feet, occasionally 6 feet
  Spacing 3 feet
  Sun or Shade ○
  Bloom Whitish or pale green, 1-inch globe, midsummer (or as early as May)
  Fruit Seed in heads, ripe in late summer
  Leaves 1 to 2 feet long, yuccalike, dormant in winter
  Native Range Post oak woods, meadows, bogs, marshes, coastal flatwoods, floodplains, eastern half of U.S., Zones 4 to 9
  Soil Acid, lime OK
  Drainage Dry to moist, seasonal flooding OK
  Root System Clump-forming
  Companion Plants Butterflyweed, black-eyed Susan/orange rudbeckia, cutleaf rudbeckia, seashore mallow, redroot, wild ageratum, pineland hibiscus, pink muhly, bluestems
  Propagation Seed, root division
  Wildlife No information

Eryngo is grown for its leaves, not its pale flowers. Use it where you want a strong vertical accent in your garden. But it needs to be a solitary focal point; several of them scattered up and down a border would be too overpowering. Where your scale is much larger, say in a corporate landscape or a meadow, a cluster would be very dramatic. Eryngo is tolerant of a wide range of habitats. It can be in dry soil with a clump of bluestem, butterflyweed, coneflowers, and black-eyed Susans, where it will usually remain relatively short. Or, it can be in an almost wet habitat with seashore mallow, redroot, wild ageratum, and pineland hibiscus, where it will always grow tall.

188. Latin Name *Eupatorium fistulosum*
(*Eupatoriadelphus fistulosus*)
Common Name Joepyeweed, queen-of-the-meadow, trumpetweed
Usual Height 5 to 7 feet, rarely 12 feet
Spacing 4 feet
Sun or Shade ○
Bloom Soft violet-purple, 6- to 14-inch heads, mid to late summer
Fruit Dry, fluffy, fall
Leaves 4 to 12 inches long, 4 to 7 whorled around purple, hollow stem in tiers, dormant in winter
Native Range Stream banks, wet hammocks, eastern U.S., Zones 5 to 9
Soil Acid, rich OK
Drainage Moist
Root System Clump-forming
Companion Plants Stokes aster, Mississippi penstemon/pink coreopsis, seashore mallow, hibiscus, cutleaf rudbeckia, wild ageratum, swamp sunflower, boltonia, fall obedient plant, New York aster
Propagation Seed, root division, softwood cuttings
Wildlife Known as a good bee plant; flowers visited by spicebush and other swallowtails, buckeye, gulf fritillary, monarch, painted lady, red admiral, and sulphur butterflies; seeds eaten by swamp sparrow
Related Species *E. purpureum,* more shade, less wet; *E. dubium*

When I saw **joepyeweed** in a friend's garden outside Memphis, it got my attention right away—even though there were scads of other blooms all around. It's tall and majestic, and, when it's in flower, it can be the star of your garden. But place it to the rear or at a place where you want a strong accent. If your clump eventually gets too large, wait until fall or early spring and then lift it out and divide it for replanting.

189. Latin Name *Hibiscus aculeatus*
Common Name Pineland hibiscus, comfort root
Usual Height 2 feet, rarely 6 feet
Spacing 3 feet
Sun or Shade ◐ ○
Bloom Cream cup, 2 to 4 inches across, fluted, with a dark red center, summer into early fall
Fruit Tan, dry, hard capsule, hairy, 1 inch, seeds ripen quickly
Leaves 3- or 5-lobed, rough, dormant in winter
Native Range Pine savannahs, marsh edges, coastal North Carolina to Texas, and up Mississippi River to Arkansas, Zones 8 to 9
Soil Acid, sand preferred
Drainage Moist, tolerates winter flooding
Root System Clump-forming
Companion Plants Stokes aster/redroot, other hibiscus, tall skullcap/swamp sunflower, cardinal flower, wild ageratum, pink muhly
Propagation Seed, self-sows
Wildlife No information
Related Species *H. coccineus,* Texas star hibiscus; *H. moscheutos,* rose mallow; *H. militaris,* halberdleaf hibiscus

Pineland hibiscus is largely unknown, but once gardeners see it, they rave about its gorgeous flowers, which range from palest yellow to rich cream with an unusual pleated texture, scalloped edges, and velvety red centers. Its short stature allows it to fit into many garden situations. This hibiscus lives five or six years and gets bushier and more full of flowers every year. Give it full sun and moist but not soggy soil in the summer. Cut it back to the ground after frost. The taller hibiscuses are more tolerant of oxygen-poor clay. **Texas star hibiscus** (Zone 8) has 8-inch flat red flowers and marijuana leaves. **Rose mallow** and **halberdleaf hibiscus** (Zones 7 to 9) are white with maroon centers, but have hybridized with Texas star to form pink or rose selections.

190. **Latin Name** *Kosteletzkya virginica*
   Common Name Seashore mallow, saltmarsh
      mallow
   Usual Height 4 to 6 feet
   Spacing 4 to 6 feet
   Sun or Shade ○
   Bloom Pink (white to lavender), 2 inches across,
      hibiscus-shaped, summer to early fall, 3 weeks to
      4 months
   Fruit Tan, dry, ring-shaped, seeds ripen very
      quickly
   Leaves 2 to 6 inches long, grayish green, dormant in
      winter
   Native Range Coastal marshes, New York to Texas
      to Cuba, Zones 7 to 10
   Soil Acid to alkaline, sand preferred, clay OK,
      saline OK
   Drainage Wet to moist, winter flooding OK
   Root System Woody crown, clump-forming
   Companion Plants Stokes aster/wild ageratum,
      cardinal flower, swamp sunflower, New England
      aster, joepyeweed
   Propagation Seed (soak the night before sowing),
      self-sows, cuttings
   Wildlife Nectar source for butterflies and
      hummingbirds

You shouldn't have any trouble growing **seashore mallow** as long as you keep it moist. We saw it everywhere. It's popular because it adds such cheery color to the garden throughout August and into the fall. The blossoms close up at night, but during the day when they open for business, they'll draw all the butterflies and hummingbirds in the immediate vicinity. Seashore mallow reaches maximum size in about five years—the age of the one in the picture. Then it declines and dies. So be sure to gather plenty of seed while it's still in its prime, and allow a seedling or two to establish so you'll have a replacement for the parent plant.

191. **Latin Name** *Lachnanthes caroliana* (*L. tinctoria*)
   Common Name Redroot
   Usual Height 12 to 18 inches, occasionally 3 feet
   Spacing 18 inches
   Sun or Shade ◑ ○
   Bloom Creamy yellow, 2- to 4-inch clusters,
      summer
   Fruit Irislike, seed ripe in late fall, red juice might
      be used as a dye
   Leaves Grasslike, 12 inches high
   Native Range Longleaf pine savannahs, flatwoods,
      bogs, coastal swales, Coastal Plain from Nova
      Scotia to Louisiana and up Mississippi River
      basin to Tennessee, Zones 6 to 9
   Soil Very acid, acid, sand preferred
   Drainage Moist, tolerates flooding
   Root System Rhizome and fibrous roots, both red,
      colonizes
   Companion Plants Barbara's buttons, pitcherplant/
      grasspink, pickerelweed, wiregrass, whitetop
      sedge, broomsedge, toothache grass, spikerush
   Propagation Seed, root division
   Wildlife Seed adored by sandhill cranes

Redroot can be grown in any garden soil as long as it's kept moist during the summer. It looks somewhat grasslike when not in bloom. Repeat that grasslike texture in your flower garden with eryngo, iris and native ornamental grasses. Redroot is relatively short, so place it up front. But sometimes it will fool you and the flowers will appear on 3-foot stems above the foliage. If you live near where sandhill cranes come to feed, plant masses of redroot in a bog garden or beside a sunny water feature, and you're sure to attract these magnificent birds.

192. Latin Name *Liatris pycnostachya*

Common Name Cattail gayfeather, Kansas gayfeather, prairie blazing star

Usual Height 2 to 5 feet

Spacing 2 feet

Sun or Shade ○

Bloom Purply pink spikes, 1 to 3 feet long, 2 weeks sometime between June and October, start blooming at the top

Fruit Silvery fluff on spikes

Leaves 1 to 12 inches long, thready

Native Range Marshes, bogs, Mississippi River basin to Midwest, Zones 6 to 9

Soil Acid, poor preferred

Drainage Moist to wet

Root System Cormlike, clump-forming

Companion Plants Mississippi penstemon/curly clematis, joepyeweed, goldenrod, swamp sunflower, wild ageratum, cardinal flower, salt cordgrass, sugarcane plumegrass

Propagation Seed in fall or spring, division of corms

Wildlife Flowers visited by swallowtails and other butterflies

Related Species *L. spicata,* spiked gayfeather, eastern third U.S.

There are many gayfeathers worth your attention. Most of those native to the Deep South have grasslike leaves and don't bloom until September and October. They grow in sandhills or other poor, dry soils. Give them rich organic matter and too much water, and their upright posture becomes floppy. One exception is **cattail gayfeather;** despite its western native habitat, it does fine in well-watered Southern gardens. Its cluster of stems, each ending in a long, narrow spike of flowers, stands up tall and proud. **Spiked gayfeather,** which also tolerates moisture, has shorter, fatter spikes and comes in white as well as a strong violet-pink. Gayfeather cultivars available in nurseries usually bloom in midsummer.

193. Latin Name *Lilium catesbaei*

Common Name Pine lily, southern red lily

Usual Height 2 feet, occasionally 3 feet

Spacing 1 foot

Sun or Shade ◐ ◑

Bloom Scarlet to orange, 5 to 6 inches across, 1 bloom to each plant, usually late summer

Fruit 2 inches, upright pod, ripe 2 to 3 months after flowering

Leaves Grasslike, 5 inches long, dormant in winter

Native Range Rare, longleaf pine savannahs, bogs, Coastal Plain from Virginia to Louisiana, Zones 7 to 8

Soil Very acid to acid, rich

Drainage Moist, tolerates winter flooding

Root System Bulb, 1 inch in diameter

Companion Plants Louisiana iris, pink coreopsis, Barbara's buttons, Stokes aster/redroot, pineland hibiscus, wild ageratum, tall skullcap/boltonia, whitetop sedge, pink muhly

Propagation Seed, scales of bulbs

Wildlife Flowers a source of nectar for butterflies

Related Species *L. superbum,* Turk's cap lily; *L. michauxii,* Carolina lily

Most lilies take a long time to reach nursery size from seed, causing some unscrupulous nursery owners to dig these endangered flowers out in the wild. However, the three that I've listed here are being propagated by individually owned Southern nurseries. **Pine lily** is the shortest and the most suitable for Coastal Plain gardens. **Turk's cap lily** (winter hardy to Zone 4) requires moisture *and* good drainage at all times. While I've never seen one over 4 feet tall, the books say it might get to 11 feet. It is loaded with dark orange, nodding flowers, and, if you're lucky, will form a colony for you. **Carolina lily** is a shorter, more drought-tolerant version of Turk's cap lily. All three lilies are native to the Florida Panhandle.

194. **Latin Name** *Lobelia cardinalis*
   Common Name Cardinal flower
   Usual Height 2 to 4 feet, occasionally 6 feet
   Spacing 1 foot
   Sun or Shade ◑ ◐ ○
   Bloom Red (white, rose), 1 to 2 inches long on 8-inch spikes, late summer to October
   Fruit Round, tan, dry, seed ripe in fall
   Leaves 2 to 10 inches, usually a winter rosette, but short-lived
   Native Range Marshes, stream banks, most of North America, Zones 4 to 10, up to 3500 feet in the Appalachians
   Soil Acid, lime OK, rich preferred
   Drainage Moist to wet
   Root System Clump-forming
   Companion Plants Swamp bluestar, crinum lily, beebalm/redroot, Barbara's buttons, boltonia, cutleaf rudbeckia, big blue lobelia
   Propagation Seed, root division, cuttings, layering
   Wildlife Flowers a source of nectar to hummingbirds and butterflies
   Related Species *L. siphilitica,* big blue lobelia

Cardinal flower blooms whenever the hummingbirds come to town. It grows taller in rich soil with lots of water, and shorter when conditions are not so lush. But no matter how tall it gets, there is only one bloom per stalk, so you'll want to cluster three to five close together. Or, you can force it to branch by cutting it to two feet in early summer. Cardinal flower is short-lived, so let it self-sow, and then transplant the seedlings in the fall or early spring to wherever you want them. **Big blue lobelia** is an even bigger favorite with hummingbirds. It is not as heat-tolerant as cardinal flower, but otherwise likes similar growing conditions.

195. **Latin Name** *Marshallia graminifolia*
   Common Name Barbara's buttons
   Usual Height 18 inches, occasionally 3 feet
   Spacing 1 foot
   Sun or Shade ◐ ○
   Bloom White to palest pink, 1-inch ball, late summer to early fall, fragrant
   Fruit Brown, dry, ripe in early fall
   Leaves Grasslike, 8 inches high, winter rosette, might be evergreen
   Native Range Pine savannahs, swamps, bogs, ditches, Coastal Plain from North Carolina to Georgia, Zones 7 to 8
   Soil Acid, rich or poor
   Drainage Moist to wet
   Root System Clump-forming
   Companion Plants Redroot, Stokes aster, pineland hibiscus/swamp sunflower, cardinal flower, wild ageratum, wiregrass, whitetop sedge
   Propagation Seed sown in fall, root division
   Wildlife Flowers visited by butterflies
   Related Species *M. trinervia, M. grandiflora, M. caespitosa,* Barbara's buttons

During the hottest part of the summer, **Barbara's buttons** will give you a refreshing two-weeks' worth of fragrant white flowers. This low-growing plant needs to be placed toward the front of the bed, where its tidy foliage can provide dependable greenery the rest of the year. It doesn't like to dry out completely, but, as with most bog plants, it also does not like being overwatered; soggy soil has no oxygen in it. There are three other native species of Barbara's buttons that you might find in a nursery, and all are worthwhile additions to your garden. *Marshallia grandiflora* has the most cold tolerance. *Marshallia caespitosa,* native to Mississippi and westward, blooms in the spring and has the most drought-tolerance.

196. **Latin Name** *Phlox carolina* complex (including hybrids with *P. glaberrima* and *P. maculata*)
Common Name Carolina phlox, summer phlox
Usual Height 1 to 3 feet, rarely 5 feet
Spacing 18 inches
Sun or Shade ◑ ◕ ○
Bloom Pink, white, lavender, or rose, early to midsummer, often until frost, fragrant
Fruit Dry, ripe shortly after flowering
Leaves 2 to 5 inches long, winter rosette
Native Range Bluffs, floodplains, pinelands, thin hardwoods, eastern U.S., Zones 6 to 8
Soil Acid, rich, lime OK
Drainage Moist preferred, tolerates seasonal flooding
Root System Clump-forming
Companion Plants Stokes aster, spiderwort, Mississippi penstemon, downy phlox, beebalm, giant rudbeckia, wild ageratum, fall obedient plant, swamp sunflower, aromatic aster
Propagation Seed, division, cuttings
Wildlife Flowers visited by butterflies, hummingbirds
Related Species *P. paniculata*, fall phlox, summer phlox

Summer phloxes are a staple in every Southern flower garden. With good reason. Nothing else has such a long bloom period, especially during the hottest part of the summer. They can also be successfully scattered in a woodland garden, where they may get only two to three hours of bright dappled sun. **Fall phlox** is the most widespread and best-known of the tall, summer phloxes, but it is prone to mildew. The **Carolina complex** is more resistant and has prettier, glossy leaves. This complicated species of summer phlox has given rise to many excellent cultivars. Use one of these hybrids or selections, or use any one of the pure species that might live close to you. They are all very easy to grow from seed.

197. **Latin Name** *Pycnanthemum tenuifolium*
Common Name Narrowleaf mountain mint, common horsemint
Usual Height 2 feet, 4 feet in rich soil
Spacing 3 feet
Sun or Shade ○
Bloom White to pale pink with purple dots, large clusters, early to midsummer, minty fragrant
Fruit Dry, black seeds ripe in early fall
Leaves Pale green, 2 inches long, thready, extremely minty aromatic, dormant in winter
Native Range Meadows, post oak woods, pinelands, eastern half U.S., Zones 4 to 9
Soil Acid, poor OK, clay OK
Drainage Moist to dry, tolerates brief winter flooding
Root System Rhizome, colonizes
Companion Plants Black-eyed Susan, lyreleaf sage, beebalm/gayfeather, joepyeweed, aster, goldenrod, broomsedge
Propagation Cuttings, root division
Wildlife Flowers visited by butterflies and bees; seeds eaten by numerous wildlife, foliage browsed by deer
Related Species *P. incanum*, silverleaf mountain mint

Narrowleaf mountain mint is a medium-sized, vase-shaped perennial that starts blooming when it is about one foot wide. In succeeding years, it gets to be three feet wide. If it continues to spread, lift and divide it to keep it vital and under control. It has a long bloom time and is a welcome addition to an herb garden. Use it as a cooking herb or a tea, and rub the fragrant leaves on yourself to repel fleas and mosquitoes. The **silverleaf mountain mint** is less polite but very showy; it has wide, silvery white leaves that are even more eye-catching than the flowers. It grows on dry banks from Zones 5 to 8.

198. **Latin Name** *Rudbeckia fulgida*
    Common Name Orange rudbeckia, perennial black-eyed Susan
    Usual Height 2 to 3 feet
    Spacing 3 feet
    Sun or Shade ○
    Bloom Golden yellow, 1 to 3 inches across, dark center, rarely late spring to midsummer, usually late summer to early fall
    Fruit Seeds ripen in cone
    Leaves 2 to 4 inches, toothed, fuzzy, winter rosette
    Native Range Woodlands, meadows, flatwoods, calcareous hammocks, eastern U.S., Zones 6 to 8
    Soil Acid, lime OK
    Drainage Moist, tolerates seasonal flooding
    Root System Colonizes, lift and divide to control
    Companion Plants Blue false indigo, beebalm, sundrops, downy phlox, eryngo, Carolina phlox/asters, doll's daisy, switchgrass, Indiangrass
    Propagation Seed or root division
    Wildlife Seeds eaten by birds
    Related Species *R. hirta,* black-eyed Susan

Common **black-eyed Susan** (*R. hirta*) acts like an annual or biennial, seeding out like crazy so you never know where it'll come up. That's why, if you want a more orderly flower garden, you might opt for perennial black-eyed Susan, a.k.a. **orange rudbeckia.** Orange rudbeckia comes in two varieties: *R. fulgida* var. *fulgida,* with numerous 1-inch flowers that bloom until frost, and *R. fulgida* var. *sullivantii,* which rarely gets over 2 feet tall and has bigger blooms—3 inches across—but fewer of them. It is the parent of the cultivar 'Goldsturm,' pictured here. 'Goldsturm' is neon-vivid; personally, I find it overpowering in a perennial garden and think it is better suited to petunias and other annual paint-by-flower displays. By contrast, the two wild varieties are more subtle and blend in well with most perennials.

199. **Latin Name** *Rudbeckia maxima*
    Common Name Giant rudbeckia, giant coneflower
    Usual Height 6 feet, occasionally 10 feet
    Spacing 2 feet
    Sun or Shade ○
    Bloom Yellow, 3 inches wide, 2-inch dark cone
    Fruit Cone fills with ripe sunflower-sized seed in midsummer
    Leaves Pale green, 8 inches long, spring rosette 18 inches wide by 12 inches tall, winter rosette smaller
    Native Range Pinelands, ditches, Louisiana, Arkansas, East Texas and southeastern Oklahoma, Zones 7 to 8
    Soil Very acid to acid
    Drainage Moist
    Root System Woody crown, clump-forming
    Companion Plants Black-eyed Susan, sabatia, lanceleaf coreopsis, downy phlox, beebalm, butterflyweed, spiderlily/wild ageratum, swamp sunflower, joepyeweed, brushy bluestem, switchgrass, Indiangrass
    Propagation Seed, division
    Wildlife Browsed by deer
    Related Species *R. laciniata,* cutleaf rudbeckia, wild goldenglow, eastern half U.S., Zones 4 to 8; *R. nitida,* shining rudbeckia

Giant rudbeckia is grown as much for its leaves as its flowers. These leaves are canna-shaped, huge, and as pale as a luna moth. As summer heats up, tall stalks appear and the pale yellow flowers, with their exaggerated dark brown cones, start to bloom. After blooming, let the rosette re-form, and then cut the stalks back. **Cutleaf rudbeckia,** which grows all over the Southeast, often in floodplains, is equally tall, but bushy and 4 feet wide. It blooms from July to October and has unusual yellow-green centers. 'Herbstsonne' is a hybrid of cutleaf rudbeckia and **shining rudbeckia.**

200. Latin Name *Rudbeckia triloba*

Common Name Three-lobed rudbeckia, brown-eyed Susan

Usual Height 3 to 5 feet

Spacing 4 feet

Sun or Shade ◑ ◐ ○

Bloom Yellow, 2 to 3 inches across, dark purply brown centers, late summer to early fall

Fruit Center dries and holds the seeds, which ripen in early fall

Leaves 2 to 4 inches long, 3-lobed, winter rosette

Native Range Pinelands, cedar brakes, meadows, eastern half U.S., Zones 5 to 8

Soil Acid, lime OK

Drainage Moist to dry

Root System Woody crown, short-lived perennial

Companion Plants Wild red columbine, lyreleaf sage, downy phlox/woodmint, fall phlox/Short's aster

Propagation Seed, self-sows

Wildlife Flowers visited by butterflies, bees, seeds eaten by birds

Although full of flowers, **three-lobed rudbeckia** is not dense and overpowering. It combines well with fall phlox, cutleaf rudbeckia, joepyeweed, boltonia, seashore mallow, and other flowers that also bloom in late summer and early fall. We saw it used very effectively at Cheekwood in Nashville, where it was allowed to scatter itself along the sunny edges of the woodland garden. It is not long-lived, so gather seed or let it self-sow. Transplant the seedlings where you want them when you do your final weeding in the garden after frost.

Carolina phlox, fire pink, and fern in July on the Blue Ridge Parkway in North Carolina.

Orange rudbeckia 'Goldsturm', phlox 'Miss Lingard', cardinal flower, and 'Gold Greenheart', a cultivar of Heliopsis helianthoides, *a native southern yellow daisy commonly called oxeye, were planted by the South Hampton Roads Chapter of the Native Plant Society of Virginia at the historic Lynnhaven House, built in 1725.*

FALL-BLOOMING GARDEN FLOWERS

Many of the midsummer flowers continue to bloom on into the fall. But, in late summer and fall, which is late August to frost, you get a small third group of flowers to keep you from getting bored. Be sure to include grasses in your fall garden also.

We caught Kitty and Neil Taylor's garden in Collierville, Tennessee, in mid-September. The golden daisies of rudbeckia 'Goldsturm,' bottom right, was a week or two past its peak and seeding out. Its taller cousin, rudbeckia 'Herbstsonne,' however, was in its second bloom and *looking terrific. Also in this section of their border garden are two long-blooming purple flowers—a native phlox (P. maculata) and joepyeweed at the left rear—along with compact holly and the leafy remains of woodland bluestar and Mississippi penstemon in the foreground.*

201. Latin Name *Aster oblongifolius*
Common Name Aromatic aster, shale aster
Usual Height 2 to 3 feet, sometimes 1 foot in wild
Spacing 3 feet
Sun or Shade ◑ ○
Bloom Blue-violet to rose, 1 inch, numerous, mid to late fall
Fruit Fluffy, late fall
Leaves 1 to 3 inches long, aromatic, winter rosette
Native Range Shale barrens, limestone outcrops, eastern half U.S., Zones 4 to 8
Soil Acid, lime OK, rich OK, rocky or sandy OK
Drainage Dry to moist
Root System Woody crown, most colonize
Companion Plants Butterflyweed, coneflowers, beebalm, sundrops, Small's penstemon, downy phlox/fall phlox, mountain mint, rudbeckias, fall obedient plant
Propagation Seed, root division, cuttings
Wildlife Flowers visited by hummingbirds, butterflies, bees; seeds eaten by cardinals, finches, grosbeaks, sparrows, thrashers, towhees, chickadees, nuthatches, titmice, wild turkeys
Related Species *A. novae-angliae,* New England aster, and many, many more

There is a selection of a blue **aromatic aster** that we saw over and over in Southern gardens. It often blooms in spring and then again all fall, makes a neat mound of foliage when not in bloom, and is impervious to drought. We saw the **New England aster** nearly as often. It is usually taller and needs more moisture. It has several cultivars that range from white to pastel to hot pink to purple. **Aster species** are numerous and there seems to be one for every imaginable habitat and style. As a general rule, a wild aster that you might dig out of the vacant lot works great in a meadow, but would be too aggressive for a flower garden. The ones you find at the nursery have been selected for good behavior and loads of flowers.

202. Latin Name *Boltonia asteroides*
Common Name Boltonia
Usual Height 2 to 6 feet
Spacing 3 feet
Sun or Shade ○
Bloom White (pink, lavender), 1^1/2 inches wide, yellow centers, early fall to frost
Fruit Seed ripe mid to late fall
Leaves 3 to 5 inches long, narrow, blue-green, winter rosette
Native Range Marshes, pinelands, Southeastern U.S., Zones 6 to 8, to Zone 3 in North Dakota
Soil Acid, rich, clay OK
Drainage Moist to dry, tolerates summer dry and winter wet
Root System Rhizomes, short-lived perennial
Companion Plants Redroot, Stokes aster/cardinal flower, wild ageratum, swamp sunflower, New England aster, joepyeweed, switchgrass, brushy bluestem
Propagation Seed, root division, cuttings
Wildlife Flowers a nectar source for butterflies
Related Species *B. diffusa,* doll's daisy

Placed among the busy reds, yellows, and purples of an autumn garden, **boltonia** looks positively serene; its cool, white daisies seem to float airily on slender pale green stems. Two cultivars—'Snowbank' and 'Pink Beauty'—are very popular in Zones 6 and 7. If you live in Zone 8, however, don't count on these two. They aren't summer hardy, and until a nursery starts growing one for you, you'll have to find your own native boltonia seed out in the wild. **Doll's daisy,** with half-size flowers, is the *Boltonia* more frequently found. Sometimes it will have almost no leaves up where the flowers are, giving it a strikingly delicate appearance. Other fall white flowers you can use with it are a white version of fall obedient plant, white *Phlox paniculata,* roundleaf eupatorium, and white asters.

203. **Latin Name** *Eupatorium coelestinum (Conoclinium coelestinum)*

Common Name Wild ageratum, mistflower, blue boneset

Usual Height 18 to 24 inches, rarely 40 inches

Spacing 2 to 3 feet

Sun or Shade ◑ ◐ ○

Bloom Lavender-blue fuzzy flowers in a flat-topped head, late summer to midfall

Fruit Dry, gray to tan, shortly after blooming

Leaves 1 to 4 inches, rough, dormant in winter

Native Range Stream banks, moist meadows, Southeastern U.S., Zones 6 to 9

Soil Acid, rich, lime OK

Drainage Moist to dry

Root System Colonizes, shallow-rooted

Companion Plants Atamasco lily/hibiscus, seashore mallow, boltonia, swamp sunflower, joepyeweed, blue lobelia

Propagation Root division

Wildlife Flowers visited by butterflies

Wild ageratum doesn't require a lot of attention. Just be sure to water it in July and August if the rains forget to appear. This native drives green-thumb gardeners nuts because it spreads aggressively. But the roots are shallow and easy to yank out. As a black-thumb gardener myself, I would much rather pull out an overly rambunctious plant than have to fret and fuss over keeping a less hardy one alive. Wild ageratum drives photographers nuts, too, because its blue color is virtually impossible to capture accurately on film. This is a relatively low grower, so put it at the feet of any of your tall autumn flowers. If it gets too floppy by June and needs staking, lop it in half instead. You can't put spring flowers on top of it because it greens up early and makes a dense groundcover wherever you allow it to spread. Cut off the old blooms when they start looking ratty.

204. **Latin Name** *Helianthus angustifolius*

Common Name Swamp sunflower, narrowleaf sunflower

Usual Height 1½ to 5 feet, rarely 10 feet

Spacing 3 feet

Sun or Shade ○

Bloom Gold, 2 to 3 inches across, dark centers, early to midfall

Fruit Seeds, ripe in late fall

Leaves 4 to 6 inches long, narrow to thready, dormant in winter

Native Range Marshes, savannahs, eastern U.S., Zones 6 to 9

Soil Acid, rich or poor OK

Drainage Moist to wet

Root System Colonizes

Companion Plants Spiderlily, Stokes aster, swamp iris, redroot/pineland hibiscus, wild ageratum, sugarcane plumegrass

Propagation Seed (self-sows), root division

Wildlife Flowers visited by butterflies; seeds eaten by mourning dove, white-winged dove, bobwhite, housefinch, goldfinch, meadowlark, white-breasted nuthatch, sparrows, and wood mouse

In East Texas, it's common to see **swamp sunflower** in magnificent 1½ to 3-foot-tall golden swaths covering a half acre or more, and accented with the coppery plumes of sugarcane plumegrass and the blue of wild ageratum. This is how landscape architect Johnny Mayronne uses it in the wonderful minibog by his home in lower Louisiana. So, naturally, I was amazed to hear that many of you in the South are using it in flower gardens. And successfully, too. Clearly, it is both easy to grow and control in that semidry environment, although it does tend to grow taller there.

205. Latin Name *Physostegia virginiana* (*Dracocephalum virginianum*)
Common Name Fall obedient plant, false dragonhead, Virginia lionsheart
Usual Height 2 to 4 feet
Spacing 1 foot wide, but spreads
Sun or Shade ◐ ◑ ○
Bloom Lavender (rose, white), 1 inch long, clustered on spikes, late summer to midfall, sometimes much earlier
Fruit Tan, dry, seed ripe in fall
Leaves 2 to 6 inches long, narrow, toothed, winter rosette
Native Range Bogs, pine savannahs, eastern half North America, Zones 3 to 8
Soil Acid, lime OK, rich OK
Drainage Moist to dry
Root System Colonizes
Companion Plants Swamp bluestar, lanceleaf coreopsis, black-eyed Susan, beebalm/skullcap, redroot, hibiscus, swamp sunflower
Propagation Root division
Wildlife Flowers visited by hummingbirds

I first knew that **fall obedient plant** was my kind of flora after I'd seen it umpteen times in old-fashioned gardens where it had obviously thrived for decades with minimal care. It spreads aggressively by the roots, but they're shallow and easily pulled out, making it an easy plant to control. In rare cases, blooms might start in June, but in most Southern gardens you can expect it to start blooming in August. Sometimes it continues flowering until frost, although not with the same enthusiasm it showed initially.

206. Latin Name *Pityopsis graminifolia* (*Chrysopsis graminifolia, Heterotheca graminifolia,* including *Pityopsis microcephala* and *P. aspera*)
Common Name Silkgrass, golden aster
Usual Height 1 foot, with 1- to 3-foot bloom stalks
Spacing 1 foot
Sun or Shade ◐ ◑ ○
Bloom Dark yellow, 1 inch across, yellow centers, late summer to late fall
Fruit Fuzzy, ripe soon after blooming
Leaves Silvery, grasslike, 4 to 12 inches long
Native Range Sandhills, post oak woods, stable dunes, pine savannahs, ridges in bogs, eastern North America, Zones 6 to 11
Soil Very acid, acid, poor and sandy preferred
Drainage Dry, moist OK if drainage is excellent
Root System Colonizes
Companion Plants Pussytoes, Texas and sandhill bluestar, baptisia/thimbleweed, dry gayfeathers, splitbeard bluestem, aromatic aster, Maryland goldenaster, pink muhly
Propagation Seed, division of clumps
Wildlife Flowers visited by butterflies
Related Species *Chrysopsis mariana,* Maryland goldenaster

Silkgrass is not well known yet, but gardeners who make its acquaintance tend to get very excited. It blooms for a long time in the fall and fits in nicely in the forefront of a flower garden because of its low-growing, silvery leaves. It also makes an attractive groundcover; its ornamental foliage is ideal for those dry, semishady spots where you want more height than you'd get from pussytoes and less height than with bracken. But don't count on many flowers in such a spot. Cut it back in February, just before the new leaves appear; that'll keep it looking its freshest. **Maryland goldenaster** has showier flowers, but its foliage isn't so special. It is often used in a sunny, well-drained flower garden.

207. Latin Name *Solidago* sp.
  Common Name Goldenrod
  Usual Height 1$\frac{1}{2}$ to 5 feet
  Spacing 2 feet
  Sun or Shade ◑ ○
  Bloom Yellow to gold, fragrant, one-sided clusters
    of tiny flowers, late summer to midfall
  Fruit Fluffy, fall, lasting into winter
  Leaves 1 to 4 inches long, aromatic of anise or
    vanilla when crushed, often a small winter rosette
  Native Range Thin post oak, turkey oak woods,
    stable dunes, eastern U.S., Zones 5b to 9
  Soil Acid, poor
  Drainage Dry to moist
  Root System Short rhizomes, clump-forming, lift
    and divide as needed
  Companion Plants Texas bluestar, blue false
    indigo, sundrops, eryngo/silkgrass
  Propagation Root division, cuttings
  Wildlife Flowers visited by butterflies and bees;
    seeds eaten by goldfinch and pine siskin
  Related Species *S. rugosa,* rough-stemmed
    goldenrod; *S. pinetorum,* early goldenrod;
    S. nemoralis, grayleaf goldenrod; *S. odora,*
    sweet goldenrod; *S. speciosa,* showy goldenrod;
    S. sempervirens, seaside goldenrod; *S. rigida,*
    stiff goldenrod; *S. ulmifolia,* elmleaf goldenrod

  Goldenrod is the one most gardeners know, but
the list of related species reflects those other sun-loving
goldenrods available in nurseries. Some bloom early, in
mid- to late summer. Some are short, some tall; some have
wide leaves, some have delicate leaves, and one has gray
leaves; some like boggy conditions, and others, like sweet
goldenrod, prefer it on the dry side. You don't have to
worry about hayfever, because all goldenrods are bee and
butterfly pollinated, but you do have to beware; some wild
ones are very aggressive.

*Sugarcane plume grass blooms amid swamp sunflower
at Gus Engeling Wildlife Management Area near
Palestine, Texas, in October.*

13

ORNAMENTAL GRASSES

Our culture has traditionally thought of grasses in only three categories: lawn grasses, forage for domestic livestock . . . and *weeds!*

It is only fairly recently that we've learned (or relearned) that grasses have value other than as football fields or pasture. Salt marshes are essential to the lifecycles of shrimp and many fish, while prairies and meadows support many land animals. A lot of work is being done in reclamation and restoration of grasslands for wildlife value.

But now we are entering into a new phase of grass use. The general public is awakening to the idea that grasses have a place in the small urban or suburban garden. It started during the last generation with the introduction of pampas grass from Argentina, which was acceptable because it was evergreen. In the last few years, the importation of African bunch grasses has taught us that fall color and tan winter color are also acceptable.

But, still, few were ready to acknowledge that our *native* grasses had any aesthetic value. It wasn't until we started getting cultivars of our native switchgrass sent back to us from Germany and England that nurserymen and landscapers finally caught on that we possess a treasury of gorgeous ornamental native grasses that are suitable for use in our landscapes.

If you garden on a small property, **use grasses as you would flowers or shrubs.** The big advantage to the grasses is that you can leave them with their dead foliage in the winter, and they are still ornamental. Little bluestem is good about retaining its rich coppery color all winter long. Switchgrass always looks good because its form is so well balanced. Wiregrass is almost evergreen, and, in some parts of its range, so is pink muhly.

Many people **use grasses mixed in with the perennial flower garden,** so I've given you choices as to what flowers will grow well with each grass. Another, more unusual but very effective use is in a **total grass garden,** so I've included ideas on which grasses will combine attractively with each other.

If you have a sunny property where you want to cut way back on mowing, consider using these tall, ornamental grasses to make a meadow, prairie, savannah, or marsh. Use **contour mowing** to make lawns or paths where you really need them, and let the rest get tall. It will save you hours and hours of hard work.

In the wild, grasses are dependent on fire to burn down trees and shrubs that would shade them out of existence. This has resulted in some grasses' getting conditioned so that they grow *only* when they have been burned. If you planted a clump of grass in your flower bed and you know that there is plenty of sun, moisture, drainage, compost, and everything else it could possibly need, but it is *still* unhappy, it might need a fire.

Choose a wet day in the winter when there is no wind, so that the danger of a spark landing somewhere else in the flower bed is minimized. Light the dry foliage of the chosen grass clump with a match, and then stand by with the water hose until it has burned down to the crown, and the thatch near the ground is all charred. Then wet it down thoroughly to make certain the fire is completely out. Your efforts should be rewarded with an exuberant flush of healthy growth in the spring.

171

A grass garden is a year-round treat of textures, but it is especially glorious when the grasses are in bloom or beginning to show their fall colors, and it's all backlit by the morning or evening sun. Many home gardeners are now using ornamental grasses as part of their flower gardens. Others are creating new grass gardens, as shown in the picture. And still others substitute grasses for shrubs or yuccas to provide a softly textured accent. Those who crave lots of sun, but are tired of mowing a large lawn, are using grasses and wildflowers combined in a meadow or imitation prairie.

This grass garden surrounds a pond in Mimi's Garden, part of the Dallas Arboretum and Botanical Garden in Dallas, Texas. On the left is Indiangrass, just coming into bloom. Much shorter, in the middle, is inland sea oats with ripening seeds. On the right are a few of the delicate flowering heads of switchgrass.

(Benny J. Simpson)

208. Latin Name *Andropogon glomeratus* (*A. virginicus* var. *glomeratus, A. virginicus* var. *abbreviatus*)
Common Name Brushy bluestem, bushy bluestem, bushy beardgrass
Usual Height 2 to 5 feet
Spacing 2 feet
Sun or Shade ○
Bloom Silky, dense, silvery green to pinkish, early fall
Fruit Very showy, white to silver, plumy, early to midfall
Leaves Narrow, dense at base, cinnamon to copper in fall and winter
Native Range Savannahs, bogs, sunny swales, eastern U.S. to California, Zones 6 to 9
Soil Acid, lime OK, rich OK, clay OK
Drainage Moist, tolerates seasonal flooding
Root System Clump-forming
Companion Plants Stokes aster, pink coreopsis, hibiscus/boltonia, wild ageratum, swamp sunflower, cardinal flower, fall obedient plant, sugarcane plumegrass, switchgrass, woolgrass, salt cordgrass
Propagation Seed, root division
Wildlife Seeds eaten by birds, insects, and mammals

Brushy bluestem is an exceptionally handsome and well behaved ornamental grass that can be used in any flower garden, as long as it doesn't get too dry in the summer. Its summer look is a 2-foot-tall bunch of slender green leaves. In the fall, it usually blooms along with cattail gayfeather, swamp sunflower, goldenrod, sugarcane plumegrass, and wild ageratum. At the first hint of frost, while the white fluffy seeds are still clinging to the stalks, the leaves and stems turn a rich coral color that stays throughout the winter. Cut it to the ground in February or March to make way for the new green leaves that will appear in midspring.

209. Latin Name *Andropogon ternarius*
Common Name Splitbeard bluestem
Usual Height 2 to 5 feet
Spacing 2 feet for garden accent, $1/2$ to 2 pounds pure live seed per 1000 square feet
Sun or Shade ○
Bloom Silvery white, in a vee, late summer to midfall
Fruit Plumy white, in a vee, early to midfall
Leaves Narrow, coppery in fall and winter
Native Range Dry, thin woodland, sandhills, old fields, stable dunes, eastern U.S., Zones 6 to 9
Soil Very acid to acid, sand
Drainage Dry, tolerates brief winter flooding
Root System Clump-forming
Companion Plants Downy phlox, sundrops, Texas or sandhill bluestar, blue or white baptisias, yuccas, conradina, Georgia basil/dry gayfeathers, silkgrass, eryngo, sandhill rosemary, little bluestem, wiregrass, pink muhly
Propagation Seed, root division
Wildlife Seeds eaten by prairie chicken, junco, wild turkey, chipping sparrow, meadow mouse; foliage browsed by white-tailed deer

I predict that **splitbeard bluestem** will become one of your favorite grasses, if it isn't already. It probably is, if you've seen it growing in masses with the autumn sun backlighting its silvery white tufts. Each little feathery seed tuft catches the light and amplifies it tremendously. This would be my first choice for a meadow grass to go along with post oaks or with longleaf pines and turkey oaks in plenty of sun. It would also place high on my list for a flower garden accent, provided my soil was sandy enough to make it happy. The leaves in winter get quite curly, and eventually turn gray and unattractive. That's the time to cut it down to within 3 inches of the ground. New leaves will appear with spring.

210. **Latin Name** *Andropogon virginicus*
    Common Name Broomsedge
    Usual Height 2 to 5 feet
    Spacing 2 feet
    Sun or Shade ◑ ○
    Bloom Not showy, late summer to late fall
    Fruit Plumy white seeds, fall
    Leaves Narrow, coppery brown in fall and winter
    Native Range Old fields, thin woods, pinelands, dunes, marsh margins, eastern North America, Zones 6 to 11
    Soil Acid, poor
    Drainage Dry to moist
    Root System Clump-forming
    Companion Plants Lanceleaf coreopsis, black-eyed Susan, purple coneflower/mountain mint, goldenrod, asters, little bluestem, splitbeard bluestem
    Propagation Seed, root division
    Wildlife Seeds eaten by field sparrow, junco, chipping sparrow, prairie chicken; foliage browsed by white-tailed deer; nesting cover for bobwhite quail
    Related Species *Schizachyrium scoparium,* little bluestem

Broomsedge is the most commonly seen native grass in the South. It is often seen in quantity in old fields, where it is very important for erosion control. That's why it is the basis for most dryland Southern meadow or prairie restoration projects. **Little bluestem** can be used in the same way, especially on clay and limestone. Its leaves and stems frequently have a bluish cast in summer, while its fall color is a very warm copper that doesn't fade all winter. It replaces wiregrass in longleaf pine habitats from Mississippi westward. Broomsedge and little bluestem require periodic burning to remain vigorous, the heat stimulates root growth in a way that annual mowing does not.

211. **Latin Name** *Aristida stricta*
    Common Name Wiregrass, pineland three-awn
    Usual Height 2 feet, 3 to 4 feet when in bloom
    Spacing 2 feet
    Sun or Shade ◐ ◑ ○
    Bloom 6 to 20 inches, brownish, airy, any time
    Fruit Yellow seed, produced only in the fall after a fire
    Leaves Semi-evergreen, 20 inches long, very narrow and folded longways to make wiry, upright leaves that become relaxed with age
    Native Range Sandhills and pine savannahs, bogs, Coastal Plain from North Carolina to Mississippi, Zones 7 to 9
    Soil Very acid, very poor
    Drainage Dry, but tolerates flooding in winter and spring
    Root System Clump-forming
    Companion Plants Longleaf pine, turkey oak, dwarf huckleberry, Texas or sandhill bluestar, baptisias, Barbara's buttons/redroot, silkgrass, bluestems, toothache grass, whitetop sedge, pink muhly
    Propagation Fresh seed, root division
    Wildlife Seeds eaten by Bachman's sparrow, foliage browsed by white-tailed deer

Wiregrass is the principal savannah grass that grows alongside longleaf pines, in both wet and dry situations, from the Carolinas to Mississippi. Its very fine foliage creates a visually soft, year-round groundcover made up of new green leaves intermixed with old withered ones. It must be burned every two to three years to maintain density, as it sets seed only after a fire. This also burns out the thatch and withered leaves, so that after a fire, old clumps are lush and completely green for a while. Individual clumps planted in a flower bed remain the same size for years.

212. Latin Name *Chasmanthium latifolium* (*Uniola latifolia*)

Common Name Inland seaoats, upland seaoats, river oats

Usual Height 2 to 5 feet

Spacing 2 to 3 feet

Sun or Shade ◑ ◑

Bloom 4- to 8-inch loose clusters, not as conspicuous as seeds

Fruit Green, dangling seed heads in summer, turning gold and tan in fall

Leaves 4 to 8 inches long, alternating up the stems, fall color is bright to pale gold with purple shadings, dormant in winter

Native Range Stream banks, moist woods, eastern half U.S., Zones 6 to 8 (sometimes, #9)

Soil Acid, lime OK, sand or clay OK, rich OK

Drainage Moist, tolerates seasonal flooding

Root System Clump-forming, self-sows vigorously

Companion Plants Itea/Turk's cap, cardinal flower, wild ageratum

Propagation Seed, root division

Wildlife No information

Related Species *C. sessiliflorum,* longleaf uniola

If you want a first-rate waist-high groundcover, you can't do better than **inland seaoats**. It's ideal under live oaks and post oaks, where you'd like to have the soft, dense, luxurious texture of ferns, but the soil is a little too dry for them to stay in top condition. Inland seaoats has a softer, leafier look than your typical grass, and can be very ornamental in a flower bed. In that case, I'd advise you to cut off all the seed heads just as they start to turn color and then use them for indoor flower arrangements. If they go to seed in your flower garden, you'll have a bonanza of them next year. **Longleaf uniola** looks quite different from inland seaoats, having thin, grasslike tufts about knee-high and, sadly, no showy seed heads. But it is almost evergreen and takes even more shade.

213. Latin Name *Dichromena colorata*

Common Name Whitetop sedge, starrush

Usual Height 6 to 12 inches, occasionally to 2 feet

Spacing 1 foot for fast cover

Sun or Shade ○

Bloom White (actually the white tops of the leaves around the flowers are the showy part), late spring to fall

Fruit Nutlets in late summer or fall

Leaves Narrow, glossy, in a grassy rosette, dormant in winter

Native Range Savannahs, bogs, coastal swales, eastern North America, Coastal Plain from Virginia to Texas, Zones 8 to 10

Soil Very acid to acid, lime OK, saline OK

Drainage Wet to moist

Root System Colonizes by rhizomes

Companion Plants Copper iris/hibiscus, seashore mallow, redroot, pine lily, Barbara's buttons, wiregrass, spikerush, sugarcane plumegrass

Propagation Root division

Wildlife Flowers pollinated by insects

Related Species *D. latifolia,* tall whitetop sedge, colorful rush

The flowers of **whitetop sedge** are little tufts in the center of long, drooping bracts. One third of each bract around the flower is white, while the lower portion is green. From a distance, a colony of whitetop sedge looks like a cluster of white stars set atop delicate, slender stems. Alone or combined with spikerush, it makes an appealing groundcover for sunny, wet to moist situations—for example, that poorly drained corner of your lawn, the ditch by the road in front of your home, or the banks of a pond. **Tall whitetop sedge** is found more often in cypress swamps or in creek swamps, and it grows a foot taller than whitetop. Sedges are aggressive, so if you use them in a bog garden, they will have to be contained by dry areas, or be shaded out where you don't want them to go.

214. Latin Name *Eleocharis montevidensis*
　　Common Name Spikerush
　　Usual Height 6 to 9 inches, occasionally 2 feet
　　Spacing 4-inch-wide tufts can spread wherever
　　　　moisture is right
　　Sun or Shade ○
　　Bloom Tiny reddish cone, spring or summer
　　Fruit Yellow or brown tiny seeds, ripe late summer
　　Leaves Bright yellow-green, strawlike, stiff, dormant
　　　　in winter or drought
　　Native Range Brackish marshes, sinks, wet sands,
　　　　North America, mostly east of the Rockies,
　　　　Zones 5 to 9, and south to Argentina
　　Soil Acid, lime OK, brackish OK
　　Drainage Moist, tolerates seasonal flooding
　　Root System Colonizes by dark red rhizomes
　　Companion Plants Copper iris/hibiscus, seashore
　　　　mallow, redroot, cattail gayfeather, cardinal
　　　　flower, wild ageratum, whitetop sedge,
　　　　woolgrass, sugarcane plumegrass, brushy
　　　　bluestem
　　Propagation Root division
　　Wildlife Seeds, stems, and roots eaten by coot, 11
　　　　species of ducks, Canada goose, snow goose, blue
　　　　goose, purple gallinule, king rail, sora, Virginia
　　　　rail, yellow rail, common snipe
　　Related Species Many *Eleocharis,* all very similar in
　　　　size, but most grow in shallow water; about a
　　　　third of those native to the South are annuals

Where you have low, wet places in your lawn,
consider using **spikerush.** Its fine-textured leaves and
bright color blend in handsomely with lawn grasses. And
because it normally stays quite short, it can also be used as
an easy-care groundcover in poorly drained spots. Want to
create a minimarsh? Plant bog flowers in the spikerush.
Or, take advantage of its soothing yellow-green
smoothness to show off a sculpture.

215. Latin Name *Erianthus giganteus*
　　Common Name Sugarcane plumegrass
　　Usual Height 5 to 6 feet, occasionally 13 feet
　　Spacing 4 feet
　　Sun or Shade ○
　　Bloom 6- to 16-inch plume, rose to copper, early
　　　　fall
　　Fruit Plume fades to peach and silver within a week
　　　　of blooming
　　Leaves 20 inches long, narrow at the base and up
　　　　the stalk, dormant in winter
　　Native Range Savannahs, marshes, coastal swales,
　　　　eastern half of North America, Zones 6 to 10
　　Soil Very acid to acid, poor or rich
　　Drainage Moist
　　Root System Clump-forming, but might colonize
　　Companion Plants Spikerush/hibiscus, swamp
　　　　sunflower, wild ageratum, joepyeweed,
　　　　switchgrass, brushy bluestem
　　Propagation Seed, root division while dormant
　　Wildlife No information
　　Related Species *E. contortus,* bent-awn plumegrass,
　　　　Zones 7 to 8

Sugarcane plumegrass blooms with as much color as
joepyeweed, which is to say, it's *very* colorful. Especially
when backlit. Although this is a marsh grass, it does quite
well in moist flower gardens. It always blooms in sync
with swamp sunflower and wild ageratum, and often at
the same time as joepyeweed, cutleaf rudbeckia, New
York aster, and cardinal flower. Besides using it in a
flower garden, you can place it on a sunny edge of a pond,
in a large bog garden, or in a semiwild swale. This is the
American version of the Italian plumegrass, *E. ravennae,*
that has been popular in Northeastern gardens for many
years. **Bent-awn plumegrass,** another native American
erianthus with good garden qualities, has white candle-
shaped plumes, purplish stems, and bronzy fall coloring.

216. **Latin Name** *Muhlenbergia capillaris* (includes
     M. expansa and *M. filipes*)
     Common Name Pink muhly, hairgrass, hair-awn
     muhly
     Usual Height 1¹/₂ to 4 feet
     Spacing 2 feet
     Sun or Shade ○
     Bloom 8- to 20-inch filmy cluster of delicate pink
     flowers, early fall
     Fruit Purplish, tiny, following flowers
     Leaves 16 inches long, narrow, rolled lengthwise
     into an upright, wiry leaf, almost evergreen
     Native Range Dry woods, sandhills, savannahs,
     bogs, coastal swales, eastern half North America,
     Zones 6 to 11
     Soil Acid, poor OK, sand or clay OK
     Drainage Moist to dry, tolerates seasonal flooding
     Root System Clump-forming
     Companion Plants Prairie phlox/eryngo, silkgrass,
     wiregrass, splitbeard bluestem (dry), or Stokes
     aster/redroot, pineland hibiscus, boltonia, brushy
     bluestem (moist to wet)
     Propagation Seed
     Wildlife No information

Pink muhly is most consistently a knock-out along
both the Atlantic and Gulf coasts, causing some (but not
all) botanists to classify the coastal stands as a separate
species, *M. filipes*. Whatever you call it, it is beautiful and
easy to grow. It prefers a moist environment and rich soil,
but it can tolerate short periods of wet or drought, and can
thrive in soils as sterile as sugar sand. Use it in a sunny
flower garden, and be sure to place it where it will be
backlit by the sun, because that's how it shows off its rich
pink color. If you have the room, plant it in masses, again
backlit, and you'll have a field of pink mist for about ten
days every autumn.

217. **Latin Name** *Panicum virgatum*
     Common Name Switchgrass
     Usual Height 3 to 4 feet, occasionally 7 feet
     Spacing 3 feet, or ¹/₂ to 2 pounds pure live seed
     per 1000 square feet
     Sun or Shade ◑ ○
     Bloom 4- to 16-inch cluster, greenish, lacy,
     midsummer to fall
     Fruit 4- to 16-inch cluster, grayish, fall and winter
     Leaves Pale bluish green in summer, rich gold (or
     red) in fall, tan and dormant in winter
     Native Range Savannahs, fresh and brackish
     marshes, dunes, North America, Zones 4 to 9
     Soil Acid, lime OK, clay OK, saline OK, sand OK,
     rich OK
     Drainage Moist, tolerates seasonal flooding
     Root System Clump-forming, also colonizes by
     rhizomes
     Companion Plants Woolgrass, salt cordgrass, pink
     muhly, spikerush, whitetop sedge, wiregrass,
     Indian grass, sugarcane plumegrass, bent-awn
     plumegrass, seashore mallow, redroot, cattail
     gayfeather, wild ageratum, New York aster
     Propagation Seed, root division while in active
     growth
     Wildlife Seeds eaten by songbirds, rails, teal, and
     geese; rhizomes eaten by deer in winter, foliage
     browsed by deer and cattle

Switchgrass is ideal for the typically overwatered
home flower garden, because it usually doesn't get top-
heavy and require staking. As with all native species that
cover a wide range, there are many varieties to choose
from. Switchgrass is very effective when it is planted in
masses on large properties. Even its dried winter foliage
and bare flower clusters are remarkably delicate and
attractive. These can be left until early spring, when the
fastidious gardener will want to cut down the old foliage
to make way for clean, fresh growth.

218. Latin Name *Scirpus cyperinus*

> **Common Name** Woolgrass, marsh bulrush, teddy-bear paws
> **Usual Height** 3 feet, occasionally 5 feet
> **Spacing** 2 feet
> **Sun or Shade** ○
> **Bloom** 6- to 12-inch cluster, red-brown, wooly, mid- to late summer
> **Fruit** Yellow-brown shortly after blooming
> **Leaves** 2-foot-tall grassy clump, dormant in winter
> **Native Range** Freshwater swamps, marshes, wet meadows, eastern half North America, Zones 4 to 8
> **Soil** Very acid to neutral, rich OK
> **Drainage** Wet to moist
> **Root System** Clump-forming, can colonize by rhizomes
> **Companion Plants** Sugarcane plumegrass, spikerush, pickerelweed, swamp sunflower
> **Propagation** Root division
> **Wildlife** Seeds eaten by ducks and other marsh birds; roots and underwater stems eaten by muskrats and geese; nesting cover for marsh wrens and blackbirds

Contrary to what you might assume from reading its native range, **woolgrass** is not limited to soggy areas or standing water. It can easily be grown in normally moist flower gardens. The brown flowers are unusual but extremely appealing. They are normally evident in late July, at the height of summer's heat, when any fresh blooms are very welcome. Woolgrass can be effectively grouped with flowers that bloom about the same time and also like moist conditions. Orange coneflower, Barbara's buttons, cardinal flower, pineland hibiscus, and joepyeweed are some of the best. For those of you interested in marsh restoration or erosion control by streams or ponds, woolgrass planted in a mass is both useful and attractive.

219. Latin Name *Sorghastrum nutans* (L.) Nash

> **Common Name** Indiangrass, woodgrass
> **Usual Height** 4 to 5 feet, occasionally 8 feet
> **Spacing** 3 to 5 feet, $^1/_2$ to 2 pounds pure live seed per 1000 square feet
> **Sun or Shade** ○
> **Bloom** Bright gold, in clusters 4 to 11 inches long, late summer to early fall, showy for about 2 weeks
> **Fruit** Tawny, seeds ripe midfall, but attractive into winter
> **Leaves** Mostly in grassy clump 18 inches tall, pale green to powder blue in summer, orange in fall
> **Native Range** Sandhills, dry banks, ditches, fields, eastern two-thirds North America, Zones 3 to 9
> **Soil** Acid, lime OK, rich preferred, clay or sand OK
> **Drainage** Moist to dry, tolerates short, seasonal flooding
> **Root System** Clump-forming
> **Companion Plants** Beebalm, coneflowers (*Echinacea* and *Rudbeckia*)/aromatic aster, sweet goldenrod, bluestems, switchgrass, wiregrass, pink muhly
> **Propagation** Seed, root division
> **Wildlife** Flowers visited by bees, seeds eaten by birds, foliage a favorite with grazing animals

It's impossible to single out just one reason why everyone falls in love with **Indiangrass.** Partly its because of its large size and soaring bloom stalks. Then there are the flowers—lustrous, bright, and beautiful, even at a distance. But they're even better up close, where you get to savor the combined yellow and dark red of each individual bloom. And then there are the leaves . . . with a satisfying crispness of texture and a clarity of color—bright green in summer and shades of pumpkin in autumn. Use this grass in any sunny flower bed, or mass it in a prairie area where you would like to mow (or burn) only once a year.

220. **Latin Name** *Spartina alterniflora*
Common Name Salt cordgrass, smooth cordgrass
Usual Height 3 to 4 feet, occasionally 8 feet, 18 inches where very salty
Spacing Solid cover where present
Sun or Shade ○
Bloom 4- to 12-inch spike of fringelike flowers, late summer to fall
Fruit Seed ripe shortly after flowering
Leaves Narrow, silvery on underside
Native Range Coastal marsh, live oak beach, Newfoundland to Texas, also South America, Zones 5 to 9
Soil Sandy, brackish to very salty
Drainage Wet to moist
Root System Colonizes by rhizomes, very deep
Companion Plants Yaupon holly, wax myrtle, winged sumac, eastern red cedar, seashore mallow, yucca, curly clematis, cattail gayfeather, goldenrod, broomsedge
Propagation Root division
Wildlife Roots eaten by geese in winter: seeds eaten by black duck, clapper rail, Virginia rail, sora, seaside sparrow, sharp-tailed sparrow; browsed by muskrat and white-tailed deer, decayed plant parts eaten by small estuarine animals

Cattail gayfeather, swamp sunflower, and salt cordgrass along the Gulf Coast in October.

Salt cordgrass is the primary grass along the seashore. The constant sea breezes bend its grass blades over, revealing pretty silver-white undersides. Where salt cordgrass is established, it makes a solid mat. Imagine these silver mats, mixed with pink and yellow flowers, and set against a richly textured evergreen shrub or yucca— now that's a truly lovely sight. I don't have any idea whether this silver-leaved grass would miss its salt and languish in a flower garden, or whether it would "eat" the whole garden for lunch. But, if you live on the coast, this grass is an important component of the wet sea marsh or a drier beach habitat, and it is invaluable for shore wildlife.

14

WATER PLANTS

The water plants in this chapter are those with the biggest flowers, or those that are best behaved and therefore the most suitable for a small water garden. None are truly floating; all must be rooted in sand or mud in shallow water.

Only two water plants in this chapter—spatterdock and fragrant waterlily—have stems that must be supported by at least a foot or two of water at all times. Their leaves and flowers either float on the water or stand barely above it, so that the overall feel is horizontal. Other native water plants that fall into this category are the tall yellow American lotus (*Nelumbo lutea*), the minute white floating heart (*Nymphoides cordata* and *N. aquatica*), mosquito fern (*Azolla caroliniana*, the tiny floating fern that can turn a cypress swamp as green as a lawn), plus many more, such as frogbit (*Limnobium spongia*), watershield (*Brasenia schreberi*), and my favorite, the carnivorous floating bladderwort (*Utricularia* spp.), which requires very acid water.

The other water plants in this chapter have self-supporting stems and do not need to be actually *in* the water, as long as the soil is wet and boggy, but filled with oxygen. They grow vertically in very shallow water, such as is found on the edges of a body of water, or they can grow in ground that is just kept moist to wet at all times.

A pond garden, because it is small and shallow, is easily overgrown by water plants—all of which are aggressive. A pond that is so covered by vegetation that no water is showing is not attractive. If you have an earth-bottomed pond, plan to weed once a year. If you have an artificial pond with liner only—18 to 24 inches deep—place the plants in pots to keep them under control. Use very dark containers that will be invisible underwater. Fill them with heavy topsoil topped with a quarter inch of gravel. Don't use

*As far as I know, only one water plant—horsetail (*Equisetum hyemale*)—is evergreen, and I didn't include it because it is so aggressive that it can climb right out of a pond and take off across the rest of the yard. Horsetail is also sometimes called "scouring rush" because it has silica in its stiff stems. For some strange reason, rabbits love to browse it. Although it can be a nightmare in a natural pond (without a rabbit to curtail it), put it in a pot in a formal, well-contained water garden, and it can be a real pleasure. This elegant water feature in the Logan Young garden in Memphis, Tennessee, shows it put to good use. The horsetail is the upright plant just by the fountain girl's right knee. This garden was designed by Greg Touliatos, who has also used pots of native tuckahoe, thalia, great bulrush (*Scirpus validus*), yellow canna (*Canna flaccida*), iris, and a cyperus from Madagascar.*

A tiny water garden, the size of a child's wading pool, at Flower Place Farm in Meridian, Mississippi, provides summer color and fresh water for visiting and resident birds. Pickerelweed sits in a pot in the pond, while titi hugs the edge where overflow makes a damp spot. An infant butterflyweed (foreground) is part of the adjacent flower garden that is watered, but never wet.

potting soil; it's too light and will float away. Submerge the tub about 18 to 24 inches deep to keep the roots cool in the summer and unfrozen in the winter. It's important that any leaves on the newly planted spatterdock not be below water level. You can control this by placing bricks under the tub to keep the leaves at or just above water line. As the plant grows, remove bricks until the tub is at the proper level.

If you want a natural, self-supporting pond garden that keeps the water clean nature's way, you will also need underwater plants, pond water rich in microorganisms, tadpoles, snails, and fish to keep oxygen circulating and mosquitoes under control. If you have to fill your pond with tap water, let the chlorine evaporate before adding plants and animals. You want the water to be murky, not crystal clear. Those with an underground spring or who live on heavy clay can have a natural pond that completely imitates a natural habitat.

If you think a pond is too much work but you are enamored with bog plants, you can easily have a bog garden. Unless the place where you want this bog garden is already low and wet all the time, you'll need to dig a swale or a sunken area—about 4 to 6 inches deep. And make sure the bottom is firm. Then, plant your bog plants in the design you want, putting highly aggressive ones in solid containers. Mulch the whole area up almost to normal ground level. Then, very slowly, so the mulch won't float out, let the hose trickle into your bog garden until it is thoroughly soggy. Repeat once a week or as needed, so that it never quite completely dries out, and fresh oxygen has a chance to get into the mulch. Many of the flowers in the flower garden chapter, such as redroot, swamp sunflower, and hibiscus, and many of the grasses, such as spikerush and sugarcane plumegrass, can be included in a bog garden.

Water plants are dormant in winter. The roots are usually safe from being frozen when buried in the mud of an earthen pond, but are vulnerable in pots if you get weather that is so cold the whole pond might freeze. Lots of oxygen in the soil and water seems to protect the plants.

Water gardens are a common feature in Southern landscapes. They range from large spring-fed ponds, where the plants can be anchored directly in sand or mud, to small artificial pools. Most water plants bloom best in sun, but some will handle lots of shade. Keep the water free of chlorine, so that it can be used and enjoyed by plants, fish, songbirds, and other forms of wildlife.

This lovely pond, at the H.L. Blomquist Garden of Native Plants at Duke University, and designed by curator Ed Steffek, is fed by two springs. In early June, it is brightened by the blooms of fragrant waterlily and lizard's tail. Water plants that bloomed earlier or will flower later are powdery thalia on the right, narrowleaf cattail and iris in front, and tuckahoe to the left of the stepping stones. Out of the water are purple coneflowers in the foreground and, as a backdrop, an oakleaf hydrangea and a portion of woodland.

221. Latin Name *Nuphar luteum* (*N. advena*)
    Common Name Spatterdock, yellow pondlily, yellow cowlily
    Usual Height 4 to 6 inches above the water
    Spacing 1 per 6 to 25 square feet, 20- to 30-quart container
    Sun or Shade ◑ ○
    Bloom Yellow, 2 to 4 inches across, 1 inch high, on stalks that are 2 to 4 inches above water, early spring to late fall
    Fruit Green, oval, fleshy, 2 inches long, underwater, fall
    Leaves Heart-shaped, 9 to 12 inches long, wavy edges, usually floating, but also might be above water or even underwater, dormant in winter
    Native Range Freshwater or tidal sloughs, stream or river edges, ponds, cypress swamps, springs, eastern half of North America, Zones 6 to 11
    Soil Underwater mud, acid, lime OK, rich OK, saline OK
    Drainage Shallow water, preferably barely moving
    Root System Large rhizome, colonizes
    Companion Plants Fragrant waterlily, submerged aquatics and other floating flowers
    Propagation Root division
    Wildlife Seeds eaten by a few ducks, crane, and Virginia rail

The photo shows **spatterdock** in an earthen pond at the Tawes Garden in Annapolis, Maryland. It was growing both at the edges, where the water was about 6 inches deep, and out into the middle, where it looked to be at least 4 feet deep. The yellow flowers tend to bloom whenever the water is warm enough. In an artificial pool without mud on the bottom, plant your spatterdock in a 20- to 30-quart black plastic tub.

222. Latin Name *Nymphaea odorata*
    Common Name Fragrant waterlily
    Usual Height Leaves floating on water, flowers 0 to 6 inches above water
    Spacing 1 per 6 to 25 square feet of water, 30-quart container
    Sun or Shade ○
    Bloom White (pink), 4 to 7 inches across, golden centers, fragrant
    Fruit Green, fleshy flattened, underwater
    Leaves Round pads, 3 to 10 inches in diameter, with a pie-slice cut out where the stem attaches, purple beneath, dormant in winter
    Native Range Freshwater ponds, marshes, swamps, eastern half North America, Zones 3 to 8
    Soil Underwater mud, acid, lime OK
    Drainage Shallow water, preferably barely moving
    Root System Large rhizome, colonizes
    Companion Plants Spatterdock, water shield, submerged aquatics and other floating flowers
    Propagation Root division
    Wildlife Seeds and vegetation eaten by sandhill crane, canvasback, mottled duck, pintail, redhead duck, ring-necked duck, lesser scaup, shoveller, blue-winged teal, wood duck, purple gallinule, muskrat, and porcupine
    Related Species *N. mexicana*, yellow waterlily; *N. elegans*, blue waterlily or everglades waterlily; *N. tuberosa*, Mississippi waterlily

Fragrant water lily is the most cold-hardy of our native waterlilies and the only one that produces a sweet scent. If its natural predators are not present, it is capable of covering the surface of a good-sized pond with a magnificent blanket of blooms. In a home water garden, restrain it by planting it in a 30-quart (or larger) tub; its roots are husky and like plenty of room. Make sure the top of the lily's root (the crown) is at the top of the soil.

223. **Latin Name** *Hymenocallis liriosme,* including
H. caroliniana, H. occidentalis, H. rotata
Common Name Spiderlily
Usual Height 2 feet above water, occasionally 4 feet
Spacing 2 to 3 feet apart or 1 per 20- to 30-quart container
Sun or Shade ◑ ◐ ○
Bloom White, 4 to 7 inches across, 2 to 6 flowers per head, fragrant, early spring
Fruit Green, fleshy seeds
Leaves 2 feet long, 2 inches wide, upright from base, glossy, dormant in winter
Native Range Swamps, bogs, floodplains, eastern U.S., Zones 6 to 10
Soil Acid, lime OK, sand or clay OK, rich preferred
Drainage Shallow fresh water, 0 to 2 feet deep
Root System 4- to 5-inch bulb, clump-forming
Companion Plants Copper and other swamp iris, yellowtop/crinum lily, Texas star hibiscus, pickerelweed, tuckahoe, powdery thalia, lizard's tail, spikerush, whitetop sedge, bulrush
Propagation Division of bulblets, seed
Wildlife Flowers visited by hummingbirds
Related Species *Crinum americanum,* crinum lily

Spiderlily's aroma is sweet, not cloying, and has the kind of wonderfully rich undertones found in very expensive perfumes. But this plant is a feast for the eyes as well; its huge flowers make it a stand-out member of a water garden community, where it blooms at the same time as Louisiana iris and the yellow and Piedmont azaleas. Spiderlily's large, glossy leaves are also quite handsome and remain so until frost. You can expand on that leafy texture by planting it with **crinum lily** (186). These two are compatible in a water garden, a bog garden, or a flower garden. As with most bulbs, spiderlily is extremely long-lived. A single plant, used as an accent, is lovely. But massed, as in the photo, it's spectacular.

224. **Latin Name** *Orontium aquaticum*
Common Name Goldenclub, neverwet
Usual Height 9 to 12 inches above water, 1 to 2 feet on land
Spacing 1 (to 3) feet apart or 1 per 10- to 20-quart container
Sun or Shade ● ◑ ◐
Bloom Tiny, in the yellow tips of the 12-inch-long white and red stems, early spring
Fruit Green
Leaves Pale green, sometimes floating, briefly dormant after a frost
Native Range Shallow streams, ponds, bogs, swamps, eastern U.S., mostly in Coastal Plain and Mississippi River basin, Zones 6 to 9
Soil Very acid, acid, rich preferred
Drainage Shallow fresh, moving water, 1 to 12 inches deep
Root System Rhizome, colonizes
Companion Plants Copper and other swamp iris, spiderlily/fragrant waterlily, spatterdock, pickerelweed, crinum lily, tuckahoe, lizard's tail
Propagation Seed (self-sows), root division
Wildlife No information

Goldenclub has beautiful leaves—fresh, smooth, and sometimes bluish—with a slightly pleated look. The flowers are unusual, not unlike colorful rat's tails. But, don't let that put you off; they're really very entertaining, and, amazingly, they hold their own with iris and spiderlily, both of which bloom at the same time. Goldenclub is not for the bog garden. It needs gently flowing, oxygen-rich water. If a pond is too sluggish, this plant will pull itself up on the bank. Keep it happy in a pool with a recirculating pump, in the flow of a seep (where it will seed out downhill), or in the protected eddy of a back-yard stream that isn't too shady. It looks its best with a little sun.

225. Latin Name *Peltandra virginica*
Common Name Tuckahoe, green arum
Usual Height 1 to 2 feet
Spacing 2 feet apart or 1 per 20-quart container
Sun or Shade ◑ ◐ ○
Bloom Greenish yellow, like an upright furled leaf, late spring
Fruit Greenish bronze, fleshy, early summer
Leaves Glossy, arrowhead-shaped, dormant in winter
Native Range Swamps, flooded woodlands, bogs, marshes, edges of water, eastern North America, Zones 5 to 9
Soil Very acid or acid
Drainage Shallow, fresh water, 0 to 12 inches deep
Root System Almost tuberous, clump-forming
Companion Plants Goldenclub/crinum lily, lizard's tail, cardinal flower, rose mallow, halberdleaf hibiscus
Propagation Root cuttings, seed
Wildlife Berries eaten by wood duck, king rail
Related Species *P. sagittifolia,* spoonflower, white arum

Tuckahoe is one of those quiet, understated, dependable plants that binds a garden together. It can be used in a semishaded bog garden or in about 6 inches of water. It's never aggressive, a rare trait among water plants. Use it for texture to fill space where you want to spotlight something taller, such as itea or cardinal flower. Or, plant tuckahoe as a thick, irregular border, both on land and in the water, to create a more natural look along the edges of an artificial pool. **Spoonflower** has a white spoon-shaped shield behind its yellow wand of flowers, making it more ornamental than tuckahoe. It grows in pineland bogs and pond cypress swamps, and is winter-hardy only to Zone 8. It is rare both in the wild and in the nursery trade.

226. Latin Name *Pontederia cordata* (including *P. lanceolata*)
Common Name Pickerelweed, pickerel rush
Usual Height 2 to 4 feet above water (or mud)
Spacing 2 feet apart or 1 per 20- to 30-quart container
Sun or Shade ◐ ○
Bloom Purple (white), 6-inch spikes, each spike blooms about a week, with new spikes appearing almost continuously from late spring to early fall
Fruit Red, sticky, summer to fall
Leaves 3 to 7 inches long, smooth, dormant in winter
Native Range Sunny edges of fresh water, eastern half U.S., Zones 4 to 9
Soil Acid, lime OK, sand or clay OK
Drainage Shallow, fresh water, 0 to 12 inches deep
Root System Clump-forming, short rhizome, can colonize
Companion Plants Spiderlily/spatterdock, fragrant waterlily, lizard's tail, powdery thalia, redroot, spikerush, switchgrass
Propagation Root division, even while in bloom
Wildlife Important to dragonflies; seeds eaten by black duck, mottled duck, other ducks, geese, and other aquatic animals

I'm especially enthusiastic about **pickerelweed,** the South's most rewarding water plant. It blooms continuously all summer, and seems to be constantly covered with dragonflies. It can be planted in a bog, in the soft mud of an earthern pond, or in a large container set into a concrete or plastic-lined pool. Easy to establish, it forms a clump that grows bigger each year, but is not considered aggressive. Pickerelweed's erect stance makes it a fine vertical accent at the side of fragrant waterlily or spatterdock.

227. **Latin Name** *Saururus cernuus*
   Common Name Lizard's tail, water dragon
   Usual Height 18 inches, occasionally 3 feet
   Spacing 2 feet or 1 per 20- to 30-quart container
   Sun or Shade ● ◐ ◑
   Bloom White, tiny on 8-inch curving spikes that bloom from the bottom up, slightly fragrant, mostly in early summer
   Fruit Ripe in summer on upright spikes
   Leaves Thick, smooth, 6 inches long, heart-shaped, dormant in winter
   Native Range Marshes, acid swamps, floodplains, shallow water, eastern half of North America, Zones 4 to 9
   Soil Very acid, acid, lime OK, rich preferred
   Drainage Shallow, fresh water, 0 to 6 inches deep
   Root System Fleshy rhizome, colonizes
   Companion Plants Crinum lily/netted chain fern, cinnamon fern, sensitive fern, tuckahoe
   Propagation Root division, seed
   Wildlife Depends on beaver ponds for increased habitats

The first thing that will attract you to this native is its endearingly funny, fuzzy tail-like flowers. But **lizard's tail** has practical virtues, too—it blooms profusely in the shade. (Crinum lily is the only other water plant that flowers so well without direct sunlight.) Lizard's tail, like pickerelweed, is very easy to grow. If you put a wisp of one in a 5-gallon container, it will be ready for division by the third year. It thrives only on the edges of very shallow water, never venturing out where it is deep and sunny. On shore, lizard's tail makes a wonderful groundcover, getting thin only where the soil is not moist all year, or where shade becomes very dense, or where it is out-competed by ferns. Lizard's tail is quite shallow-rooted, and can even be found growing on old logs and floating islands of matted vegetation.

228. **Latin Name** *Thalia dealbata*
   Common Name Powdery thalia, water canna
   Usual Height 6 to 8 feet in flower, 3- to 4-foot foliage
   Spacing 3 feet apart or 1 per 30-quart container
   Sun or Shade ○
   Bloom Rosy purple with a powdery white bloom, 4- to 6-inch spikes, early summer to midfall
   Fruit Seeds ripe in fall
   Leaves 12 to 20 inches long, canna-shaped, pale, heavy, smooth, dormant in winter
   Native Range Cypress swamps, marshes, ditches, Coastal Plain from South Carolina (rare) to Texas, north to Missouri, Zones 6 to 9
   Soil Acid, lime OK, rich preferred
   Drainage Shallow fresh water, 0 to 12 inches deep
   Root System Rhizome, colonizes
   Companion Plants Spiderlily/fragrant waterlily, spatterdock, pickerelweed, swamp sunflower, sugarcane plumegrass, brushy bluestem
   Propagation Root division, seed (self-sows)
   Wildlife No information

A shrub or tree can give height to a water garden, but they can shade out the water flowers. Many people solve this dilemma by introducing cattails. But cattails have to be very carefully contained, or they can really take over. That's why I like **powdery thalia.** It gives you the height you need, but does so with grace and color. In a large earthern pond, it can be massed with a sweep of iris or pickerelweed at its feet and waterlilies out in the deeper parts. In a more formal garden, one powdery thalia in a large container makes a striking accent. Its large, pale leaves are clustered in a rather horizontal arrangement about three feet wide and tall. These leaves are topped by a three-foot fan of bare stems, at the ends of which are strangely clustered purple flowers that face out like the heads of exotic birds. Enchanting!

SOURCES

NATIONAL ORGANIZATIONS
STATE ORGANIZATIONS

Sources

A Source Book of Useful Information on Horticulturally Useful Native or Naturalized Plants of the Southeastern United States, l985, 87 pages. Western Carolina University.

The National Wildflower Research Center's Wildflower Handbook, 1992, 301 pages. Voyageur Press, Stillwater, Minnesota.

Sources of Native Plants and Wildflowers, Virginia Native Plant Society, P.O. Box 844, Annandale, VA 22003.

Commercial Seed Sources for Southeastern Native Plants. North Carolina Botanic Garden, UNC-CH, Totten Canter 457A, Chapel Hill, NC 27514.

Some Sources of Plant Material Indigenous to Pinelands Areas. South Jersey Resource Conservation and Development Council, P.O. Box 676, Hammonton, NJ 08037.

Some Sources of Plant Material Native or Adapted to Seashore Conditions. Same as above.

National Organizations

National Wildflower Research Center
2600 FM 973 North
Austin, TX 78725

Soil Conservation Society of America
7515 Northeast Ankeny Road
Ankeny, IA 50021

The Canadian Wildflower Society
35 Bauer Crescent
Unionville, Ontario L3R 4H3

Missouri Botanical Garden
P.O. Box 299
St. Louis, MO 63166-0299

The Nature Conservancy
1800 North Kent Street, Suite 800
Arlington, VA 22209

American Association of Field
    Botanists
327 Guild Drive
Chattanooga, TN 37421

Center for Plant Conservation
Missouri Botanical Garden
P.O. Box 299
St. Louis, MO 63166-0299

Society for Ecological Restoration
University of Wisconsin
1207 Seminole Highway
Madison, WI 53711

Operation Wildflower
Rt. 2, Box 54
Selman, OK 73834

Eastern Native Plant Alliance
P.O. Box 6101
McLean, VA 22106

State Organizations

Alabama Wildflower Society
Rt. 2, Box 115
Northport, AL 35476

Arkansas Native Plant Society
Rt. l, Box 282
Mena, AR 71953

Botanical Society of Washington
    (D.C.)
Smithsonian Institution
Washington, D.C. 20560

Crosby Arboretum
P.O. Box 190
Picayune, MS 39466

Florida Native Plant Society
P.O. Box 680008
Orlando, FL 32868

Georgia Botanical Society
1676 Andover Court
Doraville, GA 30360

Kentucky Native Plant Society
Eastern Kentucky University
Richmond, KY 40475

Lichterman Nature Center
5992 Quince Road
Memphis, TN 38119-4699

Louisiana Native Plant Society
Rt. l, Box 151
Salie, LA 71070

Maryland Native Plant Society
14720 Claude Lane
Silver Springs, MD 20904

Mississippi Native Plant Society
202 North Andrews Avenue
Cleveland, MS 38732

Missouri Native Plant Society
Box 20073
St. Louis, MO 63144-0073

Native Plant Society of Texas
P.O. Box 891
Georgetown, TX 78627

North Carolina Wildflower
  Preservation Society
UNC-CH
Totten Center 457-A
Chapel Hill, NC 27514

Tennessee Native Plant Society
University of Tennessee
Knoxville, TN 37916

Virginia Native Plant Society
P.O. Box 844
Annandale, VA 22003

West Virginia Native Plant Society
West Virginia University
Morgantown, WV 26506

BIBLIOGRAPHY

Aiken, George D. *Pioneering with Wildflowers.* Putney, Vermont. 1935.

Ajilvsgi, Geyata. *Butterfly Gardening for the South.* Dallas, Texas: Taylor Publishing Company, 1990.

———*Wildflowers of the Big Thicket, East Texas, and Western Louisiana.* Kerrville, Texas: Green Horizons Press, 1979.

Armstrong, Patricia. "Bryophytes." *Wildflower Magazine,* Winter 1992. Toronto, Canada.

Barry, John M. *Natural Vegetation of South Carolina.* Columbia, South Carolina: University of South Carolina Press, 1980.

Batson, Wade T. *Landscape Plants for the Southeast.* Columbia, South Carolina: University of South Carolina Press, 1984.

———*Wild Flowers in the Carolinas.* Columbia, South Carolina: University of South Carolina Press, 1987.

Bent, Arthur C. *Life Histories of North American Birds: North American Nuthatches, Wrens, Thrashers, and Their Allies.* New York: Dover, 1948.

Bir, Richard E. *Growing and Propagating Showy Native Woody Plants.* Chapel Hill, North Carolina: University of North Carolina Press, 1992.

"Birds of the Gus Engeling Wildlife Management Area." Texas Parks and Wildlife Department. Austin, Texas.

Boyles, Roger. "Top Ten Ferns for the Southwest." Presentation given at 1992 Cullowhee Native Plant Conference, Western Carolina University, Division of Continuing Education and Summer School, Cullowhee, North Carolina.

Brown, Clair A. *Wildflowers of Louisiana and Adjoining States.* Baton Rouge, Louisiana: Louisiana State University Press, 1972.

Brown, Claud L., and L. Katherine Kirkman. *Trees of Georgia and Adjacent States.* Portland, Oregon: Timber Press, 1990.

Brown, Melvin L., and Russell G. Brown. *Herbaceous Plants of Maryland.* College Park, Maryland: University of Maryland, 1984.

Clewell, Andre F. *Guide to the Vascular Plants of the Florida Panhandle.* Tallahassee, Florida: University Presses of Florida, 1988.

Cobb, Boughton. *A Field Guide to Ferns and Their Related Species of Northeastern and Central North America.* Peterson Field Guide Series. Boston: Houghton Mifflin Company, 1963.

Conard, Henry S. *How to Know the Mosses and Liverworts.* Dubuque, Iowa: Wm. C. Brown Company, 1956.

Correll, Donovan Stewart, and Marshall Conring Johnston. *Manual of the Vascular Plants of Texas.* Vol. 6 of Contributions from Texas Research Foundation: A Series of Botanical Studies, edited by Cyrus Longworth Lundell. Richardson, Texas: University of Texas at Dallas, 1979.

Crichton-Harris, Anne. "Lowbush Blueberries." *Wildflower Magazine.* Winter, 1992. Toronto, Canada.

Cronquist, Arthur. *Basic Botany.* New York: Harper & Row, 1982.

Darke, Rick. "Native Grasses in the Landscape." Presentation given at 1991 Millersville Conference on Native Plants in the Landscape. Longwood Gardens, Kennett Square, Pennsylvania.

Deneke, C. Frederick, and Edward T. Browne, Jr. "The Vascular Flora of St. Francis County, Arkansas." Abstract, *Sida, Botanical Miscellany*, Southern Methodist University, 1987.

Dirr, Michael A. *Manual of Woody Landscape Plants*. Champaign, Illinois: Stipes Publishing Company, 1990.

Duncan, Wilbur H., and Marion B. Duncan. *Seaside Plants of the Gulf and Atlantic Coasts*. Washington, DC: Smithsonian Institution Press, 1987.

———*Trees of the Southeastern United States*. Athens, Georgia: University of Georgia Press, 1988.

Duncan, Wilbur H., and Leonard E. Foote. *Wildflowers of the Southeastern United States*. Athens, Georgia: University of Georgia Press, 1975.

duPont, Elizabeth N. *Landscaping with Native Plants in the Middle Atlantic Region*. Chadds Ford, Pennsylvania: Brandywine Conservancy, 1978.

Durand, Herbert. *Field Book of Common Ferns*. New York: G. P. Putnam's Sons, 1928.

Fontenot, William R. *Native Gardening in the South*. Carencro, Louisiana: A Prairie Basse Publication, 1992.

Foote, Leonard E., and Samuel B. Jones, Jr. *Native Shrubs and Woody Vines of the Southeast*. Portland, Oregon: Timber Press, 1989.

Gandhi, Kancheepuram N., and R. Dale Thomas. *Asteraceae of Louisiana*. Dallas, Texas: SMU Herbarium/ BRIT, 1989.

Georgia Landscape Magazine. University of Georgia, Athens. 1992.

Godfrey, Robert K. *Trees, Shrubs, and Woody Vines of Northern Florida and Adjacent Georgia and Alabama*. Athens, Georgia: University of Georgia Press, 1988.

Great Plains Flora Association. *Flora of the Great Plains*. Lawrence, Kansas: University Press of Kansas, 1991.

Grelen, Harold E., and Ralph H. Hughes. *Common Herbaceous Plants of Southern Forest Range*. United States Department of Agriculture, Research Paper SO-210, November 1984.

Gupton, Oscar W., and Fred C. Swope. *Wildflowers of the Shenandoah Valley and Blue Ridge Mountains*. Charlottesville, Virginia: University Press of Virginia, 1989.

H. L. Blomquist Garden of Native Plants. "Calendar of Bloom." Sarah P. Duke Gardens, Duke University, Durham, North Carolina, revised January 1984.

Harrison, Kit, and George Harrison. *America's Favorite Backyard Birds*. New York: Simon and Schuster, 1989.

Hightshoe, Gary L. *Native Trees, Shrubs, and Vines for Urban and Rural America*. New York: Van Nostrand Reinhold, 1988.

Hunter, Carl G. *Wildflowers of Arkansas*. Little Rock, Arkansas: Ozark Society Foundation, 1984.

Imhof, Thomas A. *Alabama Birds*. 2nd Ed. University of Alabama Press, 1976.

Johnston, Marshall C. *The Vascular Plants of Texas: A List Updating the Manual*. Dallas, Texas: University of Texas at Dallas, 1988.

Jones, Samuel B., Jr., and Leonard E. Foote. *Gardening with Native Wild Flowers*. Portland, Oregon: Timber Press, 1990.

Kral, Robert. "A New Species of Conradina (Lamiaceae) from Northeastern Peninsular Florida." Abstract. *Sida, Contributions to Botany*, Vol. 14, Number 3, August 1991.

Kelt, Douglas A. "Flowers and Colour." *Wildflower Magazine*, Fall 1992. Toronto, Canada.

Lewis, George W., and James F. Miller. *Identification and Control of Weeds in Southern Ponds*. Athens, Georgia: University of Georgia College of Agriculture, revised April 1984.

Leverett, Robert T. "Old Forest Growths." *Wildflower Magazine*, Fall 1992. Toronto, Canada.

Mahnken, Jan. *Hosting the Birds: How to Attract Birds to Nest in Your Yard*. Pownal, Vermont: Garden Way Publications, 1989.

Martin, Alexander C., et al. *American Wildlife and Plants: A Guide to Wildlife Food Habits*. New York: Dover, 1951.

McIninch, Suzanne, and E. W. Garbisch. "Oxygen Requirements of Dormant Wetland Plants." *Wildflower*, Journal of the National Wildflower Research Center, Vol. 4, No. 1, Spring/Summer 1991, Austin, Texas.

Mooberry, F. M., and Jane H. Scott. *Grow Native Shrubs in Your Garden*. Chadds Ford, Pennsylvania: Brandywine Conservancy, 1980.

Mooberry, F. M. "The Story of the Brandywine Conservancy Gardens." *Quill & Trowel*, September/October 1990.

Native Gardens. *Nursery Propagated Wild Flowers,* Fall 1992, 5737 Fisher Lane, Greenback, Tennessee 37742.

Native Plant Society of Texas. "East Texas and Its Many Ecosystems." *1992 Symposium Proceedings.* Georgetown, Texas.

Nokes, Jill. *How to Grow Native Plants of Texas and the Southwest.* Austin, Texas: Texas Monthly Press, 1986.

Odenwald, Neil, and James Turner. *Identification, Selection, and Use of Southern Plants for Landscape Design.* Baton Rouge, Louisiana: Claitor's Publishing Divisions, 1987.

Parsons, Frances Theodora. *How to Know the Ferns.* New York: Dover Publications, Inc., 1961 (original publication 1899).

Peskin, Perry. "A Week in the Georgia Sun." *Wildflower Magazine,* Winter 1992. Toronto, Canada.

Pistorius, Alan. *The Country Journal of Birding and Bird Attraction.* New York: W. W. Norton, 1981.

Powers, Valerie Sparkman, and Robert M. Hatcher. *Giving Wildlife an Edge: A Guide to Ornamental Plants for Wildlife Habitat.* Tennessee Wildlife Resources Agency, 1982.

Radford, Albert E., Harry E. Ahles, and C. Ritchie Bell. *Manual of the Vascular Flora of the Carolinas.* Chapel Hill, North Carolina: University of North Carolina Press, 1987.

Sargent, Charles Sprague. *Manual of the Trees of North America.* Vols. I and II. New York: Dover Publications, Inc., 1949.

Scott, Jane. *Field and Forest, a Guide to Native Landscapes for Gardeners and Naturalists.* New York: Walker and Company, 1984.

Simpson, Benny J. *A Field Guide to Texas Trees.* Austin, Texas: Texas Monthly Press, 1988.

Southern Perennials & Herbs. 1993 Catalog. Tylertown, Mississippi.

Steffek, Edwin F. *The New Wild Flowers and How to Grow Them.* Portland, Oregon: Timber Press, 1983.

Stolzenburg, William. "Silent Sirens." *Nature Conservancy,* May/June 1992.

Stupka, Arthur. *Wildflowers in Color.* New York: Harper & Row, 1965.

Sunlight Gardens. "Handbook & Catalogue." Andersonville, Tennessee, 1992.

United States Department of Agriculture. *USDA Plant Hardiness Zone Map.* Miscellaneous Publication Number 1475, revised 1990.

University of North Carolina. *A Guide to the University Botanical Gardens at Asheville.* 1989.

Vines, Robert A. *Trees, Shrubs, and Woody Vines of the Southwest.* Austin, Texas: University of Texas Press, 1960.

Wasowski, Sally, and Andy Wasowski. *Native Texas Plants: Landscaping Region by Region.* Houston, Texas: Gulf Publishing, 1991.

Whitcomb, Carl E. *Know It and Grow It: A Guide to the Identification and Use of Landscape Plants.* Vol. 2. Stillwater, Oklahoma: Lacebark Publications, 1983.

Wilcove, David. "Empty Skies." *Wildflower Magazine,* Fall 1992.

Wilson, Jim. *Landscaping with Wildflowers.* Boston: Houghton Mifflin, 1992.

Wyman, Donald. *Wyman's Gardening Encyclopedia.* New York: Macmillan Publishing Co., 1971.

INDEX

Farkleberry (*Vaccinium arboreum*), 72
Ferns, 118-27
Fern moss (*Thuidum delicatulum*), 111
Fetterbush (*Lyonia lucida*), 91
Fevertree (*Pinckneya bracteata*), 70
Fiddleheads, 29
Fire pink (*Silene virginica*), 135
Flame azalea (*Rhododendron calendulaceum*), 84
Flatwoods, 30
Florida anise (*Illicium floridanum*), 56
Florida azalea (*Rhododendron austrinum*), 84
Florida leucothoe (*Agarista populifolia*), 75
Florida maple (*Acer barbatum*), 42
Florida shield fern (*Dryopteris ludoviciana*), 120
Flower garden, three-season sunny, 14, 16-17
Flowering dogwood (*Cornus florida*), 65
Flowering shrubs
    low, 94-98
    under 15 feet tall, 78-87
Flowering trees, over 15 feet tall, 59-72
Flowers
    garden, 145-70
    woodland, 126-48
Flowery meadow garden, 26, 27
Fly poison (*Amianthium muscaetoxicum*), 139
Foamflower (*Tiarella cordifolia*), 117
Foliage garden, early, 23
Forest, anatomy of, 1-2
Forest floor, 1
Forests, hardwood, 6, 30
Fothergilla gardenii, 82
Fothergilla major, 82
Fragrance garden, 18, 19
Fragrant waterlily (*Nymphaea odorata*), 183
Fraser magnolia (*Magnolia fraseri*), 68
Fraxinus americana, 44
French mulberry (*Callicarpa americana*), 79
Fringed pink (*Silene polypetala*), 135
Fringed loosestrife (*Lysimachia ciliata*), 142
Fringetree (*Chionanthus virginicus*), 64
Fruit garden, early, 23
Fruiting shrubs
    low, 94-98
    under 15 feet tall, 78-87
Fruiting trees, over 15 feet tall, 59-72

G

Galax (*Galax urceolata*), 109
Galax aphylla, 109
Galax urceolata, 109
Gallberry (*Ilex glabra*), 76
Garden flowers, 145-70
Gaylussacia baccata, 95
Gaylussacia dumosa, 95
Gelsemium rankinii, 101
Gelsemium sempervirens, 101
Gentiana andrewsii, 141
Georgia bark (*Pinckneya bracteata*), 70
Georgia basil (*Calamintha georgiana*), 95
Georgia pine (*Pinus palustris*), 38
Geranium maculatum, 131
Giant coneflower (*Rudbeckia maxima*), 164
Giant rudbeckia (*Rudbeckia maxima*), 164
Gillenia trifoliata, 142
Goat's beard (*Aruncus dioicus*), 139
Golden aster (*Pityopsis graminifolia*), 169
Goldenclub (*Orontium aquaticum*), 184
Golden fleece (*Solidago sphacelata*), 143
Golden groundsel (*Senecio aureus*), 112
Golden ragwort (*Senecio aureus*), 112
Goldenrod (*Solidago* sp.), 170
Golden St. John's wort (*Hypericum frondosum*), 96
Gopherwood (*Cladrastis kentukea*), 64
Gordonia (*Gordonia lasianthus*), 35
Gordonia lasianthus, 35
Grancy Graybeard (*Chionanthus virginicus*), 64
Grasses, ornamental, 171-79
Grayleaf goldenrod (*Solidago nemoralis*), 170
Great laurel (*Rhododendron maximum*), 77
Green arum (*Peltandra virginica*), 185
Green dragon (*Arisaema dracontium*), 129
Green hawthorn (*Crataegus viridis*), 65
Groundcovers, shady, 106-17
Ground pine (*Lycopodium flabelliforme*), 110

H

Habitat(s), 1
    creating, 1-7
    for wildlife, 3-4
Habitat gardens, examples of, 5

Hair-awn muhly (*Muhlenbergia capillaris*), 177
Haircap moss (*Polytrichum commune*), 111
Hairgrass (*Muhlenbergia capillaris*), 177
Hairy alumroot (*Heuchera villosa*), 132
Hairy beardtongue (*Pentstemon laevigatus*), 153
Hairy skullcap (*Scutellaria elliptica*), 143
Halberdleaf hibiscus (*Hibiscus militaris*), 159
Halesia diptera, 67
Halesia tetraptera, 67
Hamamelis vernalis, 67
Hamamelis virginiana, 67
Hammock, 30
Hardwood forests, 6, 30
Hardwoods, 41
Hazel alder (*Alnus serrulata*), 61
Heartleaf (*Hexastylis arifolia*), 110
Hearts-a-burstin' (*Euonymus americanus*), 81
Helianthus angustifolius, 168
Hepatica americana, 116
Hepatica acutiloba, 116
Herbaceous flowers, 29
Herb garden, 18, 19
Hercules club (*Aralia spinosa*), 62
Heterotheca graminifolia, 169
Heuchera americana, 132
Heuchera villosa, 132
Hexastylis, 115
Hexastylis arifolia, 110
Hexastylis shuttleworthii, 110
Hibiscus aculeatus, 159
Hibiscus coccineus, 159
Hibiscus militaris, 159
Hibiscus moscheutos, 159
Highbush blueberry (*Vaccinium corymbosum*), 72
Hoary azalea (*Rhododendron canescens*), 84
Hophornbeam (*Ostrya virginiana*), 69
Hornbeam (*Carpinus caroliniana*), 63
Horsesugar (*Symplocos tinctoria*), 58
Hydrangea arborescens, 96
Hydrangea quercifolia, 82
Hymenocallis caroliniana, 184
Hymenocallis liriosme, 184
Hymenocallis occidentalis, 184
Hymenocallis rotata, 184
Hymenocallis spp., 158
Hypericum frondosum, 96
Hypericum hypericoides, 96

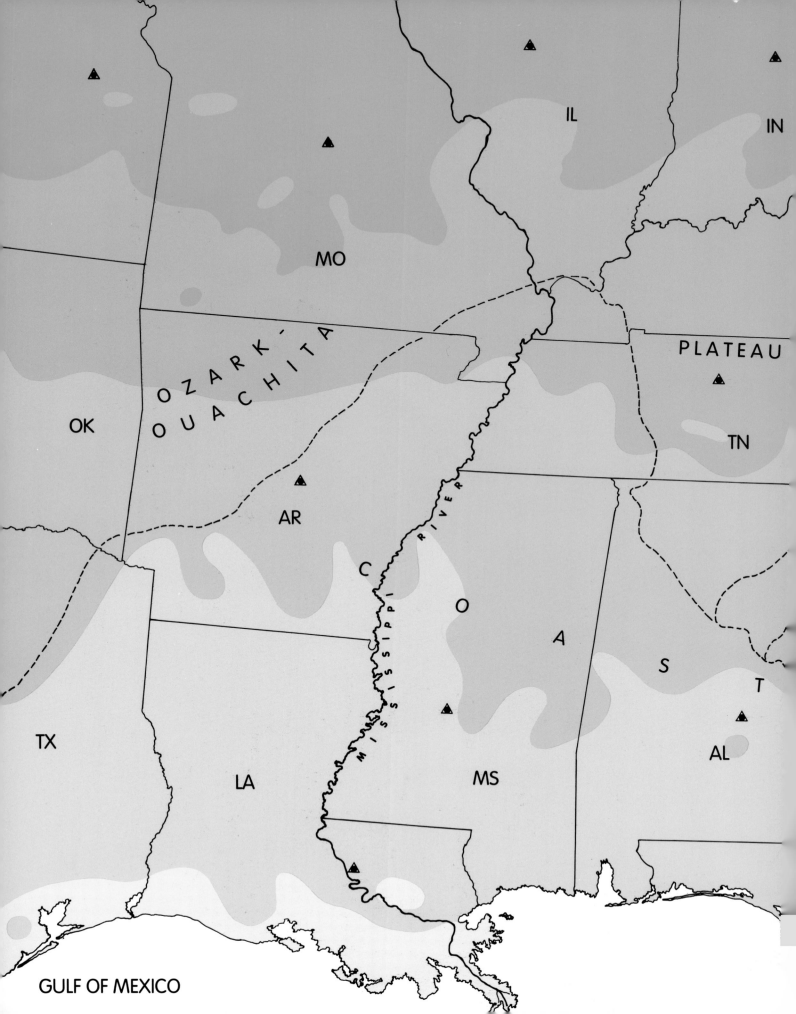

OZARK-OUACHITA

PLATEAU

OK

AR

TN

TX

LA

MISSISSIPPI RIVER

C O A S T

MS

AL

IL

IN

MO

GULF OF MEXICO